SPARKNOTES™

SAT II Writing

2003–2004 Edition

Series Editor Ben Florman

Editor Emma Chastain

Cover Design Dan O. Williams

Technology Tammy Hepps

This edition published by Spark Publishing

Spark Publishing
A Division of SparkNotes LLC
120 Fifth Avenue, 8th Floor
New York, NY 10011

02 03 04 05 SN 9 8 7 6 5 4 3 2 1

Please send all comments and questions or report errors to feedback@sparknotes.com.

Library of Congress information available upon request

Printed and bound in Canada

ISBN 1-58663-427-5

Welcome to SparkNotes™ Test Preparation

So you're planning to take the SAT II Writing test. Not only that, you're planning on getting a great score on the SAT II Writing test. You've come to the right book.

In order to help you reach your goal of extreme SAT II Writing success, the SparkNotes Guide to the SAT II Writing test provides:

The exact information on grammar and writing you need for the test. We've done the dirty work and figured out exactly what material you need to know for the SAT II Writing test, and that's what we're going to discuss in this book. Unlike other test preparation guides, we won't waste your time by presenting material you won't need to know for the test.

Critical-thinking skills and specific test-taking strategies. A thorough understanding of grammar and writing skills will serve you best on this test, but it's also extremely important to learn certain test-taking strategies. The SAT II Writing multiple-choice and essay format isn't always intuitive. In fact, a lot of the time, the format is designed to confuse the unprepared test-taker. Becoming thoroughly familiar with the test format and learning test strategies can help net you the valuable points that will distinguish you from the crowd.

Five full-length practice tests (and a study method that will teach you how to transform practice tests into powerful study tools). Practice tests can and should be an important part of your studying for any standardized test. Practice tests help you to hone your test-taking skills, become comfortable with the format and time limits of the test, and track your progress. In addition, if you follow our methods for studying the practice tests you take, the tests can become a study tool that will help you to target and overcome your weaknesses.

General information about SAT II Subject Tests. Beyond teaching you what you need to know to do well on a particular SAT II test, we think it's also important to discuss the SAT IIs in general. This first chapter of the book is dedicated to helping you figure out how the SAT II tests are used by colleges, which SAT II tests are right for you, when to take the tests, and how to register for them.

While other test prep companies actually write study guides as marketing tools to try to convince you to enroll in their expensive courses, SparkNotes' goal is to teach you so effectively that you don't need those courses. Our books are written with no hidden agenda. We simply want to help you get the best score you can.

Contents

ORIENTATION

Introduction to the SAT II Tests

Introduction to the Writing SAT II

Strategies for the Writing SAT II

SAT II WRITING REVIEW

The Essay

Identifying Sentence Errors

Improving Sentences

Improving Paragraphs

PRACTICE TESTS

Practice Tests Are Your Best Friends

ORIENTATION

Introduction to the SAT II Tests

T HE SAT II SUBJECT TESTS are created and administered by the College Board and the Educational Testing Service (ETS), the two organizations responsible for producing the dreaded SAT I (which most people call the SAT). The SAT II Subject Tests were created to act as complements to the SAT I. Whereas the SAT I tests your critical thinking skills by asking math and verbal questions, the SAT II Subject Tests examine your knowledge of a particular subject, such as Writing, U.S. History, Physics, or Biology. The SAT I takes three hours; the Subject Tests take only one hour.

In our opinion, the SAT II Subject Tests are better tests than the SAT I because they cover a definitive topic rather than some ambiguous critical thinking skills that are difficult to define. However, just because the SAT II Subject Tests do a better job of testing your knowledge of a useful subject doesn't mean the tests are necessarily easier or demand less study. A "better" test isn't necessarily better for you in terms of how easy it will be.

3

In comparison to taking the SAT I, there are good things and bad things about taking an SAT II Subject Test.

The Good

- Because SAT II Subject Tests cover actual topics like Grammar, Chemistry, and Biology, you can study for them effectively. If you don't know a topic in grammar, such as pronoun rules, you can look it up and learn it. The SAT II tests are therefore straightforward tests; if you know your stuff, you will do well on them.

- Often, the classes you've taken in school have already prepared you well for the SAT II. If you've been taking English courses for years, you've probably covered most of the topics that are tested on the SAT II English test. All you need is some refreshing and focusing, which this book provides.

The Bad

- Because SAT II Subject Tests quiz you on specific knowledge, it is much harder to "beat" or "outsmart" an SAT II test than it is to outsmart the SAT I. For the SAT I, you can use all sorts of tricks and strategies to figure out an answer. There are far fewer strategies to help you on the SAT II. Don't get us wrong: having test-taking skills *will* help you on an SAT II, but knowing the subject will help you much, much more. In other words, to do well on the SAT II, you can't just rely on your quick thinking and intelligence. You need to study.

Scoring the SAT II Subject Tests

There are three different versions of your Writing SAT II score. The "raw score" is a simple score of how you did on the test, like the grade you might receive on a normal test in school. The "percentile score" takes your raw score and compares it to the rest of the raw scores in the country, letting you know how you did on the test in comparison to your peers. The "scaled score," which ranges from 200–800, compares your score to the scores received by all students who have ever taken the SAT II.

The Raw Score

You will never know your raw score on the SAT II that you take, because the raw score is not included in the score report. But you should understand how the raw score is calculated, because this knowledge can affect your strategy for approaching the test.

Because the Writing SAT II contains an essay portion in addition to multiple-choice questions, the way its raw score is calculated differs in comparison to most SAT II tests. Calculating your Writing SAT II raw score involves a step beyond what you have to do for the other SAT II tests. Since this chapter of the book is an introduction to all SAT II tests, we're going to describe the usual way that raw scores are calculated. We'll discuss the specifics of how to calculate the Writing SAT II raw score in the next chapter, which begins our specific discussion of the Writing SAT II.

For most SAT II tests, a student's raw score is based solely on the number of questions that student got right, wrong, and left blank. A correct answer is worth one point; leaving a question blank yields no points; a wrong answer means you lose ¼ of a point.

Calculating the raw score is easy. Add up the number of questions you answered correctly and the number of questions answered incorrectly. Then multiply the number of wrong answers by ¼, and subtract this value from the number of right answers.

$$\text{raw score} = \text{\# of correct answers} - \tfrac{1}{4} \times \text{\# of wrong answers}$$

The Percentile Score

Along with the scaled score you receive from the ETS, you will get a percentile score. A student's percentile is based on the percentage of the total test-takers who received a lower raw score than he or she did. Let's say, for example, you had a friend named Zebulon, and he received a score that placed him in the 37th percentile. That 37th percentile tells him that he scored better on the SAT II than 36% of the other students who took the same test; it also means that 63% of the students taking that test scored as well as or better than he did.

The Scaled Score

The scaled score takes the raw score and uses a formula to turn that score into the scaled score from 200–800 that you've probably heard so much about.

The curve to convert raw scores to scaled scores differs from SAT II test to SAT II test. For example, a raw score of 33 on the Math Ic will scale to a 600, while the same raw score of 33 on the Math IIc will scale to a 700. In fact, the scaled score can even vary between different editions of the *same* test. A raw score of 33 on the February 2002 Math IIc might scale to a 710 while a 33 in June of 2002 might scale to a 690. These differences in scaled scores exist to accommodate for differences in difficulty level and student performance from year to year.

Colleges and the SAT II Subject Tests

We're guessing you didn't sign up to take the SAT II just for the sheer pleasure of it. That's right, you probably want to get into college, and know that the one and only reason to take this test is because colleges want or require you to do so.

Colleges care about SAT II Subject Tests for two related reasons. First, the tests demonstrate your interest, knowledge, and skill in specific topics. Second, because SAT II tests are standardized, they show how your writing (or biology or math) skills measure up to the skills of high school students nationwide. The grades you get in high school don't offer such a measurement to colleges: some high schools are more difficult than others, which means that students of equal ability might receive different grades, even in English classes that have basically the same curriculum. In contrast, since SAT II tests are national tests, they provide colleges with a definite yardstick against which they can measure your, and every other applicant's, knowledge and skills.

None of this means that SAT II tests are the primary tools that colleges use to decide whether to admit an applicant. High school grades, extracurricular activities, and SAT or ACT scores are all more important to colleges than your scores on SAT II tests. But because SAT II tests provide colleges with such a nice and easy measurement tool, they can add that extra bit of shading that can push your application from the maybe pile into the accepted pile.

When it comes down to it, colleges like the SAT IIs because the tests make the colleges' job easier. The tests are the colleges' tool. But because you know how colleges use the SAT II, you can also look at the tests as your tool. SAT II tests allow colleges to easily compare you to other applicants. This means that the SAT II tests provide you with an excellent chance to shine. If you got a 93% on your English final, and some other kid in some high school across the country got a 91%, colleges don't know how to compare the two grades. They don't know whose class was harder or whose teacher was a tough grader or whose high school inflates grades. But if you get a 720 on the SAT II Writing, and that other kid gets a 650, colleges *will* recognize the difference in your scores. Since the tests can help your application so much, and since preparing for the tests can dramatically improve your score, put some real time and effort into studying for the SAT II tests.

College Placement

Occasionally, colleges use SAT II tests to determine placement. For example, if you do very well on the Writing SAT II, you might be exempted from a basic expository writing class. It's worth finding out whether the colleges to which you are applying use the SAT II tests for placement.

Which SAT II Subject Tests to Take

There are three types of SAT II tests: those you *must* take, those you *should* take, and those you *shouldn't* take.

- The SAT II tests you *must* take are those required by the colleges you are interested in.

- The SAT II tests you *should* take are tests that aren't required, but which you'll do well on, thereby impressing the colleges looking at your application.

- The SAT II tests you *shouldn't* take are those that aren't required and which cover a subject you don't feel confident about.

Determining Which SAT II Tests Are Required

To find out if the colleges to which you are applying require that you take a particular SAT II test, you'll need to do a bit of research. Call the schools you're interested in, look at their web pages online, or talk to your guidance counselor. Often, colleges request that you take the following SAT II tests:

- The Writing SAT II test

- One of the two Math SAT II tests (either Math Ic or Math IIc)

- Another SAT II in some other subject of your choice

Not all colleges follow these guidelines, however, so you should take the time to research which tests you need to take in order to apply to the colleges that interest you.

Determining Whether You Should Take an SAT II Even If It Isn't Required

To decide whether you should take a test that isn't required you have to know two things:

1. What is a good score on that SAT II test

2. Whether you can get that score or higher

Below, we have included a list of the most commonly taken SAT II tests and the average scaled score on each. If you feel confident that you can get a score that is significantly above the average (50 points is significant) taking the test will probably strengthen your college application. Please note that if you are planning to attend an elite school, you might have to score significantly more than 50 points higher than the national average. The following table is just a general guideline. It's a good idea to call the schools that interest you, or talk to a guidance counselor, to get a more precise idea of what score you should be shooting for.

TEST	AVERAGE SCORE
Writing	590–600
Literature	590–600
American History	580–590
World History	570–580
Math Ic	580–590
Math IIc	655–665
Biology E&M	590–600
Chemistry	605–615
Physics	635–645

As you decide which test to take, be realistic. Don't just assume you're going to do great without at least taking a practice test and seeing where you stand.

It's a good idea to take three tests that cover a range of subjects, such as one math SAT II, one humanities SAT II (History or Writing), and one science SAT II. However, taking *more* than three SAT II tests is probably not necessary.

When to Take an SAT II Subject Test

The best time to take the SAT II Writing is after you've had as much time as possible in English or writing classes. This does not hold true on all of the SAT II tests—for example, it makes sense to take the Biology test right after finishing a year-long Biology course, while the material is fresh in your mind. But the Writing test is not about cramming your head full of formulas and tables; the more total time you've devoted to reading and writing, the better off you'll be. This means that you should take the SAT II Writing sometime during the end of your junior year or the beginning of your senior year.

Unless the colleges to which you are applying use the SAT II for placement purposes, there is no point in taking any SAT II tests after November of your senior year, since you won't get your scores back from ETS until after the application deadline has passed.

ETS usually sets testing dates for SAT II Subject Tests in October, November, December, January, May, and June. However, not every Subject Test is administered in each of these months. To check when the test you want to take is being offered, visit the College Board website at www.collegeboard.com, or do some research in your school's guidance office.

Registering for SAT II Tests

To register for the SAT II test(s) of your choice, you have to fill out some forms and pay a registration fee. We know, we know—it's ridiculous that *you* have to pay for a test that colleges require you to take in order to make *their* jobs easier, but, sadly, there isn't anything we, or you, can do about it. It is acceptable, at this point, to grumble about the unfairness of the world.

After grumbling, however, you still have to register. There are two ways to go about it: online or by mail. To register online, go to www.collegeboard.com and follow the instructions listed. To register by mail, fill out and send in the forms enclosed in the *Registration Bulletin*, which should be available in your high school's guidance office. You can also request a copy of the *Bulletin* by calling the College Board at (609) 771-7600, or writing to:

> College Board SAT Program
> P.O. Box 6200
> Princeton, NJ 08541-6200

You can register to take up to three SAT II tests for any given testing day. Unfortunately, even if you decide to take three tests in one day, you'll have to pay a separate registration fee for each test you take.

Introduction to the Writing SAT II

IMAGINE TWO CHILDREN, Eloise and Bartholomew, racing in the forest. Who will win—Eloise, who never stumbles because she knows the placement of every tree and all the twists and turns and hiding spots, or Bartholomew, who keeps falling down and tripping over roots because he doesn't pay any attention to the landscape? The answer is obvious. Even if Bartholomew is a little faster and more athletic, Eloise will win, because she knows how to navigate the landscape and turn it to her advantage.

This example of a race in the forest illustrates a point: in the metaphor, the structure of the SAT II is the forest, and taking the test is the competition. In this chapter we're going to describe the "landscape" of the Writing SAT II: what topics the questions cover, what the questions look like, and how the questions are organized. In the next chapter, we'll show you the strategies that will allow you to navigate and use the landscape to get the best score you can.

Chapter Contents

Content of the Writing SAT II

What does ETS test on the Writing SAT II? Not much. The essay portion of the SAT II tests your general writing skills; the multiple-choice portion tests your knowledge of the following grammar and writing rules:

- Verb Tense Agreement

- Pronoun rules

- Parallelism

- Noun agreement

- Subject-verb agreement

- Coordination and subordination

- Logical comparison

- Misplaced modifiers

- Diction

- Wordiness

- Idiom

- Sentence fragments and run-ons

- Double negatives

The SAT II Writing test does *not* cover:

- Spelling

- Punctuation

- Technical names of grammar and writing rules

Because of the limited material tested, and because you will never have to know grammar terms, you should not feel daunted or panicked as you set out to study for this test. In essence, the Writing test doesn't test your ability to understand grammar so much as it tests your ability to "hear" wrong grammar. You see, in order to do well on this test, you need to be able to identify only two things: sentences that sound strange, and sentences that sound right. On one section of the test, you'll have to know how to fix up a strange sentence so it sounds right. On the essay section, you'll have to know how to generate your own right sentences. If you can sniff out a bad sentence, you're well on your way to doing well on the Writing SAT II.

How Reading Trashy Magazines Will Help Your Score

The most important tool to cultivate before test day is your reading ear: you want to be able to "hear" errors as you read the test sentences. One excellent way to nurture your reading ear is to actually read. Regardless of whether you're looking at this book a year, a month, or a week before you plan to take the Writing SAT II, you should start reading for an hour every day. Reading instant messages, or reading the book you're assigned for English class as you simultaneously watch television—this kind of reading does not count. Read novels, or the newspaper; if you've had a terrible day and can't face the next chapter or the metro section, read a trashy magazine, but read it carefully and without distractions.

When you read something well-written, you see correct sentence structure and grammar over and over and over. Soon, correctly written sentences become familiar to you. After you read several thousand good sentences, a bad sentence will seem painfully obvious. That's the goal of all this reading: when you sit down to the Writing SAT II, you want to look at those sentences and see each error as quickly and clearly as if it were highlighted, italicized, and printed in bold.

Reading will also help you enormously on the essay. As you're writing the essay, if you have that good-sentence groove carved into your brain, all you have to do is model your sentence structure on all of the thousands of grammatically correct sentences you've read in your novels and magazines, and you'll be writing well.

General Format of the Writing SAT II

The Writing SAT II test is a one-hour-long test composed of one essay and 60 multiple-choice questions. The multiple-choice questions come in three types: 30 Identifying Sentence Error questions, 18 Improving Sentences questions, and 12 Improving Paragraphs questions. On the test, you'll encounter the different sections in the following order:

- The Essay
- 20 Identifying Sentence Error questions
- 18 Improving Sentences questions
- 12 Improving Paragraphs questions
- 10 Identifying Sentence Error questions

The Essay Section

You will have 20 minutes to plan and write one essay. After the 20 minutes are up, you will be forced to stop writing the essay, even if you're not done. If you finish writing the essay early, which is pretty unlikely, you can proceed right to the multiple-choice section of the test.

Introduction

The Multiple-Choice Questions

You will have 40 minutes to answer the 60 multiple-choice questions. In chapters to come, we will go over each of the three types of multiple-choice questions in great detail, discussing what material the different question types will cover, and the specific strategies to which each question type is vulnerable. For now, though, we just want to give you a rough idea of what the questions will look like. Below, you'll find a very brief overview of each type, including a sample question.

Identifying Sentence Errors

As the name implies, your sole task on this type of multiple-choice question involves finding errors. That's all you have to do. You don't have to fix the errors, name them, or do anything other than spot them. Commonly tested subjects on this section are subject-verb agreement and verb tense.

Questions will look like this:

> Even though the influx of people <u>has raised</u> rents citywide, <u>there is</u> many
>   (A)   (B)
>
> financial gains <u>to be had</u> from the new <u>residents</u>. <u>No error</u>
>   (C)   (D)   (E)

In this example, the correct answer is (B); the phrase *there is* uses a singular verb when it should use the plural verb *are* to match the plural subject *gains*. The original sentence has faulty subject-verb agreement.

Improving Sentences

Each question in the Improving Sentences section consists of a sentence with one portion underlined. You must decide if the underlined portion contains an error. If it does not, mark (A), no error. If it does, find the answer choice that corrects the problem.

Questions will look like this:

> In her excitement about her trip to Paris, Emily has studied French with great <u>enthusiasm, thus she completely neglects her Spanish class.</u>
>
> (A)   enthusiasm, thus she completely neglects her Spanish class.
> (B)   enthusiasm she completely neglects her Spanish class as a result.
> (C)   enthusiasm and thus has completely neglected her Spanish class.
> (D)   enthusiasm; her Spanish class neglected therefore.
> (E)   enthusiasm; her Spanish class is neglected by this.

The correct answer is (C). The original sentence is a run-on sentence, which (C) corrects by adding *and* as a conjunction.

Improving Paragraphs

For this type of question, you'll be given two short essays that are purportedly written by students. You'll read the essay and then answer six to eight questions about it. These questions fall under four categories:

1. sentence revision questions
2. sentence addition questions
3. sentence combination questions
4. analysis questions

We will show you an entire essay-and-questions sequence in the chapter devoted to Improving Paragraphs questions. Here we'll just show you some sample questions.

Sentence Revision

Which of the answer choices below is the best way of revising the underlined part of sentence 7 (reprinted below)?

Sentence Addition

Which of the sentences below, if added after sentence 10, would provide the best transition from the first paragraph to the second paragraph?

Sentence Combination

Which of the following is the best way to combine sentences 3 and 4 (reprinted below)?

Analysis

All of the following are techniques the writer uses EXCEPT:

Most Improving Paragraphs questions fall into the category of sentence revision, but most tests contain at least one question of each type.

Rules of the Test

In addition to the content and format of the test, there are some rules of the Writing SAT II that the directions will not tell you, but which are very important to know.

- **When taking the test, you can skip around between sections.** You must write the essay first, but after that, you can do the sections in any order you like. For example, if you find that the Identifying Sentence Error questions are easy for you, you can answer those thirty questions before turning to the Improving Sentences and Improving Paragraphs questions.

- **The questions on the test aren't organized by difficulty.** In other words, a difficult question about word choice might be followed by an easy question about subject-verb agreement.

- **All questions are worth the same number of points.** You will not get more points for answering a difficult question, or fewer points for answering an easy question.

These three rules greatly affect how you should approach the test. We will explain how and why in the next chapter, which discusses general strategy for the Writing SAT II, and also in the individual chapters that focus on each of the three different types of multiple-choice questions.

Scoring the SAT II Writing Test

As we said previously, because the SAT II Writing test contains an essay as well as multiple-choice questions, calculating your raw score for this test is a little more complicated than it is for other SAT II tests.

To calculate your total raw score for the Writing SAT II, you need to calculate your raw scores for the essay and for the multiple-choice, and then add the two together. Calculating your raw score for the multiple-choice is easy. Just follow the normal procedures:

$$\text{multiple-choice raw score } = \text{ # of correct answers} - \frac{\text{# of wrong answers}}{4}$$

Calculating your raw score is also easy. Take the grade that you receive on your essay, which can range between 2–12, and multiply that number by 3.43.

$$\text{essay raw score } = \text{ essay score} \times 3.43$$

The number 3.43 seems like a strange and arbitrary number, but the test writers use this multiplication by the number 3.43 to make the essay have the precise weight in your final score that they want.

Your total raw score is the sum of your multiple-choice raw score and essay raw score:

$$\text{Total Raw Score } = \text{ multiple-choice raw score} + \text{essay raw score}$$

ETS takes this raw score and converts it to a scaled score according to a special curve. We have included a generalized version of that curve in a table below. (Note that because ETS changes the curve slightly for each edition of the test, this table will be close to, but not exactly the same as, the table used by ETS.)

Raw Score	Scaled Score	Raw Score	Scaled Score	Raw Score	Scaled Score
90	800	55	650	21	450
89	800	54	640	20	440
88	800	53	640	19	440
87	800	52	630	18	430
86	800	51	630	17	430
85	800	50	620	16	420
84	800	49	610	15	420
83	800	48	600	14	410
82	800	47	600	13	410
81	790	46	590	12	400
80	790	45	590	11	400
79	790	44	580	10	390
78	780	43	570	9	390
77	780	42	570	8	380
76	770	41	560	7	380
75	770	40	560	6	370
74	760	39	550	5	370
73	760	38	540	4	360
72	750	37	540	3	360
71	740	36	530	2	350
70	740	35	530	1	340
69	730	34	520	0	340
68	720	33	520	−1	330
67	720	32	510	−2	320
66	710	31	510	−3	320
65	700	30	500	−4	310
64	700	29	490	−5	310
63	690	28	490	−6	300
62	690	27	480	−7	300
61	680	26	480	−8	290
59	670	25	470	−9	290
58	670	24	470	−10	280
57	660	23	460		
56	660	22	460		

You should use this chart to convert your raw score into a scaled score. In order to do so, you will have to grade your essay in some way. Perhaps a parent or teacher can help you, if you explain the criteria by which an essay is graded.

In addition to its function as a conversion table, this chart contains crucial information: it tells you that you can do very well on the Writing SAT II without writing a perfect essay or answering every question correctly. In fact, you could skip some questions and get some other questions wrong and still earn a "perfect" score of 800.

For example, in a test of 60 questions, you could score:

Score	Multiple-choice right	Multiple-choice wrong	Blank	Essay score
800	55	2	3	12
800	58	2	0	11
750	55	4	1	10
700	52	5	3	10
650	48	6	6	10
600	42	8	10	10
550	36	9	15	8

This chart should prove to you that when you're taking the test, you should not imagine your score plummeting with every question you can't confidently answer. You can do very well on this test without knowing or answering everything. The key is to follow a strategy that ensures that you will get to see and answer all the questions you can answer correctly, and then to intelligently guess on those questions about which you are a little unsure. We will discuss these strategies in the next chapter.

Strategies for the Writing SAT II

A MACHINE, NOT A PERSON, will score the multiple-choice questions on the Writing SAT II test. The tabulating machine sees only the filled-in ovals on your answer sheet and does not care how you came to these answers; it just impassively notes whether your answers are correct. So whether you knew the right answer immediately or just took a lucky guess, the machine will award you one point. It doesn't award extra points if you've spent a really long time getting the right answer. It doesn't award extra points if you managed to get a tricky question right. Think of the multiple-choice test as a message to you from the ETS: "We care only about your answers. We do not care about the work behind those answers."

So you should give ETS right answers, as many as possible, using whatever means possible. The Writing SAT II test not only allows you to show off your intelligence and your knowledge of writing, it allows you to show off your fox-like cunning by figuring out what strategies will allow you to best display that knowledge. Remember, the SAT II test is your tool to get into college, so treat it as your tool. It wants right answers? Give it right answers, by using whatever strategies you can.

Because the multiple-choice section of the SAT II Writing test actually contains three different types of questions, we cover type-specific strategies in the chapters devoted to the three different question types. But there are a number of strategies that apply to the entire test, and those will be covered in this chapter.

Avoid Carelessness

Avoiding carelessness probably sounds to you more like common sense than like a sophisticated strategy. We don't disagree. But it is amazing how a timed test can warp and mangle common sense.

There are two types of carelessness, both of which will cost you points. The first type of carelessness results from moving too fast, whether that speed is caused by overconfidence or fear. In speeding through the test, you make yourself vulnerable to misinterpreting the question, overlooking one of the answer choices, or simply making a careless mistake. As you take the test, make a conscious effort to approach the test calmly.

Whereas the first type of carelessness can be caused by overconfidence, the second type of carelessness results from frustration or lack of confidence. Some students take a defeatist attitude toward tests, assuming they won't be able to answer many of the questions. Such an attitude is a form of carelessness, because it causes the student to ignore reality. Just as the overconfident student assumes she can't be tricked and therefore gets tricked, the student without confidence assumes he can't answer questions and therefore gives up at the first sign of difficulty.

Both kinds of carelessness steal points from you. Avoid them.

Be Careful Gridding In Your Answers

The computer that scores SAT II tests is unmerciful. If you answered a question correctly, but somehow made a mistake in marking your answer grid, the computer will mark that question as wrong. If you skipped question 5, but put the answer to question 6 in row 5 and the answer to question 7 in row 6, etc., thereby throwing off your answers for an entire section . . . it gets ugly.

Some test-prep books advise that you fill in your answer sheet five questions at a time rather than one at a time. Some suggest that you do one question and then fill in the corresponding bubble. We think you should fill out the answer sheet whatever way feels most natural to you. Just make sure you're careful while doing it. In our opinion, the best way to ensure that you're being careful is to talk silently to yourself. As you figure out an answer in the test booklet and transfer it over to the answer sheet ovals, say to yourself: "Number 23, B. Number 24, E. Number 25, A."

Guessing and the Writing SAT II

Should you guess on the Writing SAT II? We'll begin to answer this question by posing a math question:

> Shakespeare is holding five cards, numbered 1–5. Without telling you, he has selected one of the numbered cards as the "correct" one. If you pick a single card, what is the probability that you will choose the "correct" card?

The answer is $\frac{1}{5}$, or 1 in 5. But the answer is only important if you recognize that the question precisely describes the situation you're in when you blindly guess the answer to any Writing SAT II question. When guessing blindly, you have a $\frac{1}{5}$ chance of getting the question right. If you were to guess on ten questions, you would, according to probability, get two questions right and eight questions wrong.

- 2 right answers gets you 2 raw points

- 8 wrong answers gets you $8 \times -\frac{1}{4} = -2$ raw points

Those ten answers, therefore, net you a total of 0 points. Blind guessing is a complete waste of time, which is precisely what ETS wants. They designed the scoring system to make blind guessing pointless.

Educated Guessing

But what if your guessing isn't blind? Suppose you're faced with this question:

> The yodelers <u>drew</u> lots of people, for <u>it</u> had never <u>appeared</u> on
>   (A)   (B)   (C)
> stage <u>before</u>. <u>No error</u>
>   (D)   (E)

Suppose that this question flummoxes you. The directions tell you to find the error in the sentence and pick the corresponding answer choice, but you can't seem to find the error. You stare at the question and realize that the only underlined word you confidently feel is correct is *before*. The other ones look like they might be wrong. Since you're almost certain *before* is correct, you eliminate (D). Once you've eliminated *before* as a possible answer, you have four choices from which to choose. Is it now worth it to guess? *Yes*. Probability states that if you are guessing between four choices you will get one question right for every three you get wrong. For that one correct answer you'll get 1 point, and for the three incorrect answers you'll lose a total of $\frac{3}{4}$ of a point.

$$1 - \frac{3}{4} = \frac{1}{4}$$

In other words, if you can eliminate one answer, the odds of guessing turn in your favor. You become more likely to gain points than to lose points.

The rule for guessing on the Writing SAT II, therefore, is simple: *if you can eliminate even one answer choice on a question, you should definitely guess.* And in the chapters that follow, we're going to outline plenty of strategies for eliminating at least one answer from each question.

If You're Stumped

If you cannot eliminate even one answer choice and find yourself staring at a certain question with mounting panic, throw a circle around that nasty question and move on. If you have time later, you can return to that question. Remember, answering a hard question correctly doesn't earn you any more points than answering an easy question correctly. You want to be sure to hit every easy question instead of running out of time by fixating on the really tough questions. While taking five minutes to solve a particularly difficult question might strike you as a moral victory when you're taking the test, quite possibly you could have used that same time to answer six other questions that would have vastly increased your score. Instead of getting bogged down on individual questions, you will do better if you learn to skip, and leave for later, the very difficult questions that you can't answer or that will take an extremely long time to answer.

Pacing

Good pacing allows you to take the test, rather than letting the test take you. As we said earlier, the questions on the Writing SAT II test are not organized by difficulty. You are as likely to come upon a question you can answer at the end of the test as at the beginning. As you take the test, part of your job is to make sure that you don't miss out on answering those questions near the end of the test that you could have answered if only you had more time.

By perfecting your pacing on practice tests, you can make sure that you will see every question on the test. And if you see every question on the test, then you can select which questions you will and won't answer, rather than running out of time before reaching the end of the test and therefore letting the test decide, by default, which questions you won't answer.

In large part, pacing yourself entails putting into practice the strategies we've already discussed:

- Make sure not to get bogged down on one single question. If you find yourself wasting time on one question, circle it, move on, and come back to it later.

- Answer every question for which you know the answer, and make an educated guess for every question for which you can quickly eliminate at least one answer choice.

Learning to pace yourself is a crucial part of your preparation for the test. Students who know how to pace themselves take the test on their own terms. Students who don't know how to pace themselves enter the test already one step behind.

Setting a Target Score

You can make the job of pacing yourself much easier if you go into the test knowing how many questions you have to answer correctly in order to earn the score you want. So, what score do you want? Obviously, you should strive for the best score possible, but also be realistic: consider how much you know about writing and how well you do, generally, on SAT-type tests. You should also consider what exactly defines a good score at the colleges to which you're applying: a 620? A 680? Talk to the admissions offices of the colleges you might want to attend, do a little research in college guidebooks, or talk to your guidance counselor. No matter how you do it, you should find out the average score of students at the schools you want to attend. Take that number and set your target score above it (you want to be above average, right?). Then take a look at this chart we showed you before.

Score	Multiple-choice right	Multiple-choice wrong	Blank	Essay score
800	55	2	3	12
800	58	2	0	11
750	55	4	1	10
700	52	5	3	10
650	48	6	6	10
600	42	8	10	10
550	36	9	15	8

So let's say the average score for the Writing SAT II for the school you want to attend is a 600. You should set your target at about 650. Looking at this chart, you can see that, to get that score, you need to get 48 questions right. You can get 6 questions wrong and leave 6 questions blank. You also need to get a 10 on the essay.

If you know all these numbers going into the test, you can pace yourself accordingly. You should use practice tests to teach yourself the proper pace—increasing your speed if you find that you aren't getting to answer all the questions you need to, or decreasing your pace if you find that you're rushing and making careless mistakes. If you reach your target score during preparation, give yourself a cookie and take a break for the day. But just because you hit your target score doesn't mean you should stop working altogether. In fact, you should view reaching your target score as a clue that you can do *better* than that score: set a new target 50–100 points above your original and work to pick up your pace a little bit and skip fewer questions.

By improving in manageable increments, you can slowly work up to your top speed, integrating your new knowledge of the test and how to take it without overwhelming yourself by trying to take on too much too soon. If you can handle working just a little faster without becoming careless and losing points, your score will certainly go up. If you meet your new target score again, repeat the process.

Strategies

SAT II

WRITING

REVIEW

The Essay

Unlike the rest of the Writing SAT II, the first twenty minutes of the test involve actual writing. In these twenty minutes, you will be presented with a rather general question and told to plan and write an essay. This essay portion of the exam is meant to test your ability to develop an idea over the course of a few paragraphs, using grammatical, clear prose.

The rest of this chapter will teach you how to write a good SAT II Writing test essay. Note that we said "a good SAT II Writing test essay" and not just "a good essay." The two are not quite the same thing. Good essays are as variable as snowflakes. But good SAT II Writing test essays are all very similar: the people who will read and grade your essay will be looking for precise and standard things. We will explain what those things are and show you how to give the graders exactly what they want.

The Twenty-Minute Essay

Twenty minutes is a ridiculously short amount of time in which to write an essay. In fact, we'll go on record as saying that it is impossible to write a great essay in twenty minutes. ETS knows this. They made the time allowed for essay writing so brief *because* they know this. They are creating a test that tests your ability to write, but they don't want to spend all the money it would take to hire graders to analyze and grade five-page essays. Never forget that while this essay portion of the SAT II Writing requires an essay, the essay it requires is designed by people who normally write formulaic multiple-choice questions. It should not come as any surprise that these people want the essays to be as formulaic as possible. So don't get cutesy with your essay; don't get super-creative; don't fly into flights of fancy. They want a solid essay written in a precise and particular way? Give it to them.

Essay Grades

After you've finished your test and handed it in, your multiple-choice answer sheet will be handed off to a scoring machine. Your essay, in contrast, will be graded by people. Two people, to be exact. Both of these people will read your essay and give it a score that ranges from 1 (worst) to 6 (best). The two grades are totaled, giving you a score from 2 to 12. (If the two graders give your essay grades that differ by more than two points, a third reader decides on the final score.) As the chart below indicates, your essay score counts for up to 200 of a possible 800 scaled points on the SAT II Writing.

Essay Score	Points Added to Your Scaled Score
4	40
6	80
8	120
10	160
12	200

How the Test Is Graded

So now you know the way the essay is scored. It is just as important to know who grades the test and under what conditions. If you know the process by which a test is graded, you can figure out what the graders are looking for.

As we told you, two people will read and grade your essay. Who are these two readers? They are harried high school or college teachers surrounded by thousands and thousands of test booklets. They have to read and grade these test booklets at lightning speed. In fact, these teachers hired by ETS have only three minutes to read each essay that comes into their hands. *Three minutes*! Simply because of the meager amount of time the teachers have to spend on each essay, you know two things:

1. These teachers are looking for very basic things: is your essay structured well? Is it well supported? Do the examples you use make sense? Generally, are your sentences grammatically correct? In fact, it is not a good idea to make very complicated arguments that might slow down a grader. The graders want to fly through your essay, and you should do whatever you can to help them along.

2. You have only a brief chance to make a good impression.

You can make the best overall impression by paying attention to both the big picture and the little picture. In terms of the big picture, it's crucial to make your reader feel he's in good hands by laying out a road map of the paper in your first paragraph and then by making each point very clearly as your paper develops. In terms of the little picture, it's important to write in clear, muscular, straightforward prose. Your readers will have neither the time nor the inclination to unravel an essay that makes its points subtly or wanders arbitrarily from paragraph to paragraph. They will not want to parse sentences that rely on jargon, or twist and turn and rattle on for line after line.

Holistic Grading

Creating a good overall impression will serve you particularly well because the reader is instructed to grade your essay holistically. Holistic grading means that the graders treat your essay as a whole. They don't go through the essay ticking off points for each misspelled word, each grammatical mistake, and each awkward phrase. Holistic grading means, quite simply, that the graders give your essay a grade based on their general impression of the essay. That's why they look at the big things: structure, organization, topic sentences, and prose clarity.

To make a decision about the quality of your essay, the grader looks for general patterns. If you misspell a word or two, but in general write with clear, concise, correctly-spelled prose, the grader will likely overlook your few mistakes. If you misplace a comma or spell a word wrong, it's not the end of the world. So relax.

Remember, the readers aren't looking for perfection. They don't expect perfection from an essay written in a 20-minute period. But they are looking for indications that if you were given more than 20 minutes, you would be able to write an excellent essay.

The Good News about Grading

What kind of essays get 6's? Whichever essays are the best ones that year. In other words, the readers are not comparing your essay to the writing of college students, graduate students, or professional writers and thinking, "This essay is not ready for publication in an academic journal, so it gets a 2." You'll be compared to your peers. The reader thinks something like, "This essay is good compared to the other essays I've been reading. I'll give it a 5." You can relax a little, knowing that the goal is to sound really smart and literate compared to your peers, not compared to some essay-writing god. And if you practice and follow the guidelines explained in this chapter, you *will* sound smarter and more literate than the other students in the room on test-taking day, many of whom will have done no preparation whatsoever.

The Directions

The directions for the essay section have two parts: The Topic, which is the essay subject given to you by the test, and the Standard Directions, which are the standard "how-to" directions for the section. The Topic is different on every test. The Standard Directions never change.

The Standard Directions

Get a firm grasp on the Standard Directions. Don't waste time reading these directions on the day of the test. Twenty minutes is not a very long time in which to write an essay, and there is no reason to waste time reading directions that never change.

> You have twenty minutes to plan and write an essay on the topic assigned below. DO NOT WRITE ON ANOTHER TOPIC. AN ESSAY ON ANOTHER TOPIC IS NOT ACCEPTABLE.
>
> The essay is assigned to give you an opportunity to show how well you can write. You should, therefore, take care to express your thoughts on the topic clearly and effectively. How well you write is much more important than how much you write, but to cover the topic adequately you will probably need to write more than one paragraph. Be specific.
>
> Your essay must be written on the lines provided on your answer sheet. You will receive no other paper on which to write. You will find that you have enough space if you write on every line, avoid wide margins, and keep your handwriting to a reasonable size. It is important to remember that what you write will be read by someone who is not familiar with your handwriting. Try to write or print so that what you are writing is legible to the reader.

These directions bring us to the crucial issue of . . .

Handwriting

Heavens, but these people are concerned with handwriting. Cast your mind back to that final paragraph of the directions—handwriting is mentioned no less than *three times*. This compulsive obsession with handwriting may sound superficial, but have some pity for the poor essay readers, cramped in their horrible essay-reading rooms, surrounded by thousands and thousands of test booklets. When they see an essay that looks like it was written by a drugged cockatoo, they will not bother to pore over each scribble. They will read as much as they can easily decipher and slap on a grade—a grade that probably does not fairly reflect the content of the essay.

So write neatly.

And Remember, When They Use Capital Letters . . .

They mean it. When they say, "DO NOT WRITE ON ANOTHER TOPIC. AN ESSAY ON ANOTHER TOPIC IS NOT ACCEPTABLE," they want you to sit up and take notice. So (obvious point alert) don't write on another topic. Also, be sure you're writing an *essay*. Do not try to charm the readers by writing something unique. No short stories. No epic poems. No masques in the style of Milton. Your creativity must find its outlet within the confines of the SAT II essay format.

A Note on Length

The directions would have you believe that length matters not a whit in comparison to content. Don't believe the directions. Length is important. You need to prove to the readers that you didn't spend fifteen minutes picking your cuticles and writing an invitation list for your toga party, and five minutes writing two skimpy paragraphs.

So how long does the essay have to be? Four paragraphs. Five paragraphs if you have the time. You need an introductory paragraph, two or three paragraphs that use examples to prove your point (more on examples later in the chapter), and a concluding paragraph.

The Topic

The essay directions will present you with a broad statement about morality or values and ask you to take a stance on the topic and back up that stance with examples. The statement will be something like "good people are those who help the weak" or "in times of war, conventional morals should no longer apply."

You don't get to choose between different topics. ETS gives you one topic, and that's the one you must write on. The Topic will be presented in one of three different ways:

The Essay

1. The Two-Statement Topic

Consider carefully the following statements. Then plan and write your essay as directed.

"The government should never limit personal freedoms."

"In some cases, it is necessary for the government to limit personal freedoms."

<u>Assignment</u>: In an essay, discuss <u>one</u> of the two statements above, supporting your views with an example or examples from science, art, history, literature, current events, or your own experience or observation.

2. The Single-Statement Topic

Consider the following statement and assignment. Then write an essay as directed.

"True love can overcome all obstacles."

<u>Assignment</u>: Choose one example from personal experience, current events, or history, literature, or any other discipline and use this example to write an essay in which you agree or disagree with the statement above. Your essay should be specific.

3. The Fill-in-the-Blank Topic

Consider the following statement and assignment. Then write an essay as directed.

"'Failure often teaches more than success can.' For me, an experience that proves this quote true happened when____."

<u>Assignment</u>: Write an essay that completes the statement above. Explain the reasons behind your choice.

You should approach each of the three Topic formats in a slightly different way. However, a few basic rules apply to all three formats. We'll talk about the basic scheme first, and then get into the more Topic-specific tips.

How to Write the Essay

Before you start writing your essay, you must think about its structure. Structure refers to the overall arc of your essay, the way it moves from idea to idea in order to prove a point. It is crucial to consider the arc of your essay first. If you just plunge in and start writing, you're like a foolhardy explorer who walks into a forest and wanders around helpless, cold, and hungry. However, if you think about your entire essay before you start, you're like a *smart* explorer who examines maps and aerial photos before walking into the woods, and who makes it out alive and well on the other side, toting a cauldron of leprechaun gold.

Good structure involves understanding the Topic, taking a stance, coming up with good examples, and making an outline.

Understanding the Topic

The first step to writing a successful essay is to read the Topic with extreme care. Yes, that sounds like a painfully obvious point, but it's a crucial one. Suppose the Topic says, "Censorship can never be justified." Often, Topics on this test include words like *censorship*, *justice*, *morals*, *evil*—words that you've heard many thousands of times, whose definitions seem obvious. It's exactly these seemingly obvious words that can trip you up on the essay. These words cover large, unwieldy concepts, and often lure test-takers into vagueness. If you don't *really think* about what you mean by *censorship*, you can find yourself with an assortment of paragraphs that are sort of about censorship, but also sort of about free speech, and how nice it is to live in a democratic country, and the excellence of freedom of religion.

Don't launch into your essay until you've narrowed and pinned down the topic you are going to focus on. If your topic is censorship, decide what kind of censorship you're talking about. Are you talking about censorship of the arts? Censorship of things like pornography and hate speech? Censorship in democratic countries? Censorship in undemocratic countries? Carve down the topic into something concrete and manageable.

Taking a Stance

Once you've thought hard about the Topic, you must take a stance on that Topic. There is no place for wishy-washiness in the Writing SAT II. As open-minded and I-can-see-your-point as you may be in real life, when you're writing this essay, you must take a side. Do you agree with the Topic statement, or do you disagree with it? Do not write an essay that argues one side of the issue for a few paragraphs, then grinds to a halt, spins around, and says, "on the other hand, there are many reasons why the opposite argument makes sense." Be firm. Decide if you want to agree or disagree with the Topic statement, and make your position clear to the reader.

Generating Good Examples

Once you've thought about the Topic and decided what stance you'll take on it, it's example time. Before you start writing the essay, you need to generate examples that are concrete, specific, and impressive.

Think of the examples as an opportunity to impress the readers. Bowl them over with examples from history, current events, literature, or the arts. Examples from your personal life will not impress them nearly as much as will your searing insights on the

Battle of Lexington and Concord, the novel *Things Fall Apart*, or the advisability of drilling for oil in wildlife preserves. Personal examples are okay in a pinch, but avoid using them if you can. If you have time to write a third example paragraph, and the history-current event-literature-art well has run dry, you can resort to that touching story about your granny.

Before the day of the test, think of a few examples—current and historical events, novels, or artists—that already interest you and about which you can write in reasonable detail. There's no need to make extra work for yourself by dreaming up boring examples that you'll have to research. Chances are at least a couple of the examples you prepare will work for the essay. Say you just read *Little Women* for school, liked the book, and paid a reasonable amount of attention in class. Great! You now know enough about the book to use it as an example. Of course, you'll have to tweak your example to fit the Topic. If the Topic statement says, "The strong always bully the weak," talk about Mr. March running through his family's money. If the Topic is "Some say that students are their own best teachers. Some say traditional learning is best," talk about Amy's attempt to teach herself about art in Italy. Tailor your example to fit the essay.

Writing an Outline

If you spend four or five minutes jotting down an outline, actually writing the essay will be much easier. Force yourself to think through the beginning, middle, and end of the essay before you put pen to paper. If you know where you're going with the essay before you start it, you're less likely to waste time and ink hemming and hawing, wandering off on tangents, or writing paragraphs that you belatedly realize you don't really need. Second, even if you've thought through the essay before you begin to write, by the time you come to the end of the first paragraph, you may find you've forgotten all about the structure that seemed so clear only five minutes earlier. Jotting down an outline will make you feel calm, and it will keep you on track as you write.

Your outline need not be involved. You don't need to write a sentence, or even a phrase, for each paragraph—just scribble down a few words reminding yourself of what you want each paragraph to say.

Writing on the Topic: Three Approaches

The three different ways ETS presents the Topic require three slightly different approaches. Let's go through them one by one.

The Two-Statement Topic

Here's the typical Two-Statement Topic we showed you earlier:

> Consider carefully the following statements. Then plan and write your essay as directed.
>
> "The government should never limit personal freedoms."
> "In some cases, it is necessary for the government to limit personal freedoms."
>
> <u>Assignment</u>: In an essay, discuss <u>one</u> of the two statements above, supporting your views with an example or examples from science, art, history, literature, current events, or your own experience or observation.

Understand the Topic

First, as always, make sure you understand the Topic. Here, the important phrase to consider is *personal freedoms*. This phrase demands interpretation. ETS chooses the general topic for you, but personal freedoms is a broad concept, and it's up to you to narrow it. Maybe you want to discuss the freedoms mentioned in the Constitution—bearing arms, assembling, speaking freely. Maybe you want to discuss freedom from governmental prying. Whatever personal freedoms you end up writing about, it is crucial to think about and narrow the Topic before you do anything else.

Pick a Statement

The Two-Statement Topic asks you to discuss one of the two statements, so after chewing on the terms of the Topic for a moment, you'll need to decide which statement you'd rather defend. You certainly don't have to defend the statement you actually support; pick whichever statement you think you can defend more successfully. Think of yourself as a lawyer equally skilled at defending both the clients you admire and believe in, and the clients you despise and find odious. Even if, in your innermost soul, you think the government should never limit personal freedoms, you don't necessarily have to defend the corresponding statement. If you think you could do a better job defending the statement you don't actually support—that government should sometimes limit personal freedoms—by all means, defend that one.

Choose Example(s)

In the case of the Two-Statement Topic, it's often a good idea to use two or three different examples. The directions ask you to "support your views with an example or examples from science, art, history, literature, current events, or your own experience or observation." This laundry list of suggested topics implies that multiple examples are welcome.

Write an Outline

Suppose you decide to defend the first Topic statement: "The government should never limit personal freedoms." You narrow the idea of personal freedoms to include only freedom of speech. You think of a few examples: Martin Luther King, Jr., and Jerry Falwell. Your outline will sketch out what you want each paragraph to prove. The outline might look something like this:

> intro: gov't shouldn't limit freedoms, esp. freedom of speech, b/c it would impede progress
>
> 1st paragraph: MLK Jr. wasn't silenced by gov't even tho. his views were controversial
>
> 2nd paragraph: Jerry Falwell offensive but important for him to have free speech or where do we draw the line?
>
> Conclusion: even if views are offensive to some, free speech necessary

This outline doesn't make a heck of a lot of sense, but it made sense to whoever wrote it, which is the sole purpose of an outline. No one will judge you on the clarity and beauty of your outline. It is for your sole benefit.

Write the Essay

Your first paragraph should start with a fairly broad sentence that lets the reader know, in general terms, what the essay will be about. The second and third sentences should narrow that topic and clearly lay out the main idea of the paper.

The second paragraph should begin by introducing the first example and explaining how it relates to your main idea. The body of the second paragraph should develop the example. Try to provide interesting and relevant details about the example, instead of talking about it in vague terms.

The third paragraph should begin by introducing the second example and explaining how it relates to your main idea. Like the second paragraph, the body of the third paragraph should develop the example by using interesting and relevant details.

The final paragraph, which need be no longer than two or three sentences, should provide a small summary, and should synthesize the information in some slightly new way. Do not use the final paragraph to simply repeat what you've said elsewhere in the essay. Try to broaden the scope just a little bit in the last paragraph.

Sample Essay

As you read this sample essay, pay attention to its structure, organization, examples, and prose. Look for the ways in which the essay is successful, and the places where it might need improvement. Our analysis follows the essay.

One of the benefits that Americans enjoy is the freedom of speech. Free speech is one of the most treasured personal freedoms we possess. The United States government must never limit freedom of speech, even when those speaking have a controversial or upsetting message. To limit freedom of speech would be to impede progress.

Martin Luther King, Jr. had a message that upset many people. He said, in his famous "I Have a Dream" speech, that we should judge people "not by the color of their skin but by the content of their character." He also said that black people's justifiable indignation should not lead to violence. Both of these ideas, especially the first, seem like conventional wisdom today. There is hardly anyone who would say that we should judge men and women by the color of their skin rather than the content of their character. And most people agree that nonviolent protest is the answer, rather than responding to bad treatment with physical retaliation. But at the time, Martin Luther King Jr.'s message was extremely controversial. Many people objected to the idea of equality for blacks and whites; many people objected to the idea that protest should be nonviolent. But rather than censor King, the government let him speak. In fact, King delivered his stirring "I Have a Dream" speech while standing on the steps of the Lincoln Memorial in Washington, D.C., in the heart of the government. Because he was not silenced by the government, King was able to make a huge contribution to the civil rights movement. Our nation became more morally sound because he was able to express his ideas freely.

Jerry Falwell is on the opposite end of the spectrum. He preaches messages that strike many people as full of hate and anger. He often speaks against women and homosexuals. But even though many people disagree with what Falwell stands for, the government cannot interfere with his right to free speech. He has a right to express his opinions, unpopular as those opinions may be. And even though his attitudes may be objectionable, good can come of them. Some people, when they hear his angry message, are motivated to speak out in favor of tolerance and acceptance. This speaking out may have a positive effect. So in the end, if the government limited someone like Falwell in his ability to speak freely, it would also be limiting the counterattacks of groups that work for love and tolerance. Paradoxically, objectionable speech can lead to progress.

If we want to move forward as a country, we must let everyone, inspiring or offensive, have their say. Inspiring speech leads to progress and so, less obviously, does offensive speech.

The Essay

Essay Analysis

This essay is quite good, and would probably receive a combined score of 11 or 12. It has a few problems here and there, but for the most part it is well-developed, features an interesting and readable argument, and uses clear, grammatical language.

The essay is a bit vague at the outset; the sentence *To limit freedom of speech would be to impede progress*, sort of makes sense, but what the writer has in mind is not exactly clear. However, the examples clarify the writer's main point. This initial vagueness is not the end of the world, for the readers do understand that the main idea of your paper will probably become more and more clear to you as you write. Still, you should strive to explain your main idea in all its fully developed glory right from the outset. Some students don't want to "give away" the gist of their essay right off the bat, but please: give it away. The reader does not want to be mystified, the reader wants to know immediately what you're trying to say.

There are a few minor problems with the essay. In the first paragraph, the word *freedom* gets repeated too much, in various incarnations. It's hard to avoid repeating the Topic statement over and over, but do try to find synonyms. Repetition is boring for the reader.

There are a few awkward phrasings in the second paragraph. This sentence is probably the worst offender: *And most people agree that nonviolent protest is the answer, rather than responding to bad treatment with physical retaliation*. It's never a great idea to start a sentence with *And*. Also, although it's possible to figure out the meaning of the sentence, it's a lot of work for the reader. A better way to phrase it would be: "Most people agree that it's better to respond to bad treatment with nonviolent protest than with physical retaliation."

The Jerry Falwell example works fairly well, although criticizing someone's politics, as this writer does, is always risky. It's possible that you'll get a rabid Republican reader, or a Democrat who foams at the mouth when he hears the word "conservative," so be aware that it's never absolutely safe to express political opinions. You risk annoying your reader with your politics. This writer does a minimally acceptable job of sounding neutral; he or she throws in lots of phrases like *to some people* to indicate that some people do like Falwell. Despite these diplomatic phrases, however, it's blatantly obvious that he or she is not a Falwell supporter. This is fine, but indicating your politics is a calculated risk.

The last paragraph does a nice job of tying together the essay, bringing all the points and examples into a strong conclusion.

The Single-Statement Topic

Consider the following statement and assignment. Then write an essay as directed.

"True love can overcome all obstacles."

<u>Assignment</u>: Choose one example from personal experience, current events, or history, literature, or any other discipline and use this example to write an essay in which you agree or disagree with the statement above. Your essay should be specific.

Understand the Topic

True love is the big, abstract idea in this statement. *True love* is probably an easier phrase to understand and narrow than others you'll encounter. Still, even when the topic includes phrases you've heard a million times, give some thought to how you'll hone the idea. In this case, you could do something slightly different by talking about, for example, the true love of a mother for her child—or you could stick with the more obvious interpretation and write about young lovers.

Choose an Example

The Single-Statement Topic specifically asks you to write about one example. If you can, generate an example from the arts, literature, or history.

When coming up with an example, try to avoid the most obvious ones. For instance, did you read *true love* and instantly think *Romeo and Juliet*? If that's the first work of literature that popped into mind, then chances are it also popped into the minds of thousands and thousands of other test-takers. If you can't think of anything else, it's okay to write about *R&J*, but the readers are probably going to see a couple of hundred essays that use that play as an example. Using *R&J* is dangerous for two reasons: first, the readers will be sick of hearing about the balcony scene and the feuding families. Second, since they're reading tons of essays on the same play, they will be intimately familiar with that play. This means that if you fudge a little on the details because you read *R&J* three years ago, that fudging might be obvious to the readers, because they can compare your essay to the six essays by people who read the play last Tuesday. If you write about *Middlemarch*, on the other hand, they might not be quite as quick to catch your minor slipups, and they will certainly be relieved to hear about Dorothy and Mr. Casaubon instead of Ms. Capulet and Mr. Montague. So try to choose examples that are slightly off the beaten path.

A personal example is usually less desirable than an example from history, literature, or the arts. This particular Topic presents a dangerous example pitfall: it has to do with true love, and some people will be tempted to tell their personal tales of true love. This could be disastrous. Your boyfriend or girlfriend probably should not make an appearance in the essay. Valiantly as you try to keep the tone objective and disinterested, chances are the essay will get mushy, angry, or weepy.

The Essay

Write an Outline

Suppose you decide to write about *Othello*. Your outline might look like this:

intro paragraph: true love can't conquer all

2nd paragraph: o. and d. really love each other

3rd paragraph: but race class age differences drive them apart—Iago uses differences against them

conclusion: jealousy + real diffs can ruin true love

Write the Essay

The Single-Statement Topic essay does not differ very much from the two-statement Topic essay in its execution. Like the Two-Statement, the Single-Statement essay should introduce the main idea and develop it by use of an example or multiple examples.

Sample Essay

As you read, think about what elements of the essay are successful and what elements could be improved upon.

> Although it is a cliché of popular culture that love conquers all, this is not always the case. In Shakespeare's play <u>Othello</u>, for example, Desdemona and Othello truly love one another, but their love cannot survive the influence of an evil man. Iago takes advantage of the differences in Othello's and Desdemona's class, race, age, and social rank, and shatters what seems to be a perfect marriage.
>
> Desdemona and Othello truly love one another. They dote on each other. She loves the fact that he has had many adventures and has seen strange things and can tell wonderful tales about his adventures. He loves her spirit and beauty. They can hardly stand to be apart from one another. They treat each other with respect and affection.
>
> It is unclear what motivates Iago to wreck Othello's love for Desdemona. Whether from jealousy, cruelty, boredom, or the desire to control other people, Iago turns Othello against Desdemona by suggesting that Desdemona has been unfaithful. Although Desdemona is innocent of any crime, and Iago has no evidence to bring against her, he manages to convince Othello that he has been cheated on. But it is not just Iago's cruelty that ruins true love; Iago can only convince Othello that Desdemona has strayed by highlighting the differences between the lovers. He reminds Othello that Desdemona is younger. She is a nobleman's daughter, where as Othello is a general who did well but did not come from money or class. Desdemona is white, and Othello is black. Iago plays on this difference in the first scene, using racist language to suggest that Othello and Desdemona's love is like two animals having sex, because of their different races.
>
> Shakespeare seems to be suggesting that even for a couple as in love as Othello and Desdemona, disaster can strike. He tells us that pure evil (Iago) can ruin a marriage, but so, perhaps, can the mismatched coupling of rich and poor, white and black, young and old. In <u>Othello</u>, Shakespeare describes the cynical real world we live in, not the fairy tale of modern movies that pretend love can conquer all.

Discussion

This essay would probably get a 10; it might get an 11 or 12 if both readers were feeling generous. The example works, and the writing is good. The main difficulty with this essay is that its thesis is a bit too complicated for the time and space constraints. The writer argues that Iago takes advantage of preexisting differences between Othello and Desdemona, but he or she never decides whether Iago could have split up the happy couple even if they had been from exactly the same class and race, or if their differences would have broken up their marriage even if Iago didn't exist.

The essay works for the most part, but it is a bit ambitious for this space. Small problems of grammar and syntax pop up here and there. For example, these two sentences are repetitious: *Desdemona and Othello truly love one another. They dote on each other.* One or the other would suffice. Ambiguous pronouns become a problem in the phrase *manages to convince Othello that he has been cheated on*; Iago manages to convince Othello that who has been cuckolded? We can figure out the meaning from the context, but that *he* should be *Othello*.

This is a strong essay, but remember, the readers won't necessarily reward the most complex argument; they will welcome a simple argument that is made well and clearly.

The Fill-in-the-Blank Topic

Consider the following statement and assignment. Then write an essay as directed.

"'Failure often teaches more than success can.' For me, an experience that proves this quote true happened when___."

Assignment: Write an essay that completes the statement above. Explain the reasons behind your choice.

Understand the Topic

This step is often pretty easy for Fill-in-the-Blank Topics. This particular Topic leaves some room for interpretation—are you going to talk about a moral failure? A more prosaic failure to do with the classroom or the playing field?—but the basic components, failure and success, aren't as difficult to grasp as something like personal freedoms or censorship.

Choose an Example

This is perhaps the most important step for Fill-in-the-Blank Topics, especially personal Fill-in-the-Blank Topics. Choosing a good personal example is an art. You don't want to sound prim and self-righteous; the reader will see right through an essay about how you learned a lot from your failure to save more than six people from a burning building. At the same time, you don't want to be honest to the point of self-defeat; it's a bad idea to write an essay about your failure to kick your shoplifting habit.

The readers are instructed to grade the essay on the quality of your writing, and not on its topic. But since the readers grade essays based on their holistic impression, it's not a good idea to leave a bad taste in their mouths by showing yourself in a very negative light.

Write an Outline

Personal essays can, like double- or single-statement essays, introduce a main idea and then explain it by elaborating on examples. For example, suppose you decide to write about how you learned a lot from your failure to win the race for class president. Your outline could follow the traditional main idea–elaboration model:

> intro paragraph: I learned popularity isn't everything
>
> 2nd paragraphs: students know experience is more important than popularity—they elected more experienced candidate
>
> 3rd paragraph: students reward hard work; the winning candidate deserved to win
>
> conclusion: learned about myself & how people viewed me

An alternate type of personal essay can tell a story. Instead of presenting the main idea right away, it's permissible when writing a personal essay to build suspense by revealing your main idea at the end of the essay, rather than at the beginning. Here's an outline for a personal essay that tells a story.

> intro paragraph: worst day of sophomore year was election day
>
> 2nd paragraph: I was popular, well-liked, should have won
>
> 3rd paragraph: realized that Mike won because he had more experience. Vowed to improve myself
>
> conclusion: I learned that popularity isn't everything

Write the Essay

The following sample essay breaks the mold a bit by telling a story in chronological order and stating the main idea at the end, rather than the beginning.

Sample Essay

I listened to the principal's voice in disbelief: "Mike Pacelli has won the election! Let's give a round of applause to your new class president." For a moment I thought that the principal had made a mistake. He wasn't supposed to be announcing Mike Pacelli as the new president; he was supposed to be saying *my* name. I could feel people around me looking at me with pity. It was all I could do not to burst into tears.

I had failed to win the election. It was sophomore year, and I was in shock. I had been convinced I would win by a landslide. After all, I was one of the most popular kids in school. Everyone wanted to come to my house after school, everyone screamed for me when I took the field as the goalie on the soccer team, everyone even copied what I wore. And who was Mike? I thought to myself, nobody. Sure, he'd been on the student council for years, but so what? No one like me had run against him before. I decided to join the student council as a volunteer, just to see what he had that I didn't have.

I was prepared to hate Mike, but after just a few months, I had learned more about myself from him than I ever have from anyone else. I watched him run the student council, organize events, suggest fundraisers for charity, earn money for the new auditorium—he knew how to organize and motivate people, something I realized I knew nothing about. His previous three years of experience made a huge difference, and I soon saw that I was a novice next to him. Not only that, he was genuinly nice to everyone. He didn't pick and chose who he wanted to hang out with him, the way I know I did. I saw that people came to him with problems and were much more relaxed around him than they were around me. I started to question a lot about myself. I saw why he had been elected; he deserved to be class president.

What at first seemed like a failure was actually one of the luckiest things that has ever happened to me. Yes, I failed to win the election, but because I lost I changed alot of things about myself. I made a real effort not to be snobby, and I stopped taking so many things for granted. I have a more realistic opinion of myself now, and I look up to Mike as someone I can still learn from.

Discussion

This essay would probably earn a 10 or an 11. The writer develops his story nicely, leading us through the paragraphs and keeping us interested; he starts the essay with a mildly compelling "hook," and by the end of the essay we get the main idea: popularity isn't everything, and he's a changed man.

There's something smug about the example; first we think the writer's kind of a jerk, and then we think he might be lying about how much he's changed. Still, the example works pretty well. The failure involved doesn't cast the writer in a bad light, and the lesson learned is a valuable one.

Issues of grammar and syntax: generally, the essay is light in tone and word choice. This is acceptable, because the topic is light. There are a few misspellings: *genuinly* should be *genuinely*, *chose* should be *choose*, and *alot* should be *a lot*.

The strongest element of this essay is its readability. The readers will have no problem zipping through this essay and understanding the point being made. Readability is of the utmost importance.

Writing Good Sentences

Now that we've talked about both a basic approach and a more individualized approach to the three Topics, we're going to get to the nitty-gritty of sentence construction, such as how to use apostrophes and quotation marks correctly, and how to avoid writing run-on sentences and fragments. We're also going to show you how to avoid common pitfalls like inappropriate tone, clichés, and wishy-washiness.

Learning how to get the tone right might take more work than learning how to use apostrophes correctly, but the issues we're about to discuss are crucial to making a great quick impression. You'll impress the heck out of the reader by being that rare writer who doesn't litter his or her prose with clichés or write in an overblown, faux-academic tone.

Good Grammar

There's no time or space in this book to teach you all the rules of grammar. But we can point out to you the most important rules of writing and grammar that people frequently break while writing. These rules are the backbone of good writing. They transform soggy sentences into models of clear, powerful prose.

The Passive Voice and Active Voice

People seem to think that the passive voice provides prose with a sophisticated remove, the type of prose an English butler might write. But the passive voice is actually dull and pale.

The passive voice avoids naming the performer of an action. Unless the performer of an action is unknown or unimportant, always use the active rather than the passive voice. Look at the following sentences for an example of this problem:

- **Wrong:** *The sequined bell-bottoms were chosen by Mike.*

- **Right:** *Mike chose the sequined bell-bottoms.*

In the first sentence, we don't know until the last word who chose the bell-bottoms. In the sentence that uses the active voice, we know immediately that Mike did the choosing.

The passive voice always forces you to use bland forms of the verb *to be: is, are, was,* and *were.* Avoiding the passive voice will make your writing more interesting and vivid, clarifying who is doing what, and allowing you to use interesting, strong verbs.

Passive verb use sometimes occurs when writers begin writing sentences without a clear idea of where the sentences are going. Try to hear the entire sentence in your head before you begin writing.

Avoid Using the Verb *To Be*

As we just said, the verb *to be* is fairly weak and boring. In addition to avoiding the passive voice, eliminate that bland verb *to be* from your writing as much as possible. Certainly, the verb *to be* must be used when no other verb can take its place. But a great deal of the time people use *to be* when unnecessary, leading to boring sentences like:

> *Dina was laughing in the kitchen.*

This sentence is grammatically correct, but a much more colorful version follows when you eradicate the verb *to be* and replace it with other, more action-oriented verbs:

> *Dina snorted and squealed with laughter in the kitchen.*

Use Transitions

Transitions are the sentences or words that provide the context necessary to help readers understand the flow of your argument. Transitions should take the reader gently by the hand, shepherding him through your essay. A well-placed phrase can serve as an excellent transition from sentence to sentence.

- **Showing Contrast:** *Katie likes pink nail polish. In contrast, she thinks red nail polish looks trashy.*

- **Elaborating:** *I love sneaking into movies. In addition, I try to steal candy while I'm there.*

- **Providing an Example:** *If you save up your money, you can afford pricey items. For example, Patrick saved up his allowance and eventually purchased a Boxter.*

- **Showing Results**: *Manny ingested nothing but soda and burgers every day for a month. As a result, he gained ten pounds.*

- **Showing Sequence:** *The police arrested Bob at the party. Soon after, Harvard rescinded Bob's offer of acceptance, and eventually Bob drifted into a life of crime.*

Avoid Run-On Sentences

Teachers hate run-on sentences, and for good reason: a student who writes run-on sentences shows a fundamental failure to grasp proper grammar.

A run-on sentence occurs when two independent clauses are connected without any punctuation mark or conjunction between them. Essentially, an independent clause is a fully expressed idea containing a verb and subject, which is not dependent on any other idea for its existence. Look at the following run-on:

> *I wanted to leave work early I couldn't because my boss was hovering over me.*

In the example sentence, *I wanted to leave work early* and *I couldn't because my boss was hovering over me* are both independent clauses. Each contains a subject and each contains a verb. Therefore, they cannot be joined together without a conjunction or punctuation mark.

There are two ways to fix a run-on sentence: place a conjunction between the clauses, or separate the clauses with punctuation.

To fix the example sentence using a conjunction, add a comma and the conjunction *but* between the two clauses.

> *I wanted to leave work early, but I couldn't because my boss was hovering over me.*

To fix the run-on with punctuation, add a semicolon or period.

> *I wanted to leave work early; I couldn't because my boss was hovering over me.*

> *I wanted to leave work early. I couldn't because my boss was hovering over me.*

If you have a good understanding of what a run-on sentence is, you can train yourself to avoid writing them. You should also be able to "hear" run-on sentences: they make writing sound breathless and rushed, like a babbling child.

Avoid Sentence Fragments

Sentence fragments are the opposite of run-on sentences. Run-ons are two sentences that the writer has tried to mush into one. A sentence fragment is a non-sentence that the writer is trying to pass off as a sentence. A sentence fragment has a subject, but not a correctly conjugated verb.

Sentence fragments can be difficult to recognize. They are so prevalent in advertising that they begin to seem correct:

- **Wrong:** *The platinum watch only millionaires can afford.*

The subject *watch* and the verb *afford* don't go together correctly. *Only millionaires can afford* is actually an adjectival phrase modifying the subject *watch*. Within the phrase, *afford* is connected to the noun *millionaires*. To fix this problem, you can add a properly conjugated noun:

- **Right:** *The platinum watch only millionaires can afford appears on page 6 of the magazine.*

Or you could reorganize the sentence so that *millionaires* becomes the subject and *afford* its correctly conjugated verb:

- **Right:** *Only millionaires can afford the platinum watch.*

Be particularly wary of writing sentence fragments when you begin a sentence with words like *between, before, although, while,* etc. These words have a way of leading to incomplete sentences.

- **Wrong:** *Because I say so.*

- **Right:** *Because I say so, you have to make your bed.*

- **Wrong:** *Between the third and fourth quarters, the cheerleaders that pranced out onto the parquet and did their routine.*

- **Right:** *Between the third and fourth quarters, the cheerleaders pranced out onto the parquet and did their routine.*

Proper Use of Basic Punctuation Marks

The readers of your essay will lower your grade if you show a pattern of grammatical errors. Since punctuation is an omnipresent feature in writing, misunderstanding a simple rule of punctuation leads to numerous errors and suggests that you know less than you do. Be sure to understand the basic rules of punctuation usage.

Commas

Commas exist to help the reader. Often they mark pauses you would naturally make if speaking the sentence aloud. Commas are used for a variety of reasons: to tell the reader to pause, to set off words that interrupt, to set off words not crucial to the meaning of the sentence, and to join two sentences with a conjunction. They are also used in series, in dialogue, and to set off introductory remarks.

- **Telling the Reader to Pause:** *Because Mike spilled his popcorn, the other moviegoers laughed at him.*

- **Setting Off Words that Interrupt:** *Jane, on the other hand, has never worked as a rodeo clown.*

- **Setting off Words Not Crucial to the Sentence's Meaning:** *The donut, which had been left on the counter for six days, began to smell funny.*

- **Joining Two Sentences with and, but, for, or, not:** *I wanted to go skydiving, but my mom put her foot down.*

- **After Introductory Words:** *Well, I think you're wrong about Prince.*
  No, I refuse to go to the prom with you.
  Before rollerblading, Sam ate a meatball sub.

Writing Lists

People often make comma errors when writing out lists. Commas belong only in the middle of lists, not before them (as in the first wrong sentence below) or after them (as in the second wrong sentence).

- **Wrong:** *We want, pineapples, ham, red peppers, and garlic on our pizza.*

- **Wrong:** *We want pineapples, ham, red peppers, and garlic, on our pizza.*

- **Right:** *We want pineapples, ham, red peppers, and garlic on our pizza.*

Writing dialogue

It may strike you as a little peculiar, but if you have something like *he said* or *she sighed* or *they yelled* after a piece of dialogue, you have to punctuate the dialogue with a comma, not a period. You can see why this is the rule if you look at the following sentence.

> *"Get back here." he said.*

When you hit that period after "*Get back here*" you stop; then you have to lurch back into action with *he said*. The correct formulation is:

> *"Get back here," he said.*

Semicolons

Semicolons signal a big pause. You must have two sentences on either side of a semicolon. People get this wrong a lot, so be careful. Use a semicolon in place of a period or in place of a conjunction.

- **In Place of a Period, When Two Ideas are Closely Connected:** *Alex spent his summer working at the diner; his friends came in all the time and demanded free fries.*

- **In Place of Conjunctions Like** *and, or, but,* **and** *because*: *I don't know if I want to go to Jones Beach; I'm not really in the mood for sweaty masses of people.*

Colons

Colons are used to signal definitions, commands, and lists.

- **To signal a definition:** *Hookah: a curved pipe used by a character in Alice in Wonderland.*

- **To signal a command:** *You must do as follows: turn around, and walk away.*

- **To signal a list:** *I'll tell you what I did this morning: watched cartoons, ate a leftover piece of pizza, and got in a fight with Jason.*

Using the Proper Tone

The tone of your essay is almost as important as its grammar. The tone you adopt can dramatically affect the experience of your reader. It can confuse your reader, make her trust you, or set her teeth on edge. Your grade is dependent on the impression you make, and the tone you choose will affect that impression.

You should try to write in the voice you'd use to talk to your friend's mom—a little formal, but comfortable and natural. Avoid a weighty academic tone, which will likely come off as false or pretentious rather than impressive. Similarly, don't use a casual email style. Spell words formally—no *lite* as in *Miller Lite*, no *b/c* in place of *because*. Here are some other rules of tone:

Avoid Clichés

Clichés make your writing sound trite, dull, and unimaginative. You know that person who says, "Boy, it's raining cats and dogs out there!" *every single time* it rains? You know how annoying that is? Don't be that person on the essay.

Don't Write Just to Fill Up Space

A healthy desire to make paragraphs long and impressive-sounding can lead to writing simply to fill up space. Don't do it. It's terribly easy to spot sentences that sound okay but don't mean anything. Cast such sentences into outer darkness. Expunge even those little phrases that sound good but could be said in half the space, such as "in my own personal opinion."

Mentioning Yourself

The word "I" shouldn't really appear in your essay, unless you're using a personal example. You don't need to say, "I think in war, conventional morality loses its hold on the popular imagination," to alert the reader that you're one woman with one of many valid opinions. In these essays, it's okay to act like your opinion is the only possible one. Instead of prefacing remarks with "I think," or "In my opinion," screw your courage to the sticking place and write, simply, "In war, conventional morality loses its hold on the popular imagination."

Of course, those directions that instruct you to use personal examples are a different story. For those, you should trot out those great stories about your mom and your most inspiring teacher, and the word "I" will invariably crop up.

Identifying Sentence Errors

Chapter Contents

O N IDENTIFYING SENTENCE ERROR questions, you must (as the title suggests) find errors in sentences. You don't have to fix the error, or name the error. You just have to find it.

There are two sections of Identifying Sentence Error questions on the Writing SAT II. The first is located at the beginning of the multiple-choice section and consists of 20 questions. The second one comes at the end of the multiple-choice section and consists of 10 questions. In total, there are 30 Identifying Sentence Error questions, making them the most common question type on the test (there are 18 Improving Sentences questions and 12 Improving Paragraphs questions). If you find that these questions are fairly manageable, it's a good idea to do the first Identifying Sentence Error section, and then flip to the end of your test booklet and do the last Identifying Sentence Error section. This means you'll skip the Improving Sentences and Improving Paragraphs sections, and come back to them once you've completed both of the Identifying Sentence Error sections.

This chapter will discuss the strategies needed for approaching and answering Identifying Sentence Errors, and it will explain the specific grammatical errors that most often appear on this type of question.

The Directions

Below are the official directions for Identifying Sentence Error questions. Remember to read these directions several times before the day of the test. You don't want to waste time on test day reading directions that never, ever change.

> <u>Directions</u>: The following sentences test your knowledge of grammar, usage, diction (choice of words), and idiom.
>
> > Some sentences are correct.
> > No sentence contains more than one error.
>
> You will find that the error, if there is one, is underlined and lettered. Elements of the sentence that are not underlined will not be changed. In choosing answers, follow the requirements of standard written English.
>
> If there is an error, select the <u>one underlined part</u> that must be changed to make the sentence correct and fill in the corresponding oval on your answer sheet.
>
> If there is no error, fill in answer oval E.

In addition to describing the questions you will encounter, these directions tell you two very important things. First, when ETS says *follow the requirements of standard written English*, they mean you must use the rules that govern formal writing, rather than the rules that govern the way we talk. Second, the directions inform you that some of the questions are actually correct. In fact, about ⅕ of the Identifying Sentence Error questions on the test will be grammatically impeccable. In essence, the instructions are telling you that you need the ability to "hear" bad grammar when it comes up.

Sample Question

Here's what an Identifying Sentence Error question might look like:

> The crowd, <u>which</u> clamored for the play to begin, <u>were</u> surprisingly <u>rowdy for</u> a
>   (A)   (B)   (C)
> Broadway <u>audience</u>. <u>No error</u>.
>   (D)   (E)

How to approach this question, and the right answer, will be discussed below.

Approaching Identifying Sentence Errors

1. Read the sentence and try to hear the mistake.

Sometimes all you have to do is read the sentence, and immediately you'll hear the problem. If that happens, great.

2. If you don't hear the mistake, eliminate underlined parts that are correct.

Sometimes, though, you'll read the sentence without hearing a mistake. If your initial reading of the sentence doesn't result in finding the answer, go through the underlined parts and eliminate those that are correct. Take a look at the example a few lines back. Say you read that sentence once and didn't hear a problem. You would then go through the sentence again, crossing off underlined parts that are correct. *Which*—that might be wrong. You're not sure, so keep the answer choice for now. *Were*—also could be wrong. There might be a subject-verb agreement problem. Keep it. *Rowdy for*—you feel sure there's nothing wrong with that. Eliminate answer choice (C) by crossing it out in your test booklet. *Audience*—nothing wrong with that, either. *A Broadway audience* is a grammatically impeccable phrase. Cross out (D) in your test booklet. Now you're down to (A) and (B), and it's time to move to step 3. For the moment, since you're not sure if an error exists, do not eliminate choice (E).

3. Check for errors in the remaining underlined parts.

The crowd, <u>which</u> clamored for the play to begin, <u>were</u> surprisingly <u>rowdy for</u> a
    (A)   (B)   (C)
Broadway <u>audience</u>. <u>No error</u>
    (D)   (E)

Look at your two remaining choices, (A) and (B). Answer choice (A) is *which*. Sometimes *which* is mistakenly used instead of *that*, but here, *which* is the correct choice. (Quick rule: when there's a comma, choose *which*; when there's no comma, choose *that*.) You can eliminate (A). What about (B), *were*? *Were* is a verb. Subject-verb agreement problems are commonly tested on this section of the test. What is the subject of *were*? *The crowd*. Standing between the subject and the verb is a prepositional phrase, *which clamored for the play to begin*. Get rid of that prepositional phrase for the moment, so you can more easily see whether the subject matches up with the verb. When you eliminate the phrase, you get *the crowd were*. That doesn't match. *The crowd* is a singular subject, and *were* is a plural verb. (B) is the correct answer.

4. Trust yourself. If you can't hear an error, and you can't find an error, it's probably an error-free sentence.

Remember, about ⅕ of the time the answer will be (E), no error. Sometimes you'll read the sentence, eliminate the error-free underlined parts, and find that you've crossed out every single underlined part. If this happens, don't second-guess yourself. Don't force yourself to find an error where none exists.

Common Identifying Sentence Error Grammar Mistakes

The Writing SAT II covers the same grammar from year to year. In fact, it tests the same grammar subsets on the different types of questions from year to year. For example, on Identifying Sentence Error questions, the test will cover your knowledge of pronoun errors, tense errors, subject-verb disagreement, and a handful of other errors. If you get a handle on how to find the following common errors, you'll be in great shape. Below, we discuss common errors roughly by the frequency with which they appear in Identifying Sentence Error questions.

Pronoun Errors

Nouns, remember, are words for people, places, or things. Pronouns are words that take the place of nouns—words like *she, her, hers, he, him, his, they, their, it, its, that,* and *which.* Say you begin with this sentence:

> *Bernie felt better after going on a shopping spree.*

A pronoun is a word you could use to replace the noun *Bernie*:

> *He felt better after going on a shopping spree.*

Whenever you see an underlined pronoun (*she, he, it*) in an Identifying Sentence Error question, go on high alert. Pronoun errors are the most common error type on this section of the test.

"Hearing" pronoun problems might take a little practice, because we often use pronouns incorrectly in speech. Therefore, even if a particular pronoun sounds correct, double check to make sure it follows all the rules discussed below.

What follows is a discussion of the most common pronoun pitfalls, all of which are tested on the Writing SAT II. Of these problems, by far the most frequently tested is pronoun agreement.

Pronoun Agreement

Pronouns must agree in number with the noun they refer to. If the noun is plural, the pronoun must be plural; if the noun is singular, the pronoun must be singular. This sounds straightforward enough, but spotting errors in pronoun agreement on the test gets tricky, because we make errors of pronoun agreement so frequently in speech. We tend to say things like *someone lost their shoe* instead of *someone lost his shoe* because we don't want to exclude women by saying *his*. And it's cumbersome to write *someone lost his or her shoe*. People attempt to solve these problems with the brief and gender-neutral *their*. This tactic is okay in speech, but if you see it on the test, you'll know it's an error. *Their* might be gender-neutral, but it's plural, and plural pronouns cannot replace singular nouns.

Because this error is so prevalent in common speech, and therefore *sounds* correct, you can be sure that you'll see a few questions on this topic.

The sentence below is incorrect because the pronoun and the noun don't agree in number:

> Every student in the classroom pretended to forget their homework. No error
>   (A)   (B)   (C) (D)   (E)

When you start out with a singular noun (like *student, someone, anyone,* or *no one*), you can replace it or refer to it only with a singular pronoun (like *his* or *her*). This sentence begins with the singular noun *student*, so the pronoun must be singular too. *Their* is plural, and therefore wrong in this sentence.

As we know from studying actual Writing SAT II tests, ETS will almost certainly give you a few questions with an incorrect usage of the word *their*. Sometimes, however, they test the opposite mistake. Look at the following sentence for an example of what we mean:

> Even though some possess the flexibility to change their opinions, most people
>   (A)
> vary in his or her willingness to listen to reason. No error
> (B)   (C)   (D)   (E)

In this sentence, the problem is with (C), the phrase *his or her*. The second clause in this sentence begins with the plural noun *people*; therefore, a plural pronoun must be used to refer to that plural noun. *His or her* is singular. This is a case in which *their* is correct, and *his or her* is incorrect.

Another kind of pronoun agreement question will essentially test to see if you're paying attention. On such questions as the one below, you'll get into trouble if you're reading quickly and thus fail to make sure that the pronoun matches up with the noun it's replacing.

> <u>For</u> the robber trying to decide between potential getaway cars, every car
> (A)
>
> <u>up for</u> consideration poses <u>their</u> <u>own</u> passel of problems. <u>No error</u>
> (B)   (C)   (D)   (E)

In this sentence, the pronoun *their* replaces the noun *car*. This is incorrect, because *car* is singular, and *their* is plural. If you were reading carelessly, however, you might assume that since the first part of the sentence contains the plural noun *cars*, the plural pronoun *their* is correct. Most students do fine on this kind of are-you-paying-attention pronoun agreement question; just make sure you're inspecting each pronoun with an eagle eye.

Pronoun Case

The "case" of a word refers to the function that a word performs in a sentence. The most important thing for you to understand in reference to pronoun case is the subjective and objective case.

A word that is the subject of a sentence is the main noun that performs the verb. The object of a sentence is the noun toward which, or upon which, the verb is being directed. Look at this sentence:

Joe kissed Mary.

Joe is the subject, since he performed the kiss, and Mary is the object, since she received the kiss.

When a pronoun replaces a noun, that pronoun must match the noun's case. This is important because pronouns actually have different forms, depending on their cases.

Subjective Case Pronouns	Objective Case Pronouns
I	Me
You	You
He, She, It	Him, Her, It
We	Us
They	Them
Who	Whom

In the example sentence, you would replace the subject *Joe* with the subject pronoun *he* and the object *Mary* with the object pronoun *her*.

The Writing SAT II will often test your knowledge of pronoun case in a tricky way. They'll give you phrases like *her and her cats*, *him and his friends*, etc. These phrases seek to confuse you by including two pronouns, each of which is doing separate things. They want you to reason that if one pronoun is in a certain case, then the other pronoun should be in the same case:

> <u>Her</u> and <u>her family</u> like to stay in their hotel room and <u>play</u> cards <u>whenever</u>
> (A)   (B)   (C)   (D)
> they take a trip. <u>No error</u>
>   (E)

This sample has a plural subject: *Her and her family.* You know *her and her family* is the subject since they are the ones who do the liking in the sentence; they are the performers of the verb. This sentence is tricky because the *her* in *her family* acts as an adjective, not a pronoun. Since *family* is a perfectly acceptable subject noun, that underlined portion is correct. But the initial *her* is a pronoun, and it is wrong since it is in the objective case rather than the subjective.

Now, all this might be a little too technical for you. If you already know, or can grasp, this grammar, then you're in great shape. But whether you know the grammar or not, there is a strategy that can help you decide if a pronoun is in the proper case. When you have a phrase like *her and her family*, just throw out each side of the phrase and try it out in the sentence (remembering to make the verb singular, since by throwing out one half of the subject you stopped it from being plural). Following this method, you would have two sentences, which would begin in the following two ways:

> *Her likes to stay . . .*
> *Her family likes to stay . . .*

You should immediately be able to "hear" that the first sentence is wrong and the second one is right. Suddenly it seems obvious that the first part of the original sentence should read:

> *She and her family like to stay . . .*

The Writing SAT II particularly likes to test you on phrases such as *Toto and me*, or *the wicked witch of the North and I*, because many people don't know when to use *me* and when to use *I*. A misconception exists that it's always more polite or proper to use *I*—but this is not true! Sometimes *me* is the right word to use. Look at the following sentence:

> There is usually <u>an atmosphere of</u> heated competition surrounding <u>Jesse and I,</u>
>   (A)   (B)
> especially when we <u>compete at</u> Cosmic Bowling Night <u>at the Bowladrome</u>. <u>No error</u>
>   (C)   (D)   (E)

If you saw right away that *Jesse and I* is the object in this sentence, good for you! You can confidently answer that (B) is incorrect, since it should read *Jesse and me*. If you didn't know the grammar straight off, though, you still should have been suspicious when you saw *Jesse and I* as one of the underlined portions of the sentence. Then, performing the crossing out trick on *Jesse* leaves you with *There is usually an atmosphere of heated competition surrounding I*. That sounds wrong. On this section, of course, you don't need to fix the errors, you just need to identify them, but if you were to fix this sentence you'd do it by substituting *me* for *I*. Plug that back in, and you get *There is usually an atmosphere of heated competition surrounding me*. That sounds much better.

It can also be tough trying to figure out whether *me* or *my* is the correct pronoun choice. Look at this sentence:

> When it comes to me studying for the SAT, " concentration" is my middle
> (A)   (B)   (C)
> name. No error
> (D)   (E)

Although it may sound right, *me* is actually incorrect in this sentence. If you use *me*, the phrase means *when it comes to me*, which isn't right. You're doing more than talking about yourself; you're talking about you and studying. Using *my* allows you to say *when it comes to my studying*.

Pronoun Shift

A sentence should start, continue, and end with the same kind of pronouns. Pronoun shift occurs when the kind of pronouns used changes over the course of the sentence. If you begin with plural pronouns, for example, you must use plural pronouns throughout.

> When one first begins to play tennis, it's important to work on your serve, and
>   (A)   (B)   (C)
> to wield your racket well. No error
>   (D)   (E)

This sentence presents a pronoun shift problem. If you start talking about *one*, you have to keep talking about *one* for the duration of the sentence. The sentence could read *when one first begins to play tennis, it's important to work on one's serve* or *when you first begin to play tennis, it's important to work on your serve*, but the sentence cannot combine *one* and *you*. (C) is the correct answer.

Ambiguous Pronouns

We call a pronoun ambiguous when it's not absolutely clear to whom or what the pronoun refers. We use ambiguous pronouns all the time when we're talking. In speech, you can make it clear, from context or gestures, what pronoun refers to what noun, but in writing you can't do that. Even if awkwardness is the result, you must make sure it's absolutely clear what the pronoun refers to. See if you can spot the ambiguous pronoun in the following sentence:

Sarah told Emma that <u>she</u> <u>had</u> a serious foot odor problem, <u>and that</u> medicated
             (A) (B)   (C)
spray <u>might</u> help. <u>No error</u>
    (D)   (E)

The pronoun *she* poses a problem in this sentence. Who has a problem with foot odor, Sarah or Emma? No one knows, because *she* is ambiguous. Grammatically and logically, *she* could refer to Sarah or Emma. Therefore, (A) is the correct answer.

Comparisons Using Pronouns

Your suspicions should rise when you see a comparison made using pronouns. When a pronoun is involved in a comparison, it must match the case of the other pronoun involved:

I'm fatter than <u>her,</u> <u>which</u> is good, <u>because</u> it means <u>I'll win</u> this sumo
           (A) (B)   (C)   (D)
wrestling match. <u>No error</u>
           (E)

In this sentence, *I* is being compared to *her*. These two pronouns are in different cases, so one of them must be wrong. Since only *her* is underlined, it must be wrong, and therefore the right answer.

Another way to approach comparisons is to realize that comparisons usually omit words. For example, it's grammatically correct to say, *Alexis is stronger than Bill*, but that's actually an abbreviated version of what you're saying. The long version is, *Alexis is stronger than Bill is*. That last *is* is invisible in the abbreviated version, but you must remember that it's there. Now let's go back to the sumo sentence. As in our Alexis and Bill example, we don't see the word *is* in the comparison, but it's implied. If you see a comparison using a pronoun and you're not sure if the pronoun is correct, add the implied *is*. In this case, adding *is* leaves us with *I'm fatter than her is.* That sounds wrong, so we know that *she* is the correct pronoun in this case.

Take a look at this similar sentence:

<u>Pedro</u> is a <u>better</u> pitcher <u>than</u> <u>them</u>. <u>No error</u>
 (A)   (B)   (C) (D)   (E)

Here the word *are* is implied (we use *are*, which is plural, because in this sentence the pronoun *them* is plural). Adding *are* leaves us with *Pedro is a better pitcher than them are*. Again, that sounds wrong, so we know that the sentence should read *Pedro is a better pitcher than they*, and that (D) is the right answer.

Subject-Verb Agreement

The basic rule about subjects and verbs is: if you have a singular subject, you must use a singular verb, and if you have a plural subject, you must use a plural verb. It sounds simple, and a lot of the time it is. For example, you know that it's incorrect to say *candy are good*, or *concerts is fun*.

However, in a few instances, subject-verb agreement can get hairy. There are four varieties of subject-verb problems ETS loves to test. These varieties crop up when:

1. the verb comes after the subject

2. the subject and verb are separated from each other

3. you have an *either/or* or *neither/nor* construction

4. the subject seems plural.

Remember, it's not necessary to remember the *name* of the problem—you certainly don't have to memorize that list of subject-verb agreement varieties. It's only necessary to check subjects and verbs carefully to see if they match up. Knowing the different ways subjects and verbs can go awry will help you check more efficiently.

Subject Comes After Verb

In most sentences, the subject comes before the verb. ETS will try to throw you off by giving you a sentence or two in which the subject comes *after* the verb, and the subject-verb match-up is incorrect.

<u>Even though</u> Esther created a petition to protest the <u>crowning</u> of a Prom Queen, <u>there is</u>
    (A)   (B)   (C)
many people who refused to sign, saying they support the <u>1950s-era</u> tradition. <u>No error</u>
                                                            (D)   (E)

The SAT II Writing Test frequently uses this exact formulation, so be wary if you see a comma followed by the word *there*. It's tempting to assume that just because the word *there* comes before the verb *is, there* is the subject—but it's not. Notice that in this sentence the subject is *people*. Here we see that since *people* is the subject, and *people* is plural, the matching verb must be plural. *Is* is a singular verb, and therefore incorrect in this sentence.

Even when you don't see the red flag of *there is,* don't just assume that the subject always comes before the verb. Look at the following sentence:

<u>Atop</u> my sundae, a <u>mass</u> of <u>whipped cream</u> and sprinkles, <u>sits</u> two maraschino
(A)   (B)   (C)   (D)
cherries. <u>No error</u>
        (E)

Tricky! The answer is (D), *sits*. Because we're talking about two maraschino cherries (plural subject) we need to use *sit* (plural verb). The sentence should read *Atop my sundae, a mass of whipped cream and sprinkles, sit two maraschino cherries.* Why is this tricky? The subject, *maraschino cherries,* comes after the verb, *sits*. With all the singular stuff floating around—one sundae, one mass of whipped cream—it's easy to assume that the verb should be singular, too. Look out for those backwards constructions.

Subject and Verb Are Separated

One of ETS's best-loved tricks is putting the subject here and the verb *waaaaay* over there. They hope that by the time you get to the verb, you'll have no memory of the subject.

> Sundaes with whipped cream and cherries, while good if consumed in
>   (A)   (B)
> moderation, is sickening if eaten for breakfast, lunch, and dinner. No error
>   (C)   (D)   (E)

In this sentence, they've put the subject (*sundaes*) at the beginning of the sentence, and the verb (*is*) miles away. Sometimes it helps to bracket prepositional phrases so you can see what's really going on. A prepositional phrase is a phrase that begins with a preposition like *while, although, which,* etc., which does not change the essential meaning of the sentence if removed. Prepositional phrases are often set off by commas. If you get rid of the prepositional phrase here (*while good if consumed in moderation*), you're left with *sundaes is sickening*. That sounds plain old wrong. (C) is the right answer.

Neither/Nor, Either/Or

In *neither/nor* and *either/or* constructions, if the nouns are singular, the verb must be singular, too. This can be confusing; in *neither/nor* constructions, you're always talking about two things, so it's tempting to assume that you always need a plural verb. But if the two things being discussed are singular, you need a singular verb. For example, it's correct to say, *Neither baseball nor football is fun to watch*, because if you broke the components of the sentence in two, you would get *baseball is fun to watch* and *football is fun to watch*. It's incorrect to say, *Neither baseball or football are fun to watch*, because if you break that sentence into its components, you get *baseball are fun to watch* and *football are fun to watch*.

It can be hard to hear this error, so be sure to check subject-verb match-ups carefully when you see a sentence like this one:

> Neither rummy nor solitaire measure up to hearts. No error
> (A)   (B)   (C)   (D) (E)

Even though there are two card games being discussed, both of those card games are singular nouns (one game of rummy, one game of solitaire), and therefore the verb must be singular. *Measure* is a plural verb, when it should be a singular one, so (C) is the answer.

Singular Subject that Looks Plural

There are several confusing subjects that look plural, but are actually singular. Of course, ETS hopes that you will see singular subjects and mistakenly match them with plural verbs. Such confusing subjects to watch out for are:

Anybody	*Either*
Anyone	*Group*
America	*Number*
Amount	*Neither*
Audience	*Nobody*
Each	*None*
Everybody	*No one*
Everyone	*One*

In this sentence, for example, the subject looks plural:

Nobody, not even me, are excited about the weekend. No error
  (A)   (B) (C)   (D)   (E)

Nobody is one of those subjects that sounds plural, but is actually singular. It needs to be matched with a singular verb. Look carefully at all seemingly plural subjects; make sure they're not singular subjects masquerading as plural ones. In this sentence, the answer is (C). The sentence should read *Nobody, not even me, is excited about the weekend.*

Be particularly careful with phrases like *as well as*, *along with*, and *in addition to*. Like the *neither/nor* construction, these phrases can trick you into thinking you need a plural verb. But look at the following sentence:

The leadoff hitter, as well as the cleanup hitter, are getting some
                   (A)   (B)
good hacks tonight. No error
(C)   (D)   (E)

The actual subject here is *leadoff hitter*. Since *leadoff hitter* is a singular subject, the verb must be singular, too. The presence of the phrase *as well as* does not make the subject plural. Even though there are two hitters doing well, the leadoff hitter is the only subject of this sentence. (B) is the answer; the sentence should read *the leadoff hitter, as well as the cleanup hitter, is getting some good hacks tonight.* If the sentence read, *The leadoff hitter and the cleanup hitter are getting some good hacks tonight,* are would be correct. It's that *as well as* construction that changes things.

Tense Errors

Identifying Sentence Error questions will test your knowledge of three common causes of tense errors: annoying verbs, illogical tense switches, and the conditional. Most tense errors will be pretty easy to spot; we don't make tense errors very often in speech, so when you read a tense error on the test, it will most likely "sound" wrong to you. Your ear is your most reliable way of spotting tense errors.

Annoying Verbs

By annoying verbs, we mean those verbs that never sound quite right in any tense—like *to lie*, or *to swim.* When do you lay and when do you lie? When do you swim and when have you swum? Unfortunately, there's no easy memory trick to help you remember when to use which verb form. The only solution is to learn and remember.

> *You LIE down for a nap.*
> *You LAY something down on the table.*
> *You LAY down yesterday.*
>
> *You SWIM across the English Channel.*
> *You SWAM across the Atlantic Ocean last year.*
> *You HAD SWUM across the bathtub as a child.*

You'll probably see one question that will test your knowledge of a confusing verb like *to lie.* Look at this sentence, for example:

> <u>On</u> Saturday afternoon, I <u>laid</u> in the sun <u>for an hour</u>, working on my <u>tan</u>. <u>No error</u>
> (A)   (B)   (C)   (D)   (E)

(B) is the correct answer here, because *laid* is not the correct tense in the context of this sentence. The past tense of *to lie* is *lay*, so the sentence should read *I lay in the sun.*

To lie and *to swim* aren't the only two difficult verbs. Below, you'll see a table of difficult verbs, in their infinitive, simple past, and past participle forms. You don't have to memorize all of these forms; you'll probably only see one tricky-verb question. Still, it is well worth your time to read carefully the list below and to make sure you understand especially those verbs that you've found confusing before.

Infinitive	Simple Past	Past Participle
Arise	Arose	Arisen
Become	Became	Become
Begin	Began	Begun
Blow	Blew	Blown
Break	Broke	Broken
Choose	Chose	Chosen
Come	Came	Come

Infinitive	Simple Past	Past Participle
Dive	Dived/Dove	Dived
Do	Did	Done
Draw	Drew	Drawn
Drink	Drank	Drunk
Drive	Drove	Driven
Drown	Drowned	Drowned
Dwell	Dwelt/dwelled	Dwelt/dwelled
Eat	Ate	Eaten
Fall	Fell	Fallen
Fight	Fought	Fought
Flee	Fled	Fled
Fling	Flung	Flung
Fly	Flew	Flown
Forget	Forgot	Forgotten
Freeze	Froze	Frozen
Get	Got	Gotten
Give	Gave	Given
Go	Went	Gone
Grow	Grew	Grown
Hang (a thing)	Hung	Hung
Hang (a person)	Hanged	Hanged
Know	Knew	Known
Lay	Laid	Laid
Lead	Led	Led
Lie (to recline)	Lay	Lain
Lie (tell fibs)	Lied	Lied
Put	Put	Put
Ride	Rode	Ridden
Ring	Rang	Rung
Rise	Rose	Risen
Run	Ran	Run
See	Saw	Seen
Set	Set	Set
Shine	Shone	Shone
Shake	Shook	Shaken
Shrink	Shrank	Shrunk
Shut	Shut	Shut
Sing	Sang	Sung
Sink	Sank	Sunk
Sit	Sat	Sat
Speak	Spoke	Spoken

Identifying Sentence Errors

Infinitive	Simple Past	Past Participle
Spring	Sprang	Sprung
Sting	Stung	Stung
Strive	Strove/strived	Striven/strived
Swear	Swore	Swore
Swim	Swam	Swum
Swing	Swung	Swung
Take	Took	Taken
Tear	Tore	Torn
Throw	Threw	Thrown
Wake	Woke/waken	Waked/woken
Wear	Wore	Worn
Write	Wrote	Written

Tense Switch

Nowhere is it written that you must use the same tense throughout a sentence. For example, you can say, *I used to eat chocolate bars exclusively, but after going through a conversion experience last year, I have broadened my range, and now eat gummy candy, too.* That sentence has tense switches galore, but they were logical: the sentence used past tense when it was talking about the past and present tense when it was talking about the present, and the progression from past to present made sense.

ETS will give you a sentence or two with bad tense switches. Your most powerful weapon against tense switch questions is logic. We could prattle on for paragraph after paragraph about present tense, simple past, general present, and present perfect, but remembering the millions of different tense forms, and when to use what, is both difficult and unnecessary. For the Writing SAT II, simply remember: if you don't hear an error the first time you read a sentence, and if you don't see a pronoun problem, check out the tenses and figure out if they're okay. Look at the following example:

<u>At swimming pools</u> last summer, the heat <u>will have brought</u> hundreds and
      A   B

even <u>thousands of people</u> to bathe in <u>tepid</u> chlorine. <u>No error</u>
      C   D   E

This sentence begins by talking about the past (*last summer*), but then uses the phrase *will have brought*, which is not the past tense. We're talking about a phenomenon of last summer that is now over and done with, and firmly in the past. The phrase *will have brought* doesn't fit because it suggests an ongoing phenomenon. Therefore, (B) is the correct answer.

Just look at the meaning of the sentence on these iffy tense questions, and you'll be fine.

The Conditional

The conditional is the verb form we use to describe something uncertain, something that's conditional on something else. You can memorize the conditional formula. It goes, "If . . . were . . . would." Look at this sentence:

> If I <u>was</u> queen, I <u>would</u> never <u>have to</u> <u>study for</u> a standardized test. <u>No error</u>
>   (A)   (B)   (C)   (D)   (E)

Was may sound right to you on first reading this sentence, but when in doubt, remember the formula. *Was* violates the formula and therefore is incorrect. The sentence should read, *If I were queen, I would never have to study for a standardized test.* (A) is the right answer.

Parallelism

Parallelism means making sure the different components of a sentence start, continue, and end in the same way. It's especially common to find errors of parallelism in sentences that list actions or items. In the question below, for example, the activities are not presented in the same format, which means there is an error of parallelism.

> Porter never liked <u>drinking wine,</u> <u>eating cheese,</u> or <u>to go</u> to a cocktail <u>party</u>.
>   (A)   (B)   (C)   (D)

When you see a list like this, be on the alert for an error in parallelism. In this case, the list starts out with two gerunds (*drinking, eating*) and then switches to an infinitive (*to go*). Because the list starts out with gerunds, it has to use gerunds all the way through. (C) is the correct answer.

Not all parallelism errors occur at the beginning of phrases; some occur at the end. The sentence below is incorrect because its two halves don't end in a similar way.

> The steak <u>is definitely</u> the best entree <u>on the menu,</u> and <u>the clam chowder</u> is the
>   (A)   (B)   (C)
> <u>best appetizer</u>. <u>No error</u>
>   (D)   (E)

The best appetizer where? In the nation? In the world? Because the first part of the sentence specifies *on the menu*, the second part of the sentence must also be specific. In corrected form, this sentence would read, *The steak is definitely the best entrée on the menu, and the clam chowder is the best appetizer in the world.*

Double Negative

A double negative is a phrase that uses two negative words instead of one. Double negatives are the province of television gangsters and airheads, who say things like, "I don't take no garbage." You'll probably be adept at spotting double negatives such as

"I don't take no garbage," but ETS will try to trick you into missing a double negative by using words that are negative but don't sound it, like *hardly, barely,* or *scarcely.* If you see any of those three words, you should probably smell a rat.

> Katie <u>can't scarcely</u> stand to wear her <u>gymnastics</u> leotard <u>without</u> underwear
>   (A)   (B)   (C)
> <u>underneath</u>. <u>No error</u>
>   (D)   (E)

Can't is a fairly obvious negative word, but *scarcely* is also negative, so the two cannot be used together. (A) is the correct answer.

Adverb Errors

Adverbs present problems when they're confused with adjectives and when they're used in comparisons.

Confusing Adverbs with Adjectives

Adverbs are words used to describe verbs or other adverbs. Adverbs often end in *–ly* (*breathlessly, hardily, angrily*). For example, if you're describing how you ate your spaghetti dinner, you're describing a verb (eating), so you need to use an adverb. You could say something like, "I ate my dinner *quickly.*"

Adjectives are words used to describe nouns. Again, take the spaghetti example—but this time, suppose that instead of describing the process of eating, you're describing the actual dinner. Since you're describing a noun (dinner), you need to use an adjective. You could say something like, "My spaghetti dinner was *delicious.*"

People often confuse adverbs with adjectives, especially in speech. We say things like, "I ate my dinner quick." That, however, is incorrect. Because you're describing an action, an adverb like *quickly* is required.

One frequently confused adjective/adverb pair is *well* and *good.* *Well* is an adverb, and *good* is an adjective, so one cannot be substituted for the other. Look at the following sentence:

> This <u>paper's</u> going pretty <u>good</u>, although I'm not sure <u>I'll</u> be done <u>on time</u>. <u>No error</u>
> (A)   (B)   (C)   (D) (E)

A paper can't go pretty good; it can only go pretty well. In order to describe the verb *going*, we must use an adverb like *well*, instead of the adjective *good*.

ETS will usually test adverb/adjective confusion by giving you a sentence that uses an adjective when it should use an adverb. See if you can spot the incorrect adjective use in this sentence:

No matter how careful kites are flown, they often get tangled in trees. No error
(A)   (B)   (C)   (D)   (E)

In this sentence, the adjective *careful* is used improperly to describe the verb *flown*. Because a verb is being described, *careful* should be *carefully*. The following sentence has a similar problem:

The fascinating TV special shows how quick the hungry tiger can devour her
(A)   (B)   (C)   (D)

prey. No error
(E)

This sentence uses the adjective *quick* to describe the verb *devour*; the adverb *quickly* is the right word to use. Notice that in this sentence, the adjective, *quick*, is separated from the verb, *devour*, by three words. Sniffing out the improper use of an adjective can be difficult when the verb being described is not right next to the adjective. If you see an adjective you're not sure about, don't be fooled by distracting phrases like *the hungry tiger*. Just check to see what the adjective is describing. If it's describing a verb, you'll know it's an error.

Adverb or Adjective Misuse in Comparisons

When you see a comparison or an implied comparison, check to make sure all of the adverbs and adjectives are used as they should be. How should they be used? Well, if you're comparing two items, you need to use what's known as a comparative modifier. Don't worry—you don't need to remember the phrase "comparative modifier," you just need to remember that when comparing two items, use a word that ends in *–er*, like *better, sexier, shinier,* etc. Only when comparing three or more things can you use a superlative modifier like *best, sexiest,* or *shiniest.*

ETS will probably test your knowledge of this rule by giving you a question in which a superlative modifier is used incorrectly. Look at the following example:

Of the two cars I drive, I like the Millennium Testerosa best. No error
(A)   (B)   (C)   (D)   (E)

This sentence implies a comparison between two cars. Because only two things are being compared, *best* is the wrong word. Only when comparing three or more things can you use words like *best*. You could figure this out by phrasing the comparison in a different way. You wouldn't say, *I like my Testerosa best than my Civic*, you'd say, *I like my Testerosa better than my Civic*. This rephrasing also works if you're puzzling over a sentence that compares three or more items. You wouldn't say, *After trying skydiving, hula-dancing, and pineapple-eating, I decided that I liked hula-dancing less,* because that sentence does not explain if you liked hula-dancing less than you liked skydiving, or less than you liked pineapple-eating, or less than you liked both. What you would say is, *After trying skydiving, hula-dancing, and pineapple eating, I decided that I liked hula-dancing least.* The superlative modifier *least* makes it clear that hula-dancing was the most disagreeable of all three activities.

Gerund Errors

A gerund is a word that ends in *–ing*, such as *prancing, divulging, stuffing,* etc. The infinitive form of a verb is the verb in its unconjugated form: *to prance, to divulge, to stuff,* etc. Your understanding of gerunds will usually be tested by questions that use the infinitive when they should use gerunds.

> In my family, Scrabble usually causes two or more family members to engage in a
>   (A)   (B)
> screaming match, thus preventing the game to be completed. No error
>   (C)   (D)   (E)

Your ear will help you on gerund questions. The phrase *preventing the game to be completed* might sound funny to you. This phrase should read *thus preventing the game from being completed,* changing the infinitive *to be* to the conjugated form, *being.*

Idiom

We've been talking on and on about how tough it is to spot the errors tested on this exam, because sometimes grammatical errors sound right. Well, this should make you happy: idiom errors are easy to spot because they sound wrong. In fact, there's no rule about idiom errors. You have to be able to read a sentence and think, "That sounds plain old wrong." Usually it's a prepositional phrase that's off.

> Melissa recently moved to a brand-new apartment in 108th street. No error
>   (A)   (B)   (C)   (D)   (E)

Here, the answer is (C), because we say, "I live *on* this street," rather than, "I live *in* this street." There is no specific rule that explains why we use the word *on*; it's just something you probably know from years of English-speaking.

The following is a list of *proper* idiomatic usage.

> He can't *abide by* the no-spitting rule.
>
> She *accused me* of stealing.
>
> I *agreed to* eat the broccoli.
>
> I *apologized for* losing the hamsters in the heating vent.
>
> She *applied for* a credit card.
>
> My mother pretends to *approve of* my boyfriend.
>
> She *argued with* the bouncer.
>
> I *arrived at* work at noon.
>
> You *believe in* ghosts.

I can't be <u>blamed for</u> your neuroses.

Do you <u>care about</u> me?

He's in <u>charge of</u> grocery shopping.

Nothing <u>compares to</u> you.

What is there to <u>complain about</u>?

He can always <u>count on</u> money from his mommy.

Ice cream <u>consists of</u> milk, fat, and sugar.

I <u>depend on</u> no one.

That's where cats <u>differ from</u> dogs.

It's terrible to <u>discriminate against</u> parakeets.

I have a plan to <u>escape from</u> this prison.

There's no <u>excuse for</u> your behavior.

You can't <u>hide from</u> your past.

It was all he'd <u>hoped for.</u>

I must <u>insist upon</u> it.

It's impossible to <u>object to</u> her lucid arguments.

I refuse to <u>participate in</u> this discussion.

<u>Pray for</u> me.

<u>Protect me from</u> evil.

<u>Provide me with</u> plenty of Skittles.

She stayed home to <u>recover from</u> the flu.

I <u>rely on</u> myself.

She <u>stared at</u> his chest.

He <u>subscribes to</u> several trashy magazines.

I <u>succeeded in</u> fooling him.

<u>Wait for</u> me!

<u>Work with me</u>, people!

Occasionally, the idiomatic association between words can affect the entire sentence. Take the following example:

> While the <u>principal</u> of the high school <u>is</u> mild-mannered, the vice
>   (A)   (B)
> principal <u>is often</u> accused <u>to be</u> too harsh with the students. <u>No error</u>
>   (C)   (D)   (E)

The answer to this questions is (E), because the word *accused* must take the preposition *of* rather than *to*. This means that the use of the verb *to be* is incorrect. Instead, the sentence must use *of*, and the preposition *of* must take a gerund. For this sentence to be correct, it should read:

> *While the principal of the high school is mild-mannered, the vice principal is often accused of being too*
> *harsh with the students.*

Wrong Word

You might see one or two wrong word questions on Identifying Sentence Error questions. There are tons of frequently confused words, and while it's impossible to predict which ones ETS will throw at you, it *is* possible to learn the difference between these pairs of words, even those words you always get wrong in your own writing.

We've broken down wrong words into categories: words that sound the same but mean different things (like *allusion* and *illusion*), made-up words and phrases (like *should of*), tricky contractions (like *its* and *it's*), and words commonly and incorrectly used as synonyms (like *disinterested* and *uninterested*).

Words That Sound the Same but Mean Different Things

In the following list, you'll find homonyms—words that sound the same or similar when spoken aloud, but that are spelled differently and have different meanings—*dying* and *dyeing*, for example. Because the word *die* sounds exactly the same as the word *dye*, it can be hard to remember which spelling means *expire* and which means *color*. Here is a handy list of commonly confused words, and their definitions:

allusion/illusion

An *allusion* is a reference to something.

> *Isolde's essay was littered with conspicuous <u>allusions</u> to Shakespeare and Spenser.*

An *illusion* is a deception or unreal image.

> *By clever use of his napkin, Jason created the <u>illusion</u> that he'd eaten his quiche.*

alternate/alternative

An *alternate* is a substitute.

> *When Cherry was ousted after the voting scandal, the <u>alternate</u> took her place on the student council.*

An *alternative* is a choice between two or more things.

> *The Simpsons provides an <u>alternative</u> to mindless, poorly written sitcoms.*

appraise/apprise

To *appraise* is to figure out the value of something.

> *After <u>appraising</u> the drawing, Richard informed Cynthia that she was the owner of a Picasso sketch.*

To *apprise* is to give someone information.

> *In an urgent undertone, Donald <u>apprised</u> me of the worrisome situation.*

breath/breathe

Breath and *breathe* cannot be used interchangeably. *Breath* is a noun, and *breathe* is a verb. That little *e* on the end makes all the difference. A *breath* (noun) is the lungful of air you inhale every few seconds.

> *Elena took a deep <u>breath</u> and jumped off the diving board.*

To *breathe* (verb) is the act of taking in that lungful.

> *"I can't <u>breathe</u>!" gasped Mario, clutching at his throat.*

conscience/conscious/conscientious

A *conscience* is a sense of right and wrong.

> *After he robbed the store, Pinocchio's <u>conscience</u> started to bother him.*

To be *conscious* is to be awake and alert.

> *Suddenly, Marie became <u>conscious</u> that she was not alone in the room.*

To be *conscientious* is to be dutiful and hardworking.

> *<u>Conscientious</u> Cedric completed his chores and then did his homework.*

desert/dessert

A *desert* is a place with sand and camels.

> *The cartoon figure pulled himself across the <u>desert</u>, calling out for water.*

A *dessert* is something sweet that you eat after dinner.

> *My favorite <u>dessert</u> is mint chocolate chip ice cream.*

effect/affect

There's a good chance you'll see this pair on the test, because ETS knows that differentiating between *effect* and *affect* drives students crazy. *Effect* is usually a noun. The *effect* is the result of something.

> *Studying had a profound <u>effect</u> on my score.*

Affect is usually a verb. To *affect* something is to change it or influence it.

> *My high score positively <u>affected</u> the outcome of my college applications.*

eminent/imminent

An *eminent* person is one who is well-known and highly regarded.

> *The <u>eminent</u> author disguised himself with a beret and dark glasses.*

Identifying Sentence Errors

An *imminent* event is one that is just about to happen.

> *When the paparazzi's arrival seemed <u>imminent</u>, the author ducked out the back entrance.*

lose/loose

To *lose* something is to misplace it or shake it off.

> *Michel tried to <u>lose</u> the hideous shirt his girlfriend had given him for Christmas.*

Loose means movable, unfastened, or promiscuous.

> *The <u>loose</u> chair leg snapped off, and the chair's occupant fell to the floor.*

principal/principle

The *principal* is the person who calls the shots in your high school.

> *<u>Principal</u> Skinner rules Springfield Elementary School with an iron fist, yet he still lives with his mother.*

A *principle* is a value, or standard.

> *Edward, a boy of <u>principle</u>, refused to participate in the looting.*

stationary/stationery

Stationary means immobile.

> *Nadine used her <u>stationary</u> bike as a place to hang her clothes.*

Stationery is the paper you get for Christmas from your aunt.

> *Nathaniel wrote thank-you notes on his humorous Snoopy <u>stationery</u>.*

Made-Up Words and Phrases

Here is a list of some of the words and phrases that don't actually exist, although people still incorrectly use them in their writing. These misspellings and concoctions exist mainly because they are the phonetic spellings of words and phrases we use in speech. For example, the phrase *should of* (a grammatically incorrect phrase) sounds like the way we pronounce *should have* or *should've*, which is why it creeps into people's writing.

a lot/alot

Despite widespread usage, the word *alot* does not exist. It is a made-up word that is never grammatically correct. Always use the phrase *a lot* instead.

> *Henri ate <u>a lot</u> of brie with his bread.*

could've/could of

Could've is the contraction of *could have*. People sometimes write *could of* when they mean *could've* or *could have*. Unfortunately, like *alot*, *could of* is an imaginary phrase. Never use it.

> *Matilda <u>could have</u> gone on the date, but she claimed to have a prior engagement.*

should've/should of

Should of does not exist.

> *Chadwick <u>should have</u> done his Spanish homework.*

supposed to/suppose to

Suppose to falls in the category of made-up phrases. It's often used in place of *supposed to* because when we're talking, we say *suppose to* instead of the grammatically correct *supposed to*.

> *According to the vet, Yolanda is <u>supposed to</u> brush her pit bull's teeth once a month.*

used to/use to

Use to (you guessed it) is made-up. The correct spelling is *used to*.

> *Opie <u>used to</u> play Monopoly with Anthony, but now he has put aside childish things.*

Contraction Confusion

Look into your heart. Do you write *its* sometimes and *it's* at other times, with little regard for which *its/it's* is which? If you do, cut it out.

Contractions can be confusing. Check out the following list and get them straight.

its/it's

Its and *it's* are often used interchangeably—but they are very different beasts. *Its* signals possession. *It's* is a contraction of *it is*.

It is understandable, though, why people confuse the two words. The most common way to show possession is to add an apostrophe and an *s* (*Dorothy's braids, the tornado's wrath, Toto's bark*) which is perhaps the reason why people frequently write *it's* when they should write *its*—they know they want to show possession, so they pick the word with the apostrophe and the *s*. To avoid making a mistake, when you see the word *it's*, check to make sure that if you substituted *it is* for the *it's*, the sentence would still make sense.

To sum up:

- *Its* signals possession.

> *This day-old soda has lost <u>its</u> fizz.*

- *It's* is a contraction of *it is*.

> *It's a shame that this glass of soda was left out overnight.*

their/they're/there

Their, they're, and *there* are often used willy-nilly, as if they are interchangeable, which they are not. *Their* is possessive.

> *They lost their hearts in Massachusetts.*

They're is the contraction of *they are*.

> *They're the ugliest couple in all of Boston.*

There means over yonder.

> *Look! There they go!*

whose/who's

Whose is possessive.

> *Wanda, whose California roll I just ate, is looking at me with hatred.*

Who's is a contraction of *who is*.

> *Who's responsible for the theft and ingestion of my California roll?*

your/you're

Your is possessive.

> *Your fly is unzipped.*

You're is a contraction of *you are*.

> *You're getting sleepy.*

When to Use What Word?

Below is a list of words we often—but incorrectly—use interchangeably.

aggravate/irritate

When screaming in frustration, we often say things like, "That's so aggravating!" However, this is incorrect usage. *Aggravate* is not synonymous with *irritate*. *To aggravate* is to make a condition worse.

> *Betty's skin condition was aggravated by her constant sunbathing.*

To irritate is to annoy.

> *Ambika enjoys irritating her sister by jabbing her in the leg during long car rides.*

number/amount

Use *number* when referring to a group of things that can be counted.

> Caroline concealed a <u>number</u> of gummy bears in various pockets of her jeans.

Use *amount* when referring to something that cannot be counted.

> Caroline drank a certain <u>amount</u> of soda every day.

fewer/less

Use *fewer* when referring to items that can be counted.

> Yanni complained vociferously that he had received <u>fewer</u> presents than his sister did.

Use *less* when referring to items that cannot be counted.

> Yanni's parents explained that because they loved him <u>less</u> than they loved his sister, they gave him fewer presents.

famous/infamous

As you might know, a *famous* person is someone like Julia Roberts.

> The <u>famous</u> young actor made his way up the red carpet as flashbulbs popped and girls shrieked.

An *infamous* person or thing, however, is something different. *Infamous* means notorious—famous, yes, but famous in a bad way.

> The <u>infamous</u> pirate was known the world over for his cruel escapades.

disinterested/uninterested

Even reputable daily newspapers occasionally confuse *disinterested* with *uninterested*. *Disinterest* suggests impartiality.

> Nadine and Nora need a <u>disinterested</u> third party to referee their argument.

In contrast, an *uninterested* person is one who is bored.

> Nora is completely <u>uninterested</u> in hearing Nadine's opinions.

Identifying Sentence Errors

Improving Sentences

Chapter Contents

IMPROVING SENTENCES ARE THE SECOND TYPE of multiple-choice question on the Writing SAT II. Each of the 16 Improving Sentences questions consists of a single sentence with one underlined word or phrase. Unlike Identifying Sentence Error questions, Improving Sentences questions do not require you to check out four underlined parts of the sentence to look for an error; only that one underlined part will contain an error. Your job with that underlined portion of the sentence is twofold. First, you must figure out if there is a problem with the underlined part. Then, if there is a problem, you must decide which answer choice fixes the problem. Sometimes—⅕ of the time, in fact—no error will exist.

The Improving Sentences questions are organized in one group, which is located right after the first group of Identifying Sentence Error questions and before the Improving Paragraphs questions.

The Directions

Take a look at the official instructions for Improving Sentences:

> <u>Directions</u>: The following sentences test correctness and effectiveness of expression. In choosing answers, follow the requirements of standard written English; that is, pay attention to grammar, choice of words, sentence construction, and punctuation.
>
> In each of the following sentences, part of the sentence or the entire sentence is underlined. Beneath each sentence you will find five ways of phrasing the underlined part. Choice A repeats the original; the other four are different.
>
> Choose the answer that best expresses the meaning of the original sentence. If you think the original is better than any of the alternatives, choose it; otherwise choose one of the others. Your choice should produce the most effective sentence—clear and precise, without awkwardness or ambiguity.

Notice that once again, ETS wants you to follow the rules of standard written English when you're answering these questions. The rules of standard *spoken* English aren't accepted here, so a lot of English that's passable in speech will be wrong on this test.

Also notice that because answer choice (A) is always the same as the original sentence, *you never need to waste time reading answer choice (A)*. Once you've read the question, you've also read answer choice (A). So don't waste time by rereading. Skip directly to (B).

The Good News about Improving Sentences

On this section, as on the other sections, grammar *terms* are not tested. Spelling is not tested, and, despite what the directions claim, punctuation is not tested either. A basic knowledge of punctuation might help you on some questions, but there are no questions that deal directly with punctuation in this section.

You will not have to master a huge amount of material in order to do well on this section. ETS tests your knowledge of basic grammar, which this chapter will cover. They also test the same basic grammar from year to year, which makes it easier for us to tell you what kind of questions to expect. By carefully studying actual SAT II Writing tests from past years, we have pinpointed exactly what kind of grammar questions you'll see on this section. For example, we know you'll see questions on the passive voice, run-on sentences, and misplaced modifiers; also, you'll most likely see some questions on parallelism, conjunctions, fragments, gerunds, and coordination/subordination.

Although some of the material in this chapter is new, some of the grammar we'll discuss will sound familiar, because it's grammar that ETS also tests on the Identifying Sentence Error questions.

Sample Question

Here's what an Improving Sentences question will look like:

Jenna was awarded the medal not for her academic prowess or her skill on the soccer field, <u>but for her being a participant in gym class</u>.

(A)   but for her being a participant in gym class
(B)   the reason being for her participation in gym class
(C)   the reason was her participating in gym class
(D)   but for her being participation-willing in gym class
(E)   but for her participation in gym class

How to Approach Improving Sentence Questions

When answering questions in this section, use these eight rules to help you. We briefly list the rules below and then explain them in more detail, using them to answer the sample question.

1.   Read the sentence and try to hear the problem.

2.   If there is an error, immediately eliminate (A).

3.   Before you look at the answer choices, figure out how to fix the error.

4.   Look at the remaining answer choices and try to find the correction that most nearly matches your own correction.

5.   If none of the corrections matches your own, go through the answer choices and eliminate those that repeat the mistake in the original sentence or contain a new mistake.

6.   If you're stymied, turn to your bag of cheap tricks (more on cheap tricks in a while).

7.   Once you've picked an answer choice, plug the answer back into the sentence to make sure it works.

8.   Remember, even if you only eliminate one answer choice, you must guess.

Improving Sentences

Now to apply these steps to the sample question, which is reprinted below:

> Jenna was awarded the medal not for her academic prowess or her skill on the soccer field, <u>but for her being a participant in gym class</u>.
>
> (A)   but for her being a participant in gym class
> (B)   the reason being for her participation in gym class
> (C)   the reason was her participating in gym class
> (D)   but for her being participation-willing in gym class
> (E)   but for her participation in gym class

1.   Read the sentence and try to hear the problem.

A good ear will take you far on Improving Sentences questions. If you can read a sentence and figure out what about the underlined part sounds strange or wrong, you're on your way to a right answer. You might read the sample sentence and immediately recognize that wordiness is the problem—the phrase *but for her being a participant* should be rewritten in a more compact form. If you don't come up with the specific term "wordiness," you might sense that something about the underlined part is vague and a bit convoluted. It's fine if you can't think of the term that would best describe the problem. Just getting a general sense of the problem will be very helpful.

2.   If there is an error, immediately eliminate (A).

You already know that there's a problem with this sentence. That means you can eliminate (A), since answer choice (A) always repeats the underlined part word for word. Even if you know only that there's an error of some sort, and haven't yet figured out what the error is, you can eliminate (A).

The elimination of (A) means something besides "one down, four to go." It means that even if the other four answers look like gibberish, you must guess. Remember, if you can eliminate even one answer choice, the guessing odds are in your favor.

3.   Before you look at the answer choices, figure out how to fix the error.

Once you've decided what the problem is with the underlined part of the sentence, say to yourself (silently, not aloud—you don't want to reveal your genius to other test takers in the room): "This would be a better sentence if it read something like *Jenna was awarded the medal not for her academic prowess or her skill on the soccer field, but for participating in gym class.*" That conveys the right information, but doesn't take up unnecessary space.

It is of the *utmost importance* to correct the sentence in your head *before* you look at the answer choices. Why? Because if you go right to the answer choices, and dutifully read through them one by one, by the time you get to (C), they will all sound equally confusing and wrong. The answer choices are designed to make you feel this way. If you have a solution in mind before you dive in, you can look at the answer choices calmly, and with focus.

4. Look at the remaining answer choices and try to find the correction that most nearly matches your own correction.

Your correction was, *Jenna was awarded the medal not for her academic prowess or her skill on the soccer field, but for participating in gym class*. You look at the remaining answer choices and see which one of them most nearly matches your correction:

(A)   but for her being a participator in gym class
(B)   the reason being for her participation in gym class
(C)   the reason was her participating in gym class
(D)   but for her being participation-willing in gym class
(E)   but for her participation in gym class

(E) looks most like the answer you came up with before looking at the answer choices. It's not exactly like your prepared answer—it uses *her participation* instead of *for participating*—but it's very close. Rarely will an answer choice exactly match the one you generated on your own, which is fine. The purpose of preparing your own answer first is not to find an exact match in the answer choices, but to have an idea of what you're looking for before you start reading the choices.

Of course, sometimes you won't be sure whether your own answer matches any of the answer choices closely enough. In that case, move to step #5.

5. If none of the corrections matches your own, go through the answer choices and eliminate those that repeat the mistake or contain a new mistake.

You'll usually see a few answer choices that actually repeat the mistake. Some might fix the original mistake, but in the process add a new error to the mix.

Suppose you weren't certain that (E) matched your prepared answer closely enough. In that case, you would read through the answer choices and try to determine if they repeated the first mistake or contained a new one. Answer choice (B) has a problem similar to that of the original sentence. It says, *the reason being*, which is a wordy phrase. (C) contains a new problem: the word *participating* is a gerund, but should be a noun. (D) repeats the original mistake, repeating the phrase *but for her being*; it also introduces a new problem by using the strange phrase *participation-willing*. Only (E) neither repeats the original problem nor contains a new one.

Step #6 covers cheap tricks that can help you eliminate answers when all else fails. Since we aren't stumped on this question, we'll skip the cheap tricks for now, and discuss them at the end of the chapter.

7. Plug your answer back into the sentence to make sure it works.

> Jenna was awarded the medal not for her academic prowess or her skill on the soccer field, but for her participation in gym class.

Sounds good. This step shouldn't normally cause you to reevaluate your work; it's just a quick check to make sure the answer choice actually sounds okay in the context of the sentence.

Common Improving Sentences Grammar Errors

There are four errors that will crop up again and again on Improving Sentences questions:

- Passive voice
- Run-on sentences
- Misplaced modifiers
- Parallelism problems

You will probably also see a few questions on conjunctions, coordination and subordination, fragments, and gerunds.

You won't have to know the names of these errors. For Improving Sentences questions, you'll just have to know how to spot them and then choose the answer choice that best fixes the error.

No Error

Before we get started on the discussion of common errors, it's worth reiterating that about ⅕ of the answers on this section will be (A)—"no error." In fact, answer choice (A) usually appears with more frequency than any of the common errors listed below. This doesn't mean you should go nuts and make your bubble sheet one long line of (A)s. It just means you shouldn't feel worried if, every so often, you can't find an error.

Passive Voice

In sentences that use the active voice, the subject does the action. For example, in the sentence *My dog ate a bunch of grass*, we know who ate a bunch of grass: the dog. The passive voice, in contrast, identifies the performer of the action late or even never. For example, the sentence *A bunch of grass was eaten* leaves the reader unsure of who or what did the eating. When you see the words *is, was, were, are*, etc., be on the alert: you could have passivity on your hands. The passive voice is one of the most common errors on this section of the exam.

> After Timmy blithely dropped his filthy knickers in the hamper, <u>the offensive garment was washed by his long-suffering mother</u>.
>
> (A) the offensive garment was washed by his long-suffering mother
> (B) his long-suffering mother washed the offensive garment
> (C) the washing of the offensive garment took place by his long-suffering mother
> (D) long-suffering, the offensive garment was washed by his mother
> (E) he left the offensive garment for his long-suffering mother who washed it

Here we see passive voice in all of its buck-passing ugliness. The passive voice avoids naming the performer of an action. In this sentence, for example, we don't know until the last word who washed Timmy's drawers. The phrase *was washed* suggests that someone, anyone, God maybe, did the cleaning. This avoidance of naming the performer is the reason people object to the passive voice, and the reason it is wrong on the test. If you see a sentence in which you're not sure who is performing an action until the end of the sentence, or perhaps never sure at all who performs it, you might have a passive voice problem.

In order to fix the passive voice, the performer of the action must get a place of prominence. We must realize that Timmy's mother did the load of laundry. Both answers (B) and (E) fix the passive voice problem, but (E) is wordy and redundant, so (B) is the right answer.

By the way, do you see why it is of paramount importance that you correct the error in your own mind *before* reading the answer choices? If you read the answer choices all the way through, by the time you get to (E), they've swirled together into a mass of meaningless syllables.

Wordiness

Wordiness is the crime you commit when writing your papers at 1 A.M. the night before they're due. It's all that meaningless junk you type in a desperate bid to fill up space. We list wordiness as a subset of the passive voice because on the Writing SAT II the two problems often exist simultaneously in the same sentence. On some questions, it's difficult to say whether the passive voice or wordiness is the more pressing problem. Of course, you don't need to worry about what to call the problem, you just have to figure out how to fix the sentence.

Pierre observed the diners and motels of middle America, and <u>these are sights that are depicted</u> in his trendy paintings.

- (A)   these are sights that are depicted
- (B)   the depiction of these sights is
- (C)   these sights having been depicted
- (D)   his depiction of these sights
- (E)   depicted these sights

This sentence is both wordy and passive. The underlined part could be said in half the space—it's wordy. You could easily remove a few words without changing the meaning of the sentence at all. For example: *Pierre observed the diners and motels of middle America, and these sights are depicted in his trendy paintings*. But even in that succinct version, another problem remains: the underlined phrase does not make it clear that Pierre depicted the sights. The phrase *sights that are depicted* makes it sound like a disembodied hand put paint on canvas.

If you encountered this question on the test, you could immediately eliminate (A) if you realized there was a problem. Both (B) and (C) repeat the original mistakes. They are wordy and they avoid identifying Pierre as the performer of the action. Answer choice (D) looks much better; it's short and there are no red-flag phrases or words, such as *having been* or *is*, that suggest the passive voice. Suppose you suspect that (D) is the right answer; if you plug it back into the sentence, as you should always do, you get, *Pierre observed the diners and motels of middle America, and his depiction of these sights in his trendy paintings*. This newly created sentence is actually a fragment, and therefore grammatically unacceptable.

So we come to (E): brief, clear, to the point, and entirely devoid of the passive voice. Does it check out? *Pierre observed the diners and motels of middle America, and depicted these sights in his trendy paintings*. Yes. (E) both avoids wordiness and names Pierre as the performer of the action.

Run-On Sentences

You'll probably see one or two run-on sentences on this section of the test. A run-on sentence is comprised of two complete sentences jammed together. For example, this is a run-on sentence:

I walked into the pet store and asked the clerk if she had any talking parrots, this made her roll her eyes.

Both halves of this sentence could function alone:

I walked into the pet store and asked the clerk if she had any talking parrots. This made her roll her eyes.

Because each half of the sentence is complete on its own, the two halves cannot be joined together with a comma.

There are a number of ways to fix a run-on sentence. One of the most common remedies, at least on the Writing SAT II, is the insertion of a semicolon. A semicolon signals that both sides of the sentence are grammatically separate, but closely related to one another. For example, this sentence could be fixed simply by replacing the comma with a semicolon:

> *I walked into the pet store and asked the clerk if she had any talking parrots; this made her roll her eyes.*

There are other acceptable methods for correcting run-on sentences, although on this test, the semicolon is certainly the most common. Suppose you see this run-on sentence:

> *In her incredible eagerness to cheer her team to victory, Amy the cheerleader has lost her voice, therefore her performance at the games is a silent one.*

One way of correcting run-ons is to add the conjunction *and*:

> *In her incredible eagerness to cheer her team to victory, Amy the cheerleader has lost her voice and therefore her performance at the games is a silent one.*

Finally, you can correct run-ons by making one clause subordinate to the other. This sounds complicated, but take a look at this uncorrected run-on sentence:

> *The student council attempted to lure people to the dance with free food, most people attended the hockey game.*

"Making one clause subordinate to the other" is simply a fancy way of saying you can correct this sentence by making the relationship between the two clauses more clear. This sentence suggests that despite the student council's efforts, people didn't go to the dance because they went to the hockey game. This means we can correct this run-on by adding a word that makes this relationship clear:

> *Although the student council attempted to lure people to the dance with free food, most people attended the hockey game.*

Take a look at the following example:

> The police reprimanded everyone <u>at the party, they didn't seem very sympathetic to the fact that it was our senior year</u>.

(A)   at the party, they didn't seem very sympathetic to the fact that it was our senior year

(B)   at the party, seemingly the fact that it was our senior year did not make them sympathetic

(C)   at the party without being sympathetic to the fact that it was our senior year

Improving Sentences

(D)   at the party they didn't, despite the fact that it was our senior year, seem very sympathetic

(E)   at the party; they didn't seem very sympathetic to the fact that it was our senior year

Here we have a classic run-on. The two parts could stand alone:

The police reprimanded everyone at the party. They didn't seem very sympathetic to the fact that it was our senior year.

Remember, the question-writers will usually fix run-ons by exchanging the comma for a semicolon. In this case, (E), which uses the semicolon method, is the correct answer.

Note that you could also correct the question above by turning the second half into a subordinate clause:

Since they reprimanded everyone at the party, the police didn't seem very sympathetic to the fact that it was our senior year.

Alternatively, you could have inserted the word *and* between the two clauses:

The police reprimanded everyone at the party, and they didn't seem very sympathetic to the fact that it was our senior year.

In most instances, the answer choices will only include one of these methods for fixing a run-on sentence. If both methods appear among the answer choices, you can be sure that one of those two answers will introduce some new, unrelated error.

Here's another example of an Improving Sentences run-on:

The crème brûleé is delicious <u>at that bistro I recommend you try it after your meal</u>.

(A)   at that bistro I recommend you try it after your meal
(B)   at that bistro, and I recommend you try it after your meal
(C)   after your meal, it can be tried at that bistro
(D)   and it can be tried after your meal at that bistro
(E)   at that bistro, after your meal is when I recommend you try it

(B) is correct. It fixes the run-on by adding a comma and *and*. (D) might have tempted you; it starts promisingly with *and*, but it introduces the new problem of the passive voice, and avoids mentioning who should try the crème brûleé.

Misplaced Modifier

A modifying phrase is a phrase that explains or describes a word. In grammatical English, modifiers are usually placed right next to the word they are explaining or describing. When modifiers are placed far away from the word they're describing, the sentence can become confusing. Sometimes, as in the following sentence, it becomes unclear what word the modifying phrase is referring to.

> *Eating six corn dogs, nausea overwhelmed Jane.*

This sentence is problematic, both grammatically and logically. We can logically infer that Jane was doing the eating, but because the modifying phrase is so far from the word it's intended to modify, figuring out the meaning of the sentence takes a lot of work. And grammatically, one meaning of the sentence is that nausea ate six corn dogs. That is not the meaning the writer intended, but it makes grammatical sense.

When you see a modifier followed by a comma, make sure the word the modifier describes comes right after the comma. A corrected version of this sentence could read:

> *After eating six corn dogs, Jane was overwhelmed with nausea.*

The phrase *eating six corn dogs* describes Jane and her behavior, so Jane's name should come right after the phrase.

Another way to correct the sentence:

> *Nausea overwhelmed Jane after she ate six corn dogs.*

Take a look at this sample question:

> Having an exorbitant price and a severely trendy cut, Marcel snatched up the designer jeans as soon as he spotted them.

(A) Having an exorbitant price and a severely trendy cut, Marcel snatched up the designer jeans

(B) Marcel who chose them for their exorbitant price and severely trendy cut snatched up the designer jeans

(C) The jeans' exorbitant price and severely trendy cut led to Marcel's snatching them up

(D) Despite their exorbitant price and severely trendy cut, Marcel snatched up the designer jeans

(E) Based on their exorbitant price and severely trendy cut, the jeans were chosen by Marcel

The correct answer here is a bit tricky to determine. There is a problem with the original sentence. Because the name Marcel immediately follows the modifier *having an exorbitant price and a severely trendy cut*, the sentence implies that Marcel is overpriced, rather than the jeans. Because we know a problem exists, therefore, we can eliminate (A).

(B) can be eliminated because it is convoluted and difficult to follow. (C) can be eliminated for the same reason; the phrase *Marcel's snatching them up* is particularly unlovely. (E) looks better, but the phrase *the jeans were chosen* needlessly uses the passive voice. (D) is the correct answer. It is not the classic means of fixing a misplaced modifier, but it works. Most importantly, in the correct answer, the phrase *exorbitant price and severely trendy cut* modifies *designer jeans* rather than *Marcel*. Of secondary importance is the fact that the correct answer solves another problem with the original sentence, which is the phrase *having an exorbitant price and severely trendy cut*; that word *having* does not clearly express the relationship between the jeans' characteristics and Marcel's purchase. In the correct answer, the word *despite* does clearly express that relationship. *Despite* suggests that even though the jeans have a few major problems, Marcel bought them anyway.

Parallelism

We covered parallelism in the Identifying Sentence Error chapter, but we'll give it a brief review again here since it is likely to show up in the Improving Sentences questions. In a sentence, all of the different components must start, continue, and end in the same, or parallel, way. It's especially common to find errors of parallelism in sentences that list actions or items. In the list below, for example, the rules are not presented in the same format, which means there is an error of parallelism.

> *In the pool area, there is no spitting, no running, and don't throw your cigarette butts in the water.*

The first two forbidden things end in *-ing* (*-ing* words are called gerunds), and because of that, the third forbidden thing must also end in *-ing*. If you start with gerunds, you must continue with gerunds all the way through a sentence.

> *In the pool area, there is no spitting, no running, and no tossing your cigarette butts in the water.*

Here is a sample Improving Sentences parallelism question:

The unlimited pass allowed Gene to use the subway as much as he wanted <u>and he could transfer</u> to the bus for free.

(A)   and he could transfer
(B)   as well as transferring
(C)   so he could transfer
(D)   and a transfer
(E)   and to transfer

The description of the pass's powers begins with an infinitive, *to use*. Therefore, on the other side of that *and*, we should find another infinitive. Instead, the original sentence has the unparallel phrase *he could transfer*. (E), the correct answer, balances both sides of the equation by substituting *to transfer*. In its corrected form, the sentence is made nicely parallel and balanced by the two infinitives:

> *The unlimited pass allowed Gene to use the subway as much as he wanted and to transfer to the bus for free.*

Often, Improving Sentences questions will test parallelism by switching the infinitive to a gerund.

> Swimming for six miles after eating a big sandwich produces the same results <u>than to have</u> the flu.

> (A)   than to have
> (B)   than if you have
> (C)   as if you have
> (D)   as having
> (E)   as it does when having

The correct answer here is (D). The infinitive *to have* must be replaced by the gerund *having*.

Conjunction

Conjunctions are connecting words such as *and, but, or, which*, etc. They provide means of linking two parts of a sentence together. Suppose you have two sentences:

> *Abigail leaped over the fence. She was able to do this because she was riding a horse.*

A conjunction such as *which* enables you to connect the two halves of the sentence:

> *Abigail leaped over the fence, which she was able to do because she was riding a horse.*

Improving Sentences questions will test you on conjunctions by including sentences in which the conjunction doesn't make logical sense. For example:

> Jane Austen wrote a novel called <u>*Emma* and it depicts</u> the relationship between a snotty but lovable rich girl and her meek, slightly annoying friend.

> (A)   *Emma* and it depicts
> (B)   *Emma*, being the depiction of
> (C)   *Emma*, it depicts
> (D)   *Emma* that depicts
> (E)   *Emma*, and depicting in it

The right answer is (D). In this sentence, the conjunction *that* expresses the function of the novel more elegantly than the phrase *and it* does.

Improving Sentences

Fragment

A few paragraphs ago, we talked about run-ons, which are commonly tested errors in this section. Fragments are almost the opposite of run-on sentences. Whereas run-ons are sentences with too many clauses squashed together, fragments have no independent clause, and therefore are incomplete sentences.

The bad-cop vice principal growling at terrified students in the office.

    (A)   The bad-cop vice principal growling
    (B)   The bad-cop vice principal having growled
    (C)   Growling, the bad-cop vice principal
    (D)   It is the bad-cop vice-principal
    (E)   The bad-cop vice principle growls

The problem here is with *growling*, an incomplete verb form. The original sentence sets up—and never fulfills—an expectation in the reader. We think, "The bad-cop vice principal growling at terrified students *what*?" We expect the sentence to continue.

The sentence would be complete if, say, it read, *The bad-cop vice principal growling at terrified students was notorious for his brutal tactics*. The answer choices don't expand on sentences in quite this way, but the correct answer, (E), does take away the problem of expectation. When we read *The bad-cop vice principal growls at terrified students*, we don't expect the sentence to continue. He growls and that's the end of the story.

Coordination/Subordination

Don't worry if you've never heard of coordination and subordination. Remember, you don't need to recognize grammar terms, you just need to recognize the problem when you see it.

Bad coordination happens when two clauses are joined together with a word that misrepresents their relationship. For example:

J.C. made T-shirts but he designed the logos himself.

    (A) but he designed the logos himself
    (B) however, he designed the logos himself
    (C) and he designed the logos himself
    (D) since he designed the logos himself
    (E) and yet, he designed the logos himself

Here we see that J.C. creates his own T-shirts. He also designs logos for the T-shirts. So should the word *but* express the relationship between these two activities? No, because the two activities are closely related. The word *but* would make sense only if the sentence said something like *J.C. made T-shirts, but other than that he sat around playing Mario Kart all day*. If you get to the middle of a sentence and it takes a turn you weren't expecting, look for a coordination error.

In this question, we can eliminate (B) because the word *however* is also a bad choice when joining these two clauses. It expresses the same kind of relationship as does the word *but*. We can eliminate (E) for the same reason. Answer (D) isn't quite as bad as (B) and (E), but *J.C. made T-shirts since he designed the logos himself* doesn't make that much sense. J.C. doesn't make T-shirts *because* he designs the logos, he makes T-shirts *and* designs the logos, which is exactly what (C) says. Answer (C) conveys the idea that the two halves of the sentence go together. Read the sentence once to make sure it makes sense: *J.C. made T-shirts and he designed the logos himself*. Lovely.

Subordination problems happen when there are two subordinate clauses and no main clause. When you see the words *although*, *because*, *if*, *since*, or *so that*, you know that a subordinate clause is on the way. Don't worry if you've never heard the phrase "subordinate clause" before. As an English speaker, you already know where subordinate clauses go and how they should sound. If you see one clause that starts with *although*, *because*, *if*, *since*, or *so that*, and then another clause that starts with one of these words, you'll hear the screwiness loud and clear:

> Because Teddy thought his first date with Maria went well, <u>so that he called her every day for the next week</u>.

> (A) so that he called her every day for the next week
> (B) although he called her every day for the next week
> (C) because he called her every day for the next week
> (D) he called her every day for the next week
> (E) and he called her every day for the next week

You don't need to know that this sentence is an example of bad subordination. You just need to see that the two parts of the sentence don't go together. Why don't they? Because there's something strange about the middle of the sentence. You hit the comma, and then the sentence takes an unexpected turn.

The first part of the sentence sets us up: Because Teddy thought his first date with Maria went well, we expect something along the lines of *he invited her out again* or *he kissed her on her front porch*, right? Instead, we get the phrase *so that*. That sounds funny. So (A) is wrong, because immediately we heard a problem. In (B), the word *although* gives us exactly the same sort of problem as existed in the original sentence. Same with (C), *because*. (D) looks good (and is the right answer). In (E), the word *and* doesn't go with the *although* that starts the sentence. Read (D) into the sentence to make sure: *Because Teddy thought his first date with Maria went well, he called her every day for the next week*. Looks good.

On coordination and subordination questions, the only important thing is to think of yourself, the reader. Did you feel a twinge of surprise when you hit the middle of the sentence? Did the sentence veer off in a weird and unexpected direction? If so, look for an answer choice that makes you, the reader, feel like you're on firm ground.

Improving Sentences

Cheap Tricks

We put the cheap tricks at the end of this chapter because they are to be employed *only* in cases of desperation. Use them when you cannot eliminate even one answer choice, or when you've eliminated all but two answer choices and find yourself wasting precious minutes agonizing over which answer choice is the correct one.

Before we begin discussing the cheap tricks, we must add a further caveat: *do not apply the cheap tricks blindly.* They don't work all of the time, and they shouldn't be relied upon too heavily. For example, we advise you to avoid answer choices that include gerunds, answers that change the content of the sentence, and long answers; but sometimes the right answer will include a word that ends in *–ing*, sometimes the right answer will seem like it changes the meaning of the original sentence, and sometimes the right answer will be long. The cheap tricks can improve your odds of correctly answering a question on which you're stumped, but they aren't foolproof.

That said, let's dive into the bag of cheap tricks. Suppose that you find yourself stymied by this question:

> Brent's cowboy hat looks pretty silly, <u>seeing as how he lives in Manhattan</u>.
>
> (A) seeing as how he lives in Manhattan
> (B) since he lives in Manhattan
> (C) considering him living in Manhattan
> (D) seeing that he lives in Manhattan
> (E) after all he doesn't live in the West

You invoke the first rule (read the sentence and try to hear the problem) and hear something funny about the phrase *seeing as how.* Let's say you're not sure how to fix it. Even though you don't immediately think of a solution, since you know a problem does exist, you remember that you can automatically eliminate (A) because that choice repeats the underlined part of the sentence. You then call on another rule, and eliminate any answer choices that repeat the original mistake. In this case, that means eliminating answer choice (D), which repeats the problematic word *seeing.*

Let's say you now find yourself stuck. (B), (C), and (E) look equally good to you. It's time to call on the dirty tricks that will allow you to outwit the ETS question-writers.

Cheap Trick #1: cross out answer choices that begin with words ending in –ing.

In the case of the sentence *Brent's cowboy hat looks pretty silly, seeing as how he lives in Manhattan*, employing the trick means you'd read the word *considering* and alarm bells would go off. That means you can eliminate answer (C), *considering him living in Manhattan*. In cases like this one, *-ing* words (for the record, they're called gerunds) are often awkward. If you read the sentence and have no idea which answer choice is right, get rid of the one with a word like *considering*.

Cheap Trick #2: cross out answer choices that change the content of the sentence.

Be suspicious of answer choices that fiddle with the meaning of the sentence. (E) is the obvious suspect in our sample question: *after all he doesn't live in the West*. There's a better reason than the cheap trick to eliminate (E): if you substitute (E) into the original sentence, you get *Brent's cowboy hat looks pretty silly, after all he doesn't live in the West*, which is a run-on sentence and therefore grammatically incorrect. If you didn't spot the run-on, though, and were in a panic, you could have eliminated (E) anyway, thanks to Cheap Trick #2. The sentence we started out with had to do with New York, and how ridiculous one looks sporting a cowboy hat in Manhattan. (E) brings up the West—new territory. Remember, the directions explicitly instruct you to *choose the answer that best expresses the meaning of the original sentence*, so an answer choice that messes with the original meaning should be eliminated.

Cheap Trick #3: brevity is the soul of a right answer

When you find yourself staring blankly at two or three answer choices, bewildered and sweaty, go with the shorter answer choice. ETS likes to keep the right answers concise. (B) is not only the right answer, it's nice and short: *since he lives in Manhattan*.

Improving Sentences

Improving Paragraphs

The IMPROVING PARAGRAPHS section of the test consists of two essays. Each essay is accompanied by about six questions that will test your ability to improve awkward sentence construction, analyze individual sentences or the essay as a whole, and add sentences to improve clarity or make transitions smoother. Occasionally, a question will test your ability to combine two sentences into one.

On the test, the two Improving Paragraphs essays and their accompanying questions are located after the Improving Sentences questions and before the second group of Identifying Sentence Error questions.

Chapter Contents

Directions

Take a look at the official directions for Improving Paragraphs:

Directions: Each of the following passages is an early draft of an essay. Some parts of the passages need to be rewritten.

Read each passage and answer the questions that follow. Some questions are about particular sentences or parts of sentences and ask you to improve sentence structure and word choice. Other questions refer to parts of the essay or the entire essay and ask you to consider organization and development. In making your decisions, follow the conventions of standard written English. After you have chosen your answer, fill in the corresponding oval on your answer sheet.

In plain English: some questions will ask you to deal with fixing or combining individual sentences, and some will ask you to deal with the essay as a whole.

The Essays

The two Improving Paragraphs essays are not long. Both essays usually contain three paragraphs. The test writers want the essays to seem like drafts of student essays. This means that the essays will not be difficult to read. For the most part, the essays use simple sentence construction and a straightforward prose style. This simplicity is good, because it means you won't have to waste a lot of time poring over the essays. The questions after the essay will focus on the errors.

The Questions

Unlike the previous two multiple-choice sections, Improving Paragraphs does not focus on grammar. Although remembering the grammar rules we've talked about in previous chapters will occasionally prove helpful, these questions will focus on improving the utility and clarity of writing, rather than on fixing grammar.

There are four kinds of Improving Paragraphs questions:

1. **Sentence Revision questions.** Sentence revision questions are by far the most common question type—about 7 of the 12 Improving Paragraphs questions will cover sentence revision. As their name suggests, sentence revision questions require you to revise an entire sentence, or a portion of one. Revision questions will ask you things like which word should be added to clarify the meaning of a particular sentence, or which multiple choice answer is the best revision of a phrase.

2. **Sentence Addition questions.** Sentence addition questions will ask you which sentences or phrases should be added in order to make a smoother transition or clarify meaning.

3. **Sentence Combination questions.** Combining sentence questions, as you might guess, will ask you to pick the best way to combine two or more sentences.

4. **Essay Analysis questions.** Analysis questions will ask you things like which sentence best sums up the essay, or how a particular sentence functions.

We'll cover each of these types of questions in greater detail later in the chapter.

How to Approach the Questions

The four question types (sentence revision, essay analysis, sentence addition, and sentence combination) should each be approached a bit differently, but there are five standard steps for dealing with all types of Improving Paragraphs questions:

1. Quickly read the essay.

2. Read the question.

3. Reread the sentences before and after the "problem" sentence.

4. Come up with your own revision/analysis/addition/combination.

5. Look for the answer choice that comes closest to your own answer.

These steps are fairly simple, but there are important things to note about each one.

1. Quickly read the essay.

This first step never varies: before looking at the questions, read the essay. Spend about a minute (really, just a minute) reading the essay. A minute is not that long, but you won't need long to get through the essays. They aren't lengthy, and their prose is not that difficult. The goal of the quick read-through is to get a general idea of what the essay is about, and figure out the point of each paragraph.

It's a mistake to read the essay looking for errors and imagining how you would fix them. Because the essay has more sentences than the questions can cover, it's a waste of time to examine each sentence carefully. You won't be asked about every single sentence, so let the questions themselves tell you which sentences you should examine for problems, rather than reading the essay and trying to anticipate the questions.

2. Read the question.

This is an obvious step, but it is important to give the question a very careful read-through. On sentence revision questions, for example, you'll see a sentence from the essay reprinted; sometimes the entire sentence will need revision, while sometimes only an underlined portion of the sentence will need work. If only a portion of the sentence is underlined, you don't want to make unnecessary work for yourself by combing through the entire sentence looking for errors.

Look at this example:

1. How would sentence 4, reproduced below, be best revised?

> *I love eating pizza for <u>dinner, even more I love</u> eating it for breakfast.*

Since only a portion of this sentence is underlined, you know that you need examine only the underlined part for errors and do not need to think too much about the parts that aren't underlined.

3. Reread the sentences before and after the "problem" sentence.

"Context matters" is a good motto for this section of the test. Because you'll read the essay before you tackle the questions, you'll have a general understanding of what the essay is about. But in order to answer the individual questions, you'll have to go back to the relevant part of the essay and reread the problem sentence (the sentence mentioned in the question) more carefully. It's also crucial to read the context sentences (the sentences before and after the problem sentence). Sometimes the context can help you rewrite the sentence. Suppose you go back to the essay, and read these sentences around the problem sentence:

> *Her mother told Emily to make the bed. Another chore her mother <u>told her to do was to</u> take out the garbage. Emily reluctantly complied.*

Here, the first and second sentences convey similar information, but the second (problem) sentence is wordy and awkward, and the first sentence is clean and succinct. Therefore, you can take the first sentence as a model for the revision of the second sentence.

4. Come up with your own revision first.

As in the other multiple-choice sections, in Improving Paragraphs questions it's important to generate your own answer before you read the answer choices. The answer choices are there to confuse you. Preparing your own answer will allow you to keep a cool head as you read the answer choices.

Say you read the context sentences and see that the first sentence works well. You model the revision on that successful first sentence and come up with:

> *Her mother also told Emily to take out the garbage.*

Now, go to the answer choices and follow the fifth step:

5. Look for the answer that comes closest to your own answer.

Say the answer choices read:

(A)   Another chore her mother told her to do was to take out the garbage.
(B)   Her mother additionally asked her to do the chore of taking out the garbage.
(C)   Also, take out the garbage, her mother asked.
(D)   Then, her mother told Emily to take out the garbage.
(E)   She also asked Emily to take out the garbage.

(D) comes closest to the revision you prepared before you looked at the answer choices, so that should be your choice.

With these five basic rules in mind, we're going to take you through each of the four question types and discuss their features and quirks. We list the question types in order of the frequency with which they occur on the test—sentence revision, essay analysis, sentence addition, and sentence combination.

Sentence Revision Questions

You might be asked to revise a sentence for a variety of reasons.

Revising Awkward Sentences

Most revising sentences questions will have you untangling confusing or unwieldy syntax. These are two typical ways the test will pose this sort of sentence revision question:

> Which of the following best revises the underlined portion of sentence 3, which is reprinted below?

> Which is the clearest version of the underlined portion of sentence 2?

Revising Ambiguous Sentences

Many revising sentences questions will require you to make ambiguous wording more specific. The following question asks you to add one word in order to clear up ambiguity:

> In the context of the third paragraph, sentence 9 could be made more precise by adding which of the following words after "*That*"?

Some questions will ask you to change one vague phrase. For example:

> The phrase "*this thing*" in sentence 5 is made most specific in which of the following revisions?

Revising Unclear Sentences

Other revising sentences questions will ask you to add a phrase or word that clarifies an unclear sentence. Look at this question:

> Which is the best word or phrase to add after "*The movie theater*" in order to connect sentence 3 (reprinted below) to the rest of the first paragraph?

Improving Paragraphs

Sentence Addition

Frequently, the purpose of adding a sentence, even if this purpose is not explicitly stated in the question, is to smooth a rough transition. Therefore, when you see a sentence addition question and are preparing your own answer, try to see how you could improve the transition from paragraph to paragraph or from sentence to sentence.

Here are two sample sentence addition questions:

> Which of the following sentences should be added after sentence 7 in order to link the second paragraph to the rest of the essay?

> Which of the following sentences should be inserted at the beginning of the third paragraph, before sentence 10?

Sentence Combination

Some questions will ask you to combine two or, occasionally, three sentences. For combining sentences questions, you need only reread the sentences you've been asked to combine. Context does not usually matter. Here are two typical sentence combination questions:

> Which of the following is the best way to combine and revise sentences 5 and 6?

> How should the underlined portions of sentences 4 and 5, which are reprinted below, be revised so that the two sentences combine into one?

Frequently, you'll combine the sentences by using a comma and a conjunction (a conjunction is a word like *and, but, so,* etc.) You can also combine sentences using semicolons and colons. All of the different combination methods are discussed below.

Some rare sentence combination questions will require you to look at context:

> In order to vary the repetitive sentence structure of the sentences in the first paragraph, how should sentences 8 and 9 be combined?

On a question like this, you must look back at the relevant paragraph so that you know what repetitive sentence structure the question is asking you about.

Comma and Conjunction

Say the question asks you to combine these two sentences:

> *She accidentally flushed her ring down the toilet. The plumber got it back for her.*

One way of combining these two sentences is to use a comma and a conjunction. In this case, using a comma and a conjunction gives you a sentence like this:

> *She accidentally flushed her ring down the toilet, but the plumber got it back for her.*

Be sure the conjunction you choose makes sense. The revision below is grammatically correct, but logically flawed:

She accidentally flushed her ring down the toilet, because the plumber got it back for her.

The word *because* does not make sense, since it suggests that the woman in question flushed her ring down the toilet a second time as a result of the plumber initially retrieving it.

Semicolon

If two sentences are closely related, you can combine them with a semicolon. Say you begin with these two sentences:

Margaret recently met her future mother-in-law. Problems ensued immediately.

Using a semicolon, the combination is:

Margaret recently met her future mother-in-law; problems ensued immediately.

Expressing a Logical Relationship

Some sentence combination questions will ask you to combine two sentences in a way that makes their relationship more clear. As always, it's true that it's a good idea to prepare your own answer. It's also true that on this specific type of question, the answer choices can do a lot of the grunt work for you. They'll make it clear what kind of logical relationship the test writers see between the two sentences, and you'll simply have to pick the grammatically and logically correct answer choice. Look at this example:

> To vary the pattern of sentences in the first paragraph, which of the following is the best way to combine sentences 2 and 3 (reprinted below)?
>
> *My sister eats cottage cheese and grapes for lunch. I eat tacos.*
>
> (A) While my sister eats cottage cheese and grapes for lunch, tacos are what I'm eating.
> (B) In contrast to my sister eating cottage cheese and grapes for lunch, I will be eating tacos.
> (C) My sister was eating cottage cheese and grapes for lunch, I was eating tacos.
> (D) My sister eats cottage cheese and grapes for lunch and I am not the same because I eat tacos.
> (E) Unlike my sister, who eats cottage cheese and grapes for lunch, I eat tacos.

The correct answer is (E). As you can see, all of the answer choices express the basic logical relationship between the two sentences: the speaker is drawing a contrast between her sister's eating habits and her own. Only answer choice (E), however, expresses this contrast grammatically. (A) has a parallelism error; it begins by saying *my sister eats*, so the second half of the sentence should say *I eat*, so that both halves of the sentence use present tense. However, the second half of the sentence reads *I'm eating*. (B) has a tense problem; the sister is eating in the present tense, but the speaker is eating sometime in the future. This changes the original meaning of the two sentences, in which both people are eating at the same time. Answer choice (C) is a run-on sentence. Answer choice (D) is awkward and wordy because of the phrase *and I am not the same*.

Essay Analysis

A few questions will require you to analyze the essay as a whole. Sometimes, after reading an analysis question, you'll find that you don't even need to glance back to the essay in order to figure out the right answer. In some cases, though, you will need to go back and reread a few sentences. This question asks about the essay in general terms:

> Which sentence best summarizes the main idea of the passage?

It would be a waste of time to skim the essay again in order to figure out the answer to this question. Analysis questions that ask about the entire essay can be answered simply by relying on the quick read-through you do as the first step. If you get a general idea of the essay's content on that read-through, you're well-equipped to answer a question like this.

The following is a different variety of question, but one that also asks you to analyze the entire essay:

> The writer uses all of the following techniques EXCEPT:
>
> (A) using concrete examples
> (B) using an anecdote to illustrate his thesis
> (C) discounting those who disagree with his opinion
> (D) stating and then disproving a theory
> (E) making reference to a work of fiction

Clearly, this kind of question does not allow you to prepare your own answer; you will have to look right to the answer choices. Before you do that, however, circle the word EXCEPT. This question is worded in a confusing way: it is asking you to *eliminate* all those techniques that the writer actually uses. The correct answer, therefore, will name the one technique that does not appear in the essay.

When answering this question, go back and find the lines that use the concrete examples mentioned in (A), the anecdote mentioned in (B), and so on. If you find lines that utilize the technique mentioned, cross out the corresponding answer choice in your test booklet.

Analyzing a Single Sentence

Some analysis questions will ask you to analyze one sentence. These questions will require you to go back to the essay and read the sentences before and after the problem sentence. Look at this question, for example:

Sentence 4 works to

(A) suggest a hypothetical situation
(B) ask the reader to question the usefulness of theater
(C) let the writer appear modest
(D) contradict a widely held assumption about theater
(E) reveal the writer's confusion about theatrical productions

In order to determine the function of sentence 4, you would return to the relevant paragraph and read sentences 3, 4, and 5. Then, before looking at the answer choices, you would decide for yourself what sentence 4 works to do. If you're having trouble generating your own answer on this kind of question, the answer choices can help you out quite a bit. If you pay attention to the language each answer choice employs, some of them will strike you as obviously wrong. Perhaps the author doesn't sound *modest* at all; perhaps she's not revealing her *confusion* or contradicting a *widely held assumption*.

Here is another kind of single-sentence analysis question:

The writer could best improve sentence 8 by

(A) admitting the flaws in his theory
(B) giving concrete examples
(C) explaining his own opinion
(D) bringing up new problems
(E) explaining modern theater

For this question it is possible to prepare your own answer first. Read sentences 7, 8, and 9, and see if you can determine the problem with sentence 8 before you look at the answer choices.

Sample Improving Paragraphs Essay

Below you'll find a sample essay followed by six typical questions. Take a shot at answering the questions yourself before you look at the answers and detailed explanations that follow.

(1) In one scene in a short story I recently read, the main character goes back in time and happens to bring a few gold pieces back to the present with him. (2) The gold pieces turn out to be incredibly valuable. (3) This short story reminded me of the baseball card collecting craze, it being an interesting facet of American pop culture. (4) Buying and saving baseball cards means spending very little money on something that might turn out to be worth big bucks in the future.

(5) My dad collected baseball cards when he was a kid, and no one back then thought they'd be worth anything. (6) Someone like my dad used up his allowance every week just because he wanted to collect all of his favorite players—Roy Campanella, in my dad's case. (7) By dedicating the bulk of his weekly income to adding player after player to his collection, my father declared his dedication to the players.

(8) Baseball is a high-grossing sport, and so baseball card collecting has become one. (9) Everyone has heard of one baseball card in its original wrapping commanding an absurdly high price, and now everyone is positive that his or her shoebox full of old baseball cards contains at least one card worth millions. (10) But if my dad had that one card, he won't know it. (11) Way before he realized it, his mother had gotten rid of them.

1.   Which sentence best summarizes the main idea of the passage?

    (A)   sentence 1
    (B)   sentence 2
    (C)   sentence 3
    (D)   sentence 4
    (E)   sentence 7

2.   In context, which revision does sentence 3 most need?

    (A)   Add *In point of fact* at the beginning.
    (B)   Delete the phrase *short story*.
    (C)   Delete the words *it being*.
    (D)   Replace the comma with a dash.
    (E)   Replace *reminded* with *reminds*.

3.   Which of the following sentences should be added before sentence 5, at the beginning of the second paragraph?

    (A)   But there were people who didn't collect baseball cards with money in mind.
    (B)   Clearly, early capitalism is a good idea.
    (C)   In the collecting world, everyone has a different story.
    (D)   Let me relate to you my own father's plan to garner money.
    (E)   Some pastimes have benefits you can't discern at first.

4.   Which of the following best revises sentence 8, which is reproduced below?

Baseball is a high-grossing sport, and so baseball card collecting has become one.

    (A)   (as it is now)
    (B)   Growing to be more and more like the sport that makes its existence possible has been baseball card collecting.
    (C)   They say that baseball is now a highly profitable industry, as is this pastime.
    (D)   Like the sport itself, baseball card collecting has become a highly profitable industry.
    (E)   At last, like the highly profitable industry of baseball, baseball card collecting is wholly changed.

5.   Of the following, which best revises the underlined part of sentence 10, which is reproduced below?

But if my dad had that one card, he won't know it.

   (A)   card, he would never realize it.
   (B)   card; he would never realize it.
   (C)   card, how could he realize it?
   (D)   card, my dad won't ever realize it.
   (E)   card—he never realized it.

6.   In the context of the paragraph, which is the best revision of sentence 11, which is reproduced below?

Way before he realized it, his mother had gotten rid of them.

   (A)   (as it is now)
   (B)   Years before he realized his cards could be valuable, his mother had gotten rid of them.
   (C)   Years before he has realized about the cards, his mother has gotten rid of them.
   (D)   It was years before he realized about the cards that his mother got rid of them.
   (E)   His mother gets rid of the cards years before he realizes about them.

Answers and Explanations

What follows is a detailed discussion of each question and answer.

1. (D)

This is an essay analysis question that asks you about the essay as a whole. After reading the essay once, you should have a fairly good idea of its main idea. And happily, the test writers put this question first, which means you've just finished reading the essay and it is fresh in your mind. The only real work involved in this question is going back and reading the sentences that are mentioned by number in the answer choices. Before you do that, however, tell yourself what you think is the main idea of the essay—something like, *Collecting baseball cards can turn out to be very profitable*. This doesn't have to be a finely honed sentence. It's just a rough sketch, so that you have an idea of what you're looking for as you tackle the answer choices.

   Sentence 1 reads, *In one scene in a short story I recently read, the main character goes back in time and happens to bring a few gold pieces back to the present with him.* That deals with the anecdote the writer uses to introduce his main idea; it is too specific to be the main idea sentence. Eliminate it.

   Sentence 2 reads, *The gold pieces turn out to be incredibly valuable.* This is even more specific than the first sentence. You can also eliminate (B). Sentence 3: *This short story reminded me of the baseball card collecting craze, it being an interesting facet of*

American pop culture. This sounds better; at least it mentions baseball card collecting, which is the main idea of the essay. However, it sounds like a transition between the anecdote and the main thrust of the essay, rather than a summation of the main idea. Leave it for now, since it sounds better than the first two.

Sentence 4 reads, *Buying and saving baseball cards means spending very little money on something that might turn out to be worth big bucks in the future.* This sentence sounds very much like the answer choice you generated on your own; it talks about card collecting, and it also mentions the idea that you can make money on card collecting. Sentence 4 is a better choice than sentence 3, which is a transition sentence and is not specific about the monetary benefits of card collecting.

Look at (E), just to be sure it's not a better answer choice than (D). *By dedicating the bulk of his weekly income to adding player after player to his collection, my father declared his dedication to the players.* (E) is too specific; the passage's main point is not to explain the initial reason that kids take up card-collecting, but to explain what happens years after the collection is begun.

2. (C)

Here we have a classic sentence revision question. Sentence 3 reads, *This short story reminded me of the baseball card collecting craze, it being an interesting facet of American pop culture.* If you saw right away that the problem here was with the phrase *it being*, great—all you need do is find the correct answer choice, (C), and move on to the next question. If you can hear the problem phrase right away, trust your ear—don't waste a lot of time worrying that you got the answer too quickly. If you didn't hear the problem right away, however, go through each of the answer choices and try out the suggested change.

Making the changes suggested by (A), you get *In point of fact, this short story reminded me of the baseball card collecting craze, it being an interesting facet of American pop culture.* If you don't look at the context, there doesn't seem to be anything particularly wrong about this sentence, except perhaps that it's a bit wordy. If you look at it in context, however, you can see that adding *in point of fact* is illogical: *The gold pieces turn out to be incredibly valuable. In point of fact, this short story reminded me of the baseball card collecting craze, it being an interesting facet of American pop culture.* The phrase *in point of fact* signals that the writer is about to elaborate on a point he's begun in the last sentence, but sentence 3 is actually a departure from sentence 2, not an elaboration on it. You can eliminate (A).

If you make the changes suggested by (B), you get, *This reminded me of the baseball card collecting craze, it being an interesting facet of American pop culture.* Removing the phrase *short story* merely makes the word *this* vague. It does not improve the sentence.

(C) gives you *This reminded me of the baseball card collecting craze, an interesting facet of American pop culture.* This is the correct answer choice because it removes a superfluous phrase without making the sentence ungrammatical.

(D) gives you *This reminded me of the baseball card collecting craze—an interesting facet of American pop culture.* A dash is used to signal an abrupt transition or a new thought; however, here, the phrase that comes after the comma is not a transition or a new thought, it is an elaboration on the baseball card collecting phase, so a dash is inappropriate.

Finally, (E)'s changes: *This reminds me of the baseball card collecting craze, it being an interesting facet of American pop culture.* This revision neither worsens nor improves the sentence. On rare occasions, you will find yourself in this dilemma: you will have two answer choices that seem to work, and you will have to decide between them. In this situation, ask yourself which answer choice makes a positive change, and which one is just acceptable. Get in the heads of the ETS people. They instruct you to choose the best answer choice; which one would they consider the best? Here, (C) is a better answer choice than (E) because it makes a needed revision to the sentence, whereas (E) just avoids making things worse.

3. (A)

This is a sentence addition question that requires a firm grasp of context. Read sentences 4 and 5: (4) *Buying and saving baseball cards means spending very little money on something that might turn out to be worth big bucks in the future.* (5) *My dad collected baseball cards when he was a kid, and no one back then thought they'd be worth anything.*

Remember, the right answer to sentence addition questions is almost always the one that smooths a rough transition. If you can generate your own transitional sentence and then see which answer choice matches it, great. If not, try out the suggested sentences and see which one works.

Choice (A): *Buying and saving baseball cards means spending very little money on something that might turn out to be worth big bucks in the future. But there were people who didn't collect baseball cards with money in mind. My dad collected baseball cards when he was a kid, and no one back then thought they'd be worth anything.* (A) is the correct answer. It provides a smooth transition between the idea that people can make a lot of money from their collections, and the specific story of the writer's father.

Let's take a glance at the other answer choices.

Choice (B): *Buying and saving baseball cards means spending very little money on something that might turn out to be worth big bucks in the future. Clearly, early capitalism is a good idea. My dad collected baseball cards when he was a kid, and no one back then thought they'd be worth anything.* This sentence isn't terrible, but the phrase *early capitalism* is strange, and sounds pretentious without meaning much. Also, it doesn't tie together the two sentences, as (A) does.

Choice (C): *Buying and saving baseball cards means spending very little money on something that might turn out to be worth big bucks in the future. In the collecting world, everyone has a different story. My dad collected baseball cards when he was a kid, and no one back then thought they'd be worth anything.* This new sentence is okay, but it's more vague than the correct answer, and once again it doesn't do a good job of knitting together sentences 4 and 5. Also, the phrase *collecting world* is a little ambiguous; we're talking about baseball card collecting, not collecting in general.

Choice (D): *Buying and saving baseball cards means spending very little money on something that might turn out to be worth big bucks in the future. Let me relate to you my own father's plan to garner money. My dad collected baseball cards when he was a kid, and no one back then thought they'd be worth anything.* The problem with (D) is mainly one of tone. The writer takes a relaxed, chummy tone throughout this essay, and this new sentence has a highfalutin', serious tone that clashes with the rest of the prose. Contrast the sentence suggested by (D), which uses the words *father* and *garner*, with sentence 5, which uses the words *dad* and *kid*. (D) is inappropriately formal.

Choice (E): *Buying and saving baseball cards means spending very little money on something that might turn out to be worth big bucks in the future. Some pastimes have benefits you can't discern at first. My dad collected baseball cards when he was a kid, and no one back then thought they'd be worth anything.* As with (B) and (C), there's not a lot wrong with this sentence besides the fact that it doesn't do the job as well as answer (A) does. (E) relates almost entirely to sentence 5, without referring back to sentence 4 at all, whereas the correct answer refers to both in equal measure.

4. (D)

This is another classic sentence revision question. You might be able to hear right away that this sentence could be improved. The phrase *has become one* is vague. Preparing your own answer, in this case, can entail no more than realizing that phrase is vague, and looking for an answer choice that clears up the vagueness. Also, once you see that the sentence needs improvement, you can eliminate (A), which keeps the sentence as it is.

(B) is okay in content, but awkward in execution. The phrase *baseball collecting* should go at the beginning of that sentence. Placed at the end, as it is, it sounds like an afterthought and impedes understanding.

(C) changes the meaning of the original sentence; it implies that baseball has only recently become a profitable industry, which the original sentence does not.

(D) is the correct answer. It clears up that vague phrase *has become one*. The *one* is specified and called *a highly profitable industry*.

(E) sounds strangely melodramatic. The original sentence does not claim that base-ball card collecting is *wholly changed*, as if a vast transformation has taken place, so neither should the revised version.

5. (D)

Here we have yet another revision question, this one asking you to revise a part of a sen-tence. The verb tense in the original sentence is not right. The first half of the sentence sets up a conditional sequence, but the verb is simple past tense: *if my dad had* and *won't know it* don't fit together. Of the answers, only (A) and (D) solve this problem. But (A) introduces a new problem by creating a mismatched pronoun. The plural *they* cannot act as a pronoun for the singular *my dad*. Choice (D) must be the right answer.

All of the other answer choices fail to fix the problem and introduce additional pro-noun errors.

6. (B)

Again, a sentence revision question. The problem with the initial sentence is the phrase *way before he realized it*, which is extremely vague. Look at the sentence in context: *(9) Everyone has heard of one baseball card in its original wrapping commanding an absurdly high price, and now everyone is positive that his or her shoebox full of old base-ball cards contains at least one card worth millions. (10) But if my dad had that one card, he won't know it. (11) Way before he realized it, his mother had gotten rid of them.* In your revision, you want the vague phrase *way before he realized it* to be replaced by something more specific about realizing that his cards could be worth something.

Choice (B) is the correct answer. It replaces *way before he realized it* with the more specific phrase *years before he realized his cards could be valuable*.

If you didn't initially see that (B) was correct, you could have eliminated wrong answers. Answer (A) can be eliminated, since you know there is something wrong with the sentence. (C) has a tense problem; since everything in the sentence is happen-ing in the past tense, *he has realized* should be *he realized*, and *has gotten rid of them* should be *got rid of them*. (D) is awkward, and difficult to follow. (E) has a tense prob-lem, like (C); *his mother gets rid* should be *his mother got rid*. She got rid of the cards in the past, not in the present.

PRACTICE
TESTS

Practice Tests Are Your Best Friends

Believe it or not, the Writing SAT II test has some redeeming qualities. One of them: reliability. The dear old thing doesn't change much from year to year. You can always count on a bunch of questions about subject-verb agreement and tense in the Identifying Sentence Errors section. You'll always see run-on sentences, passive voice, and parallelism errors tested in the Improving Sentences section. Revision questions will abound in the Improving Paragraphs section, and come hell or high water, you'll always have to write an essay in response to a statement.

Obviously, different editions of the Writing SAT II aren't *exactly* the same; individual questions will never repeat from test to test. But the subjects that those questions test, and the way in which the questions test those subjects, *will* stay constant.

This constancy can be of great benefit to you as you study for the test. To show how you can use the similarity between different versions of the Writing SAT II test to your own advantage, we provide a case study.

Using the Similarity of the Writing SAT II for Personal Gain

Suppose you sit down in a quiet room and spend an hour taking the practice test. Once you've completed the test, you flip to the back of the book and check your answers.

You get to question 10 and notice that you got it wrong. You look back at the question, and see that number 10 asked about this sentence:

> At a crucial juncture in the movie, someone reached for their box of candy and loudly removed the plastic packaging.

You chose (E), no error, which turns out to be the wrong answer. As you puzzle over the question, you realize that you don't understand why you got the answer wrong. The sentence looks perfectly fine to you! You start paging through this very book, looking for tips on the Identifying Sentence Errors section. Seeing that tense errors are common in this section, you check for a tense error in the sentence. No dice. Reading on, you find a tip: look out for the pronoun *their*, which people often use incorrectly in speech in an effort to avoid using a gender-specific singular pronoun. You realize that you didn't catch the error in number 10 (which should read, by the way, *At a crucial juncture in the movie, someone reached for his or her box of candy and loudly removed the plastic packaging*) because you didn't understand that *their* is incorrect in that context because *someone* is singular and so must be matched with a singular pronoun. You now promise that you will exercise extra caution when you see *their* in a sentence. Also, you now feel confident and smart, because you understand one of the rules governing pronouns.

Analyzing Your Post-Practice Test Performance

Sometimes you'll answer a question wrong not because you weren't paying attention, and not because you were rushing, but because, as in the example above, you truly didn't understand the material being tested. When you are checking over your practice test, it's crucial to figure out *why* you got wrong what you got wrong. It's a bad idea to simply see that you got an answer wrong and continue on your merry way. It's a good idea to do what the hypothetical you did when faced with question number 10: go back to the question and figure out why you got it wrong, and what you need to know to get it right.

Skeptical readers might say, "Sure, but I'll never see that question again. I'll never have to examine that sentence about the rude moviegoer on the real Writing SAT II, so isn't figuring out my mistake a waste of time?"

No! It's definitely *not* a waste of time. The reason: if you take the time to learn why you got a question wrong, and to learn the material you need to know to get it right, you'll probably remember what you've learned the next time you're faced with a similar question. And chances are excellent that you will be faced with a similar question. Sure, you won't see exactly the same sentences you saw on the practice test, but you'll see sentences that test exactly the same rules. Learn the rules when you're checking your practice tests, and you'll remember the rules when you're taking the real thing.

But What if I Get a Lot of Questions Wrong on the Practice Test?

What if you take a practice test and get a whole bunch of questions wrong, and it turns out you're shaky not just on pronoun rules, but on parallelism and run-on sentences and tense errors and misplaced modifiers? Instead of throwing up your hands in despair and flopping down on the couch to watch TV, make yourself identify all of the questions you got wrong, figure out why you got them wrong, and then teach yourself what you should have done to get these questions right. If you can't figure out your error, find someone who can. *Study* your completed practice test.

Think about it. What does an incorrect answer mean? That wrong answer identifies a weakness in your test taking, whether that weakness is an unfamiliarity with a particular topic or a tendency to be careless. If you got fifteen questions wrong on a practice test, then each of those fifteen questions identifies a weakness in your knowledge about the topics the Writing SAT II tests. But as you study each question and figure out why you got that question wrong, you are actually learning how to answer the very questions that will appear, in similar form, on the real Writing SAT II. You are discovering your SAT II Writing weaknesses and addressing them, and you are learning to understand not just the knowledge behind the question, but the way that ETS asks its questions as well.

True, if you got fifteen questions wrong, the first time you study your test will take quite a bit of time. But if you invest that time and study your practice test properly, you will be eliminating future mistakes. Each successive practice test you take should have fewer errors, meaning you'll need to spend less time studying those errors. Also, and more importantly, you'll be pinpointing what you need to study for the real Writing SAT II, identifying and overcoming your weaknesses, and learning to answer an increasing variety of questions on the specific topics covered by the test. Taking practice tests and studying them will allow you to teach yourself how to recognize and handle whatever the Writing SAT II has to throw at you.

Taking a Practice Test

Now you know a bit about what to do when you're finished taking the test. Let's backtrack and talk about what to do while you're actually taking the practice test.

Controlling Your Environment

Although a practice test is practice, and no one but you needs to see your scores, you should do everything in your power to make the practice test feel like the real Writing SAT II. The closer your practice resembles the real thing, the more helpful it will be.

Practice Tests are
Your Best Friends

When taking a practice test, follow these rules:

Take the tests timed. Don't give yourself any extra time. Be stricter with yourself than the meanest proctor you can think of. Also, don't give yourself time off for bathroom breaks. If you have to go to the bathroom, let the clock keep running; that's what'll happen on the real SAT II.

Take the test in a single sitting. Training yourself to endure an hour of test taking is part of your preparation.

Find a place to take the test that holds no distractions. Don't take the practice test in a room with lots of people walking through it. Go to a library, your bedroom, a well-lit closet, anywhere quiet. Otherwise your concentration won't be what it should be and your practice test won't reflect your true capabilities, or your true weaknesses.

These are the rules of taking practice tests. Now, having stated them, we can relax a little bit: don't be so strict with yourself that studying and taking practice tests becomes unbearable. The most important thing is that you actually study. Do whatever you have to do in order to make your studying interesting and painless enough that you actually do it.

Ultimately, if you can follow all of the above rules to the letter, you will probably be better off. But, if following those rules makes studying excruciating, find little ways to bend them that won't interfere too much with your concentration.

Practice Test Strategy

You should take each practice test as if it were the real Writing SAT II. Don't be more daring than you would be on the actual test, guessing blindly even when you can't eliminate an answer; don't carelessly speed through the test. Don't flip through this book while taking the practice exam just to sneak a peek. Follow the rules for guessing and for skipping questions that we outlined in the chapter on strategy. The more closely your attitude and strategies during the practice test reflect those you'll employ during the actual test, the more predictive the practice test will be of your strengths and weaknesses and the more fruitful your studying of the test will be.

Scoring Your Practice Test

After you take your practice test, you'll no doubt want to score it and see how you did. When you do your scoring, don't just write down how many questions you answered correctly and incorrectly and tally up your score. Instead, keep a list of every question you got wrong and every question you skipped. This list will be your guide when you study your test.

Studying Your . . . No, Wait, Go Take a Break

Go relax for a while. You know how to do that.

Studying Your Practice Test

After grading your test, you should have a list of the questions you answered incorrectly or skipped. Studying your test involves going through this list and examining each question you answered incorrectly. When you look at each question, you shouldn't just look to see what the correct answer is, but rather why you got the question wrong and how you could have gotten the question right. Train yourself in the process of getting the question right.

Why did you get the question wrong?

There are three main reasons why you might have gotten an individual question wrong.

Reason 1: You thought you knew the answer, but actually you didn't.

Reason 2: You managed to eliminate some answer choices and then guessed among the remaining answers; sadly, you guessed wrong.

Reason 3: You knew the answer but made a careless mistake.

You should know which of these reasons applies to every question you got wrong.

What could you have done to get the question right?

The reasons you got a question wrong affect how you should think about it while studying your test.

If You Got a Question Wrong for Reason 1, Lack of Knowledge: A question answered incorrectly for Reason 1 identifies a weakness in your knowledge of the material tested on the Writing SAT II. Discovering this wrong answer gives you an opportunity to target your weakness. When addressing that weakness, make sure that you don't look solely at that question; study the rule governing that question, too. Say you get an Improving Paragraphs question wrong that asks you to combine two sentences. Don't just note that the right answer involved combining the sentences using a comma and a conjunction; study the other ways you can combine sentences, and look at the ways people commonly combine sentences incorrectly. Remember, you will *not* see a question exactly like the question you got wrong. But you probably *will* see a question that covers the same topic as the practice question. For that reason, when you get a question wrong, don't just figure out the right answer to the question—learn the broader topic of which the question tests only a piece.

If You Got a Question Wrong for Reason 2, Guessing Wrong: If you guessed wrong, review your guessing strategy. Did you guess smartly? Could you have eliminated more answers? If yes, why didn't you? By thinking in this critical way about the decisions you made while taking the practice test, you can train yourself to make quicker, more decisive, and better decisions.

If you took a guess and chose the incorrect answer, don't let that sour you on guessing. Even as you go over the question and figure out if there was any way for you to have answered the question without having to guess, remind yourself that if you eliminated at least one answer and guessed, even if you got the question wrong, you followed the right strategy.

If You Got a Question Wrong for Reason 3, Carelessness: If you discover you got a question wrong because you were careless, it might be tempting to say to yourself, "Oh I made a careless error," and assure yourself you won't do that again. That is not enough. You made that careless mistake for a reason, and you should try to figure out why. Whereas getting a question wrong because you didn't know the answer constitutes a weakness in your knowledge about the test, making a careless mistake represents a weakness in your *method of taking the test*. To overcome this weakness, you need to approach it in the same critical way you would approach a lack of knowledge. Study your mistake. Reenact your thought process on the problem and see where and how your carelessness came about: were you rushing? Did you jump at the first answer that seemed right instead of reading all the answers? Know your error and look it in the eye. If you learn precisely what your mistake was, you are much less likely to make that mistake again.

If You Left the Question Blank

It is also a good idea to study the questions you left blank on the test, since those questions constitute a reservoir of lost points. If you left the question blank, then a different thinking applies. A blank answer is a result either of:

1. Total inability to answer a question

2. Lack of time

In the case of the first possibility, you should see if there was some way you might have been able to eliminate an answer choice or two and put yourself in a better position to guess. In the second case, look over the question and see whether you think you could have answered it. If you definitely could have, then you know that you are throwing away points and probably working too slowly. If you couldn't, then carry out the above steps: study the relevant material and review your guessing strategy.

The Secret Weapon: Talking to Yourself

Yeah, it's embarrassing. Yeah, you might look silly. But talking to yourself is perhaps the best way to pound something into your brain. As you go through the steps of studying a question, you should talk them out. When you verbalize something, it makes it much harder to delude yourself into thinking that you're working if you're really not.

We are serious about this advice. Of course, it is just a suggestion. We can't enforce it and, anyway, we don't want to. But it is a nice little study trick. And it will help you.

WRITING TEST I

Part A

Time — 20 minutes

You have twenty minutes to plan and write an essay on the topic assigned below. DO NOT WRITE ON ANOTHER TOPIC. AN ESSAY ON ANOTHER TOPIC IS NOT ACCEPTABLE.

The essay is assigned to give you an opportunity to show how well you can write. You should, therefore, take care to express your thoughts on the topic clearly and effectively. How well you write is much more important than how much you write, but to cover the topic adequately you will probably need to write more than one paragraph. Be specific.

Your essay must be written on the following two pages. You will find that you have enough space if you write on every line, avoid wide margins, and keep your handwriting to a reasonable size. It is important to remember that what you write will be read by someone who is not familiar with your handwriting. Try to write or print so that what you are writing is legible to the reader.

Consider the following statement and assignment. Then write the essay as directed.

"I have experienced many difficulties, but the most difficult situation I have ever had was when ____."

Assignment: Write an essay that completes the statement above. Explain the reasons behind your choice.

DO NOT WRITE YOUR ESSAY IN YOUR TEST BOOK. You will receive credit only for what you write on your answer sheet.

WHEN YOUR SUPERVISOR ANNOUNCES THAT TWENTY MINUTES HAVE PASSED, YOU MUST STOP WRITING THE ESSAY AND GO ON TO PART B IF YOU HAVE NOT ALREADY DONE SO. IF YOU FINISH YOUR ESSAY BEFORE THIS ANNOUNCEMENT, GO ON TO PART B AT ONCE.

BEGIN WRITING YOUR ESSAY ON THE ANSWER SHEET.

WRITING TEST

Part A

Time — 20 minutes

WRITING TEST

Part A

Time — 20 minutes

WRITING TEST

Part B

Time — 40 minutes

<u>Directions:</u> The following sentences test your knowledge of grammar, usage, diction (choice of words), and idiom.

Some sentences are correct.
No sentence contains more than one error.

You will find that the error, if there is one, is underline and lettered. Elements of the sentence that are not underlined will not be changed. In choosing answers, follow the requirements of standard written English.

If there is an error, select the <u>one underlined part</u> that must be changed to make the sentence correct and fill in the corresponding oval on your answer sheet.

If there is no answer, fill in answer oval Ⓔ.

EXAMPLE:

<u>The other</u> delegates and <u>him</u> <u>immediately</u>
   A   B   C

accepted the resolution <u>drafted by</u> the
                           D

neutral states. <u>No error</u>
                E

SAMPLE ANSWER:

Ⓐ ● Ⓒ Ⓓ Ⓔ

---

1. Everyone in my English class, <u>in spite of</u> the teacher's
                      A

   generous <u>curve,</u> <u>have done</u> incredibly <u>poorly</u> on all of the
          B   C   D

   tests this term. <u>No error</u>
              E

2. Foxholes, <u>otherwise</u> known as trenches, <u>proved critical</u>
            A   B

   in the First World War, because <u>it offered</u> soldiers a
                          C

   <u>useful</u> escape from a newly invented weapon: the
    D

   machine gun. <u>No error</u>
           E

3. A <u>gifted</u> figure skater, Michelle Kwan <u>has won</u> more
     A   B

   medals for the United States <u>as any</u> figure skater
                       C

   <u>before her time</u>. <u>No error</u>
        D   E

4. The first college in New York, founded in 1754

   <u>with a grant</u> from King George II, <u>was originally</u> <u>called</u>
     A   B   C

   King's College, and <u>is now known as</u> Columbia College.
                    D

   <u>No error</u>
    E

GO ON TO THE NEXT PAGE →

5. The politically apathetic writer <u>was surprised</u>
                                        A

   to find himself <u>accused</u> <u>to be</u> a Communist
                      B   C

   <u>by</u> Senator Joseph McCarthy. <u>No error</u>
   D   E

6. The Colonial house had a <u>kind of an</u> armoire <u>rare</u>
                               A   B

   for <u>its</u> intricate carving and original <u>handles</u>. <u>No error</u>
       C   D   E

7. The most <u>deadly</u> American forest fire occurred in the
               A

   late nineteenth century in Peshtigo, Wisconsin;

   <u>thousands died</u> as firefighters attempted to
         B

   <u>battle the blaze</u>, slow the fire's spread, and
         C

   <u>giving first aid</u> to the injured. <u>No error</u>
         D   E

8. <u>All the cats</u> who normally <u>pick through</u> Mr. Lopez's
      A   B

   garbage cans have finally <u>stopped coming</u>, because
                                C

   <u>it has</u> been empty for days. <u>No error</u>
   D   E

9. The historian could not decipher the document

   <u>that had been</u> unearthed, <u>because</u> water damage had
      A   B

   <u>made the writing</u> <u>not hardly</u> legible. <u>No error</u>
   C   D   E

10. V.S. Naipaul was born <u>of</u> Indian parents, lives
                           A

    <u>in England</u>, writes <u>fiction and essays</u>, and has been
    B   C

    awarded the Booker and Nobel <u>prizes</u>. <u>No error</u>
                                    D   E

11. Patricia had <u>knew</u> Jim <u>for many years</u> <u>before</u>
                   A   B   C

    <u>she became</u> his friend. <u>No error</u>
    D   E

12. <u>Whenever</u> I make pasta, I <u>get</u> a stomachache <u>from</u>
       A   B   C

    eating it too <u>quick</u>. <u>No error</u>
                  D   E

13. J.S. Bach <u>was first married</u> to his cousin Maria Barbara
                         A

    Bach, <u>who bore him</u> seven children; <u>later he married</u>
                B   C

    Anna Magdalena Wülken, who bore him

    <u>thirteen children.</u> <u>No error</u>
          D   E

14. This <u>year's</u> <u>performance of</u> *Hamlet* <u>was well</u> advertised
       A   B   C

    and drew a much larger audience than <u>last year</u>.
                                       D

    <u>No error</u>
       E

15. <u>The medieval knight</u>, generally heavily armored
          A

    soldiers who competed <u>in jousts</u> and tournaments,
                       B

    <u>traveled</u> the countryside <u>in search of</u> honor and
     C   D

    fortune. <u>No error</u>
              E

16. <u>Every technician</u> on the space shuttle took <u>their last</u>
         A   B

    look around the machine and declared <u>the shuttle fit</u>
                                          C

    <u>for the mission.</u> <u>No error</u>
         D   E

17. <u>Maintaining his alliance</u> with Winston Churchill and
              A

    Chiang Kai-shek, Franklin Delano Roosevelt

    <u>pledged to oppose</u> Japan until Japan <u>surrendered</u>
          B   C

    <u>unconditionally.</u> <u>No error</u>
         D   E

18. <u>Over</u> the past ten years, the rapid increase in the power
     A

    of computers <u>will have</u> <u>drastically improved</u> the ability
                 B   C

    of meteorologists to <u>predict</u> the weather with accuracy.
                    D

    <u>No error</u>
       E

19. The protagonist <u>finds himself</u> apologizing not because
                 A

    <u>he is</u> genuinely sorry, but because his lust for money
     B

    stops him <u>to do</u> anything that <u>would cause him</u> to lose
            C   D

    cash. <u>No error</u>
         E

20. Mr. Brown <u>called</u> a family meeting <u>to discuss</u> <u>feasible</u>
           A   B   C

    <u>solutions toward</u> Jimmy and Eric's fight. <u>No error</u>
        D   E

GO ON TO THE NEXT PAGE →

WRITING TEST

Directions: The following sentences test correctness and effectiveness of expression. In choosing answers, follow the requirements of standard written English; that is, pay attention to grammar, choice of words, sentence construction, and punctuation.

In each of the following sentences, part of the sentence or the entire sentence is underlined. Beneath each sentence you will find five ways of phrasing the underlined part. Choice A repeats the original; the other four are different.

Choose the answer that best expresses the meaning of the original sentence. If you think the original is better than any of the alternatives, choose it; otherwise choose one of the others. Your choice should produce the most effective sentence—clear and precise, without awkwardness or ambiguity.

EXAMPLE: SAMPLE ANSWER:

Laura Ingalls Wilder published her first book
and she was sixty-five years old then.

(A) and she was sixty-five years old then
(B) when she was sixty-five
(C) at age sixty-five years old
(D) upon the reaching of sixty-five years
(E) at the time when she was sixty-five

---

21. The store was known for its knives and watches, but the difficulty was in its not being known for its clothing.

   (A) the difficulty was in its not being known for its clothing
   (B) the difficulty it had was in the fact that it hadn't been known for its clothing
   (C) it was not known for its clothing
   (D) it had been known for its clothing
   (E) having difficulty in not being known for its clothing

22. The puzzle of Stonehenge seeming almost like a cliché of a mystery, especially since its parody in the film *This is Spinal Tap*.

   (A) The puzzle of Stonehenge seeming almost like a cliché
   (B) The puzzle of Stonehenge having seemed almost like a cliché
   (C) Seeming almost like a cliché, the puzzle of Stonehenge
   (D) Stonehenge, the puzzle that seems almost like a cliché
   (E) The puzzle of Stonehenge seems almost like a cliché

23. American women were allowed to vote for the first time in 1920, they helped elect Warren G. Harding.

   (A) American women were allowed to vote for the first time in 1920
   (B) American women, who were allowed to vote for the first time in 1920
   (C) When American women were allowed to vote for the first time in 1920
   (D) When American women, who were allowed to vote for the first time in 1920
   (E) American women, voting for the first time in 1920

GO ON TO THE NEXT PAGE

24. Being one of the premier pianists of his generation, critics applauded Glenn Gould for his definitive recording of the Goldberg Variations.

    (A) Being one of the premier pianists of his generation, critics applauded Glenn Gould
    (B) Critics applauded Glenn Gould, one of the premier pianists of his generation,
    (C) Glenn Gould's status as one of the premier pianists of his generation resulted in the applauding of him by critics
    (D) The fact that Glenn Gould was one of the premier pianists of his generation, which meant that critics applauded him
    (E) Critics who applauded Glenn Gould being one of the premier pianists of his generation

25. Many older women develop osteoporosis this is largely due to insufficient calcium intake in early years.

    (A) osteoporosis this
    (B) osteoporosis, which
    (C) osteoporosis; and this
    (D) osteoporosis which
    (E) osteoporosis, that

26. There was a long line outside the new club, and the club hadn't received any publicity yet.

    (A) and the club
    (B) even though the club
    (C) even so the club
    (D) but, the club
    (E) so the club

27. The private investigator took pictures of Adela hailing a cab, eating dinner at a steakhouse, and having a drink at Z Bar.

    (A) and having a drink
    (B) and while she was having a drink
    (C) also when she had a drink
    (D) and while she drank
    (E) and during the time when she consumed a drink

28. In a famous experiment, subjects administered what they thought were severe electric shocks, exhibiting a willingness to comply with authority that is disturbing.

    (A) a willingness to comply with authority that is disturbing
    (B) which is disturbing and it shows a willingness to comply with authority
    (C) a willingness that is disturbing in its willingness to comply with authority
    (D) this is disturbing in showing their willingness to comply with authority
    (E) seeing as how they demonstrated a disturbing willingness to comply with authority

29. Josephine Baker danced topless and walked her leopard on the streets of Paris, and these are the sort of colorful escapades for which she is remembered.

    (A) Josephine Baker danced topless and walked her leopard on the streets of Paris, and these are the sorts of colorful escapades for which she is remembered
    (B) Josephine Baker, who danced topless and walked her leopard on the streets of Paris, is remembered for these and other colorful escapades
    (C) People remember Josephine Baker for colorful escapades such as dancing topless and walking her leopard on the streets of Paris
    (D) Remembered for colorful escapades such as dancing topless and walking her leopard on the streets of Paris, is Josephine Baker
    (E) Josephine Baker, topless dancer and walker of her leopard on the streets of Paris, is remembered for these and other colorful escapades

30. The film *Holiday Inn* is set in a small town in Connecticut, starring both Bing Crosby and Fred Astaire.

    (A) *Inn* is set in a small town in Connecticut, starring
    (B) *Inn* is, being set in a small town in Connecticut, starring
    (C) *Inn*, had its setting in a small town in Connecticut which stars
    (D) *Inn*, set in a small town in Connecticut, stars
    (E) *Inn*, which is set in a small town in Connecticut and which stars

GO ON TO THE NEXT PAGE

31. The idea that literary criticism should focus on the contradictions and gaps in a text gained prominence as a result of Jacques Derrida's influential writings.

    (A) The idea that literary criticism should focus on the contradictions and gaps in a text gained prominence as a result of Jacques Derrida's influential writings
    (B) The idea that gained prominence as a result of Jacques Derrida's influential writings was that of focusing on the contradictions and gaps
    (C) Gaining prominence as a result of Jacques Derrida's influential writings, they thought that literary criticism should focus on the contradictions and gaps in a text
    (D) Prominent as an idea a result of Jacques Derrida's influential writings was for literary criticism to focus on the contradictions and gaps in a text
    (E) As a result of Jacques Derrida's influential writings, they gained the idea that literary criticism should focus on the contradictions and gaps in a text

32. Alice wrote and directed a play and it depicted an unhappy poet loosely modeled on Sylvia Plath.

    (A) a play and it
    (B) a play; and it
    (C) a play that depicted
    (D) a play, being that it depicted
    (E) a play, it depicted

33. When compared to their current counterparts, Elvis's lyrics, music, and his dancing seem unobjectionable, and even conservative.

    (A) Elvis's lyrics, music, and his dancing seem unobjectionable
    (B) the lyrics, music, and the dancing of Elvis seem impossible to object to
    (C) the lyrics, music, dancing, of Elvis seem unobjectionable
    (D) Elvis's lyrics, music, and dancing seem unobjectionable
    (E) it is difficult to object to Elvis's lyrics, music, and his dancing

34. Consuming large quantities of soda and tea has the same effect as to drink lots of coffee.

    (A) as to drink lots of coffee
    (B) than to drink lots of coffee
    (C) as drinking lots of coffee
    (D) as it does to drink lots of coffee
    (E) than drinking lots of coffee

35. Experts insist that regular exercise and a nutritious diet help people maintain a healthy weight.

    (A) maintain a healthy weight
    (B) cause the weight to be maintained healthfully
    (C) make weight a healthy maintenance
    (D) weigh healthy
    (E) to be maintaining a healthy weight

36. Opposing the tariff on moral grounds was the right thing to do under the circumstances.

    (A) Opposing the tariff on moral grounds was the right thing to do under the circumstances
    (B) On moral grounds, opposing the tariff was the right thing to do under the circumstances
    (C) Under the circumstances, opposing the tariff on moral grounds was the right thing to do
    (D) It was the right thing to do, opposing the tariff on moral grounds under the circumstances
    (E) On moral grounds, it was the right thing to do to oppose the tariff under the circumstances

37. Some people claim that acting instinct and natural talent are just as useful as an expensive education at a theater academy.

    (A) as useful as
    (B) as useful than
    (C) as it is useful to have
    (D) as useful as if one gets
    (E) as of use as

38. Sun-dried tomatoes are a delicious addition to food; they are great in pasta sauce, on crackers, or in salads.

    (A) food; they are great in pasta sauce
    (B) food, they are great in pasta sauce
    (C) food, and pasta sauce is one of the dishes in which they are great
    (D) food; pasta sauce, in which they are great
    (E) food; it is great in pasta sauce

GO ON TO THE NEXT PAGE →

WRITING TEST

Questions 39-44 are based on the following passage.

(1) *Recently, the Internet has come into wide use.* (2) *For example, today most people rely on email, a convenient Internet-based method of communication.* (3) *Electronic versions of the paper, provide a handy alternative version to the traditional print versions of newspapers.* (4) *Also, lots of people use the Internet to check stock quotes, pay bills, and make reservations.*

(5) *Even though Internet use is becoming more and more common, some people are still intimidated by the thought of Internet navigation.* (6) *They assume it will prove too complicated.* (7) *Because they worry they won't be able to use the Internet, people don't even try to.*

(8) *This is a shame.* (9) *The Internet makes life easier.* (10) *If we didn't have the Internet, wouldn't we lose a lot?* (11) *Not only would communication become more time-consuming, and transactions of all kinds would take much longer.* (12) *Also, the sense that we are all connected by our computers would diminish.* (13) *The Internet is now woven into the fabric of our everyday lives.* (14) *You who are intimidated by it, we should recall that the Internet can be as simple to operate as a modern-day version of pen and paper.*

39. Which of the following sentences should be added after sentence 1?

(A) Issues of Internet privacy have come to the fore in recent days.
(B) Personally, I don't enjoy navigating the Internet.
(C) Many people utilize one or more of its functions on a daily basis.
(D) Like the cell phone, use of the Internet has become ubiquitous.
(E) Music-sharing programs are under fire from government and musicians.

40. Which of the following phrases should be inserted after *electronic versions of the paper* in sentence 3 in order to connect sentence 3 to the rest of the paragraph?

(A) most assuredly
(B) another Internet convenience
(C) on the other hand
(D) in contrast
(E) it is clear

41. Which of the following words should be added after *this* in sentence 8 in order to make the sentence more precise?

(A) Internet
(B) communication
(C) case
(D) stock quote
(E) reluctance

GO ON TO THE NEXT PAGE

42. Sentence 10 works to

    (A) undercut the writer's initial assertion
    (B) ask a hypothetical question
    (C) suggest that the Internet actually has several serious drawbacks
    (D) reveal that the writer's stance wavers
    (E) allow the reader to question the convenience of the Internet

43. Which of the following best revises the underlined part of sentence 11, which is reprinted here?

    Not only would communication become more time-consuming, records, and transactions of all kinds would take much longer.

    (A) but many of the transactions would require much more time
    (B) however transactions of all kinds take much longer
    (C) but so would transactions of all kinds
    (D) and to take longer for transactions of all kinds
    (E) and they would need more time to do transactions of all kinds

44. In context, which of the following best revises the underlined part of sentence 14, which is reprinted here?

    You who are intimidated by it, we should recall that the Internet can be as simple to operate as a modern-day version of pen and paper.

    (A) (As it is now)
    (B) You who it scares would do well to recall that the Internet
    (C) Recall that you are intimidated that the Internet
    (D) We are intimidated by the Internet because it
    (E) People who are intimidated by the Internet should recall that it

GO ON TO THE NEXT PAGE

Questions 45-50 are based on the following passage.

(1) *I'm a guy who used to think ballet was little more than fluttering around a stage in a tutu, flapping your arms.* (2) *I thought that any skinny girl with a little grace could do it.* (3) *Sure, guys could take ballet classes.* (4) *Their friends would make fun of them for it.*

(5) *I've played football since I was in fourth grade.* (6) *My friends like to sit around watching TV and eating nachos.* (7) *I feel guilty if I'm not running six miles a day.* (8) *People think I'm crazy, but I think football would be a great way of getting a college scholarship.* (9) *One day my coach approached me and said my game would really improve if I worked on flexibility and agility.* (10) *He said I should try taking a ballet class.* (11) *I'm surprised by his suggestion.* (12) *I decided to take his advice.* (13) *I signed up for a class.* (14) *I've never been so shocked in my life as I was the first day I went to class.* (15) *It was extremely hard.* (16) *I was in a beginner class and I still couldn't do anything.* (17) *The worst part was that unlike in football, in ballet you can't reveal how hard you're working.*

(18) *After six weeks of class, I could see an improvement in my football performance.* (19) *However, even though I improved on the field, my ballet performance was still so poor that I wasn't allowed to participate in the recital.*

45. Which of the following is the best way to revise and combine the underlined parts of sentence 3 and sentence 4, which are reprinted below?

    Sure, guys could take <u>ballet classes. Their friends</u> *would make fun of them for it.*

    (A) ballet classes, and their friends
    (B) ballet classes, however their friends
    (C) ballet classes, so their friends
    (D) ballet classes, but their friends
    (E) ballet classes, seeing as how their friends

46. Which sentence should be added after sentence 4 in order to improve the transition from the first paragraph to the rest of the essay?

    (A) I can't remember a time when I didn't think this way about ballet.
    (B) However, a recent experience led me to change my opinion about ballet.
    (C) Nothing about ballet appealed to me.
    (D) I think the steps and routines in ballet look easy.
    (E) My older sister sometimes invited me to come to her ballet class.

47. Which of the following is the best way to combine sentence 6 and sentence 7 (which are reprinted below) in order to make their relationship to one another more clear?

    My friends like to sit around watching TV and eating nachos. I feel guilty if I'm not running six miles a day.

    (A) My friends are sitting around watching TV and eating nachos, I was running six miles a day.
    (B) In contrast to my friends, who like to sit around watching TV and eating nachos, I feel guilty if I'm not running six miles a day.
    (C) While my friends like to sit around watching TV and eating nachos, I'll be feeling guilty if I'm not running six miles a day.
    (D) In contrast to my friends who like to sit around watching TV and eating nachos, I was feeling guilty if I wasn't running six miles a day.
    (E) My friends like to sit around watching TV and eating nachos and I'm different than them because I feel guilty if I'm not running six miles a day.

GO ON TO THE NEXT PAGE

48. In context, which of the following best revises sentence 11, which is reprinted below?

    I'm surprised by his suggestion.

    (A) (as it is)
    (B) His suggestion is surprising to me.
    (C) However, I'm surprised by his suggestion.
    (D) His suggestion was surprising me.
    (E) I was surprised by his suggestion.

49. Which of the following best revises and combines sentence 12 and sentence 13, which are reprinted below?

    I decided to take his advice. I signed up for a class.

    (A) (As they are)
    (B) After deciding to take his advice, I signed up for a class.
    (C) After deciding to take his advice, I then proceeded to sign up for a class.
    (D) Signing up for a class after I decided to take his advice.
    (E) After deciding to take his advice, it was then that I signed up for a class.

50. The writer uses all of the following techniques EXCEPT:

    (A) telling a story
    (B) providing examples
    (C) undermining the viewpoint described in the first paragraph
    (D) drawing contrasts
    (E) setting up a hypothetical circumstance

GO ON TO THE NEXT PAGE

WRITING TEST

Note: The remaining questions are like those at the beginning of Part B.

Directions: For each sentence in which you find an error, select the one underlined part that must be changed to make the sentence correct and fill in the corresponding oval on your answer sheet.

If there is no answer, fill in answer oval Ⓔ.

EXAMPLE:

The other delegates and him immediately
    A   B   C

accepted the resolution drafted by the
                       D

neutral states. No error
            E

SAMPLE ANSWER:

Ⓐ ● Ⓒ Ⓓ Ⓔ

---

51. The artist said all of her early paintings were
              A

   rejected by art dealers and museums because it was
      B   C

   considered too experimental. No error
            D   E

52. Faneuil Hall in Boston was once used as a meeting place
             A   B

   for revolutionaries and is now a tourist attraction that
                 C   D

   features shops and restaurants. No error
                  E

53. The chef said he finds inspiration more from
          A

   memories of his mother's cooking and not from food
      B   C   D

   trends of the moment. No error
              E

54. Beneath a thin layer of stone lies the bones of
                A

 specimens of a species of fish whose origins
                B

 remain mysterious to scientists. No error
  C   D   E

55. During July, Disney World and Universal Studios,
   A

   which are among the most frequently visited theme
    B C

   parks in the country, were clogged with visitors.
                  D

   No error
    E

56. Given the choice between cats and dogs, many people
   A

   like cats best, even if they don't dislike dogs. No error
       B   C   D   E

57. Novelist George Eliot is perhaps most infamous for
              A   B

   her novel *Middlemarch*, which follows a woman named
                     C

   Dorothea as she endures an unhappy marriage.
              D

   No error
    E

GO ON TO THE NEXT PAGE ▶

58. The daylight saving time system <u>used by</u> most states
                                        A

    <u>to provide</u> more hours of light and <u>save energy</u> <u>is</u> not
     B   C   D

    used in Arizona, Hawaii, and parts of Indiana. <u>No error</u>
                                                        E

59. The entire delegation, except for the ambassador

    <u>himself,</u> <u>were on board</u> the plane <u>that arrived</u> late
     A   B   C

    yesterday <u>in</u> Los Angeles. <u>No error</u>
              D   E

60. Maria Callas <u>was known</u> more for her dramatic
                   A

    abilities than <u>most opera singers</u>, and her followers
                    B

    <u>also admired</u> the drama of her romantic <u>attachments</u>.
     C   D

    <u>No error</u>
     E

S T O P

IF YOU FINISH BEFORE TIME IS CALLED, YOU MAY CHECK YOUR WORK ON THIS TEST ONLY.
DO NOT TURN TO ANY OTHER TEST IN THIS BOOK.

Answers to SAT II Writing Practice Test I

Question Number	Correct Answer	Right	Wrong	Question Number	Correct Answer	Right	Wrong
1.	C	___	___	31.	A	___	___
2.	C	___	___	32.	C	___	___
3.	C	___	___	33.	D	___	___
4.	E	___	___	34.	C	___	___
5.	C	___	___	35.	A	___	___
6.	A	___	___	36.	C	___	___
7.	D	___	___	37.	A	___	___
8.	D	___	___	38.	A	___	___
9.	D	___	___	39.	C	___	___
10.	E	___	___	40.	B	___	___
11.	A	___	___	41.	E	___	___
12.	D	___	___	42.	B	___	___
13.	E	___	___	43.	C	___	___
14.	D	___	___	44.	E	___	___
15.	A	___	___	45.	D	___	___
16.	B	___	___	46.	B	___	___
17.	E	___	___	47.	B	___	___
18.	B	___	___	48.	E	___	___
19.	C	___	___	49.	B	___	___
20.	D	___	___	50.	E	___	___
21.	C	___	___	51.	C	___	___
22.	E	___	___	52.	E	___	___
23.	C	___	___	53.	D	___	___
24.	B	___	___	54.	A	___	___
25.	B	___	___	55.	E	___	___
26.	B	___	___	56.	B	___	___
27.	A	___	___	57.	B	___	___
28.	E	___	___	58.	E	___	___
29.	C	___	___	59.	B	___	___
30.	D	___	___	60.	B	___	___

Calculating Your Score

Your raw score for SAT II Writing test is a composite of your raw score in the multiple-choice section and your score on the essay. Once you have determined your composite score, use the conversion table on page 17 to calculate your scaled score. To Calculate your raw score, count the number of questions you answered correctly on the multiple choice: _____

A

Count the number of questions you answered incorrectly, and multiply that number by $\frac{1}{4}$:

_____ X $\frac{1}{4}$ = _____
B   C

Subtract the value in field C from value in field A: _____

D

Round the number to the nearest whole number: _____

E

Take your score for the Essay (ask a teacher to grade your essay or grade yourself) and multiply it by 3.43:

_____ X 3.43 = _____
F   G

Add the number in field E to the number in Field G: _____

H

Round the number in field H. This is your Writing SAT II score: _____

Student Essays

Total Score: 12 (each reader gave the essay a 6)

Although I have experienced many difficulties, my aunt's breast cancer was perhaps the most difficult experience I have ever undergone.

It was January 2nd; I was thirteen years old, and had just come into the kitchen after an afternoon of sledding at a golf course near my house. I was sitting on the rug, taking off my boots and peeling off my gloves and scarf, when my mother came into the room. I could tell from her face that something was horribly wrong. "Honey," she said, leaning against the fridge, "I just talked to Elizabeth. It's not good news."

Over the next couple of months, my family and I watched the deterioration of my mother's sister. She got more and more sick.

Part of the reason the experience was such a harrowing one was that before her illness, Aunt Liz was the most vivacious, daring person I knew. She hated to see me sitting around watching TV, and it drove her crazy when my mother forbid me from doing something because it was dangerous. Once she snuck me out of the house and we went parasailing. I asked her if it was OK, and she laughed and said, "Don't be such an old lady!"

Her sickness changed her completely, at least in my eyes. For a while she seemed the same as she always had, and then suddenly she lost all of her energy. She never came flying into our driveway in her red car, ready to whisk me off on some adventure; she never called me up and laughed at my dumb stories. She lost her hair, her weight, her glowing skin.

I behaved like a child. I was angry all of the time. I felt cheated. I hadn't done anything wrong, so why was my favorite aunt being taken away from me? I was even angry at Aunt Liz sometimes. I wanted her to get better, and I actually resented her for being sick.

Then one day, after my mother and I had gone to the hospital to visit Aunt Liz, everything changed. We were in the car on the way home, and I was crying and shouting at the same time. "It's not FAIR!" I said. "I have the worst life!" My mother quietly asked, "Are you the one who's sick?" "No," I said, still angry. My mother told me that in that case, I was lucky. She said that I was being selfish, and that Liz needed my love and kindness, not my anger and self-concern. My mother was so obviously right, but I had never really considered my own behavior. After she said that, I realized I was acting badly, and I resolved to change my behavior.

It didn't happen all at once, but eventually I think I succeeded in being more concerned with Aunt Liz than with myself. Today, my aunt is back to her usual self, she's even more happy and energetic than she was before she got breast cancer. And although the experience was the single most difficult one I have ever dealt with, at the same time it was the most rewarding, because I appreciate my aunt more than ever, and because it changed me from a selfish little kid to someone with a bit of concern for others.

Discussion:

This writer took as her subject matter her aunt's bout with breast cancer. An essay about cancer has the potential to look like a pathetic attempt to win the sympathy of the reader, and this essay is cheesy at moments; still, it is far better to tell a slightly cheesy story than it is to write about how the most difficult experience of your life was lying to a cop after being pulled over in a stolen car.

Even though this essay sometimes gets sappy, it avoids pious posturing. While you don't want to write about your grand auto-theft hijinks, you also want to avoid tooting your own horn for six paragraphs. The reader won't appreciate an entire essay about how wonderful and smart you are. It's good to reveal your wonderfulness and smartness in the course of your essay, but be subtle about it. This writer does well to let her wonderfulness seep through the cracks, instead of trumpeting it. In a display of modesty, she talks about how she acted selfishly—but the subtle indication is that now, she's a lovely, unselfish young adult. This essay successfully blends self-deprecation with self-glorification.

Sometimes, as in this sample essay, personal essays will almost structure themselves. This is because oftentimes the personal essay takes an anecdote or a story as its subject matter, which lends itself to a chronological structure. This writer does a nice job of unfolding her story. The fourth paragraph is not part of the chronological story, but it is well placed and does not disrupt the flow of the story.

Note too that there are a few grammatical errors in this essay. Remember, it is possible to get a 12 on the essay even if there are a few grammatical errors. For example, in the fourth paragraph, this writer uses the made-up word snuck (it should be *sneaked*). Also, the sentence that begins *Today, my aunt is back to her usual self* is a run-on sentence. The readers don't expect perfection. It's problematic if you demonstrate a pattern of grammatical errors, but a few mistakes won't prevent you from getting an excellent score.

Total Score: 4 (each reader gave the essay a 2)

I have experienced many difficulties, the difficulty that I think was the hardest was when I broke up with my girlfriend Amelia. We started "going out" in fourth grade, two little kids, we kissed under the swing set. I was head over heals for her. Now a few weeks ago she calls me and tells me she just doesn't love me anymore. What! I said. I'm shouting into the phone. I can't believe she's telling me over the phone. I can't believe she's breaking up with me, but I really can't believe she doesn't even have the guts to tell me in person.

This reminds me of a play we recently read in my English class called Romeo and Juliet. By William Shakespeare. Romeo and Juliet couldn't be together because their families hate each other, and say they can't be together. I know Amelia's mother has always hated me. For stupid reasons, I have bad table manners according to her and she doesn't like it that I wear a baseball hat indoors. But my family likes Amelia, in fact I think they were more upset than me when we broke up.

I can't believe we broke up. My heart is like a dessert without her in my life.

Discussion:

According to ETS, essays that receive a total score of 4 are those that demonstrate "some incompetence." This essay gets a 4 because it has serious problems with organization, examples, grammar, diction, and sentence structure.

The subject matter this writer chooses is not appropriate. A statement like this one, which asks for a personal example, provides an opportunity to cast yourself in a good light. By choosing to write about the experience of being dumped, this writer misses an opportunity to show the readers what a mature, wonderful person he is. The sad breakup story, as this writer tells it, is too shallow for the Writing SAT II essay.

There is no clear organizational strategy guiding this essay. The essay reads almost like a stream-of-consciousness piece. It seems that the writer simply wrote down whatever he was thinking, jumping from a summary of his relationship with Amelia to an uncomfortably intimate account of his reaction to their breakup to a mini-synopsis of Romeo and Juliet to resentful details of Amelia's mother's dislike of him. The writer does not bother to organize his thoughts into paragraphs; he simply lets his train of thought dictate the organization of the essay.

This essay is rife with grammatical errors. The writer demonstrates not that he made a few careless errors because of the time constraint, but that he has systematic problems with run-on sentences, fragments, tense switches, and misspelled words. The first sentence is a run-on: *I have experienced many difficulties, the difficulty that I think was the hardest was when I broke up with my girlfriend Amelia.* The second sentence is also a run-on: *We started "going out" in fourth grade, two little kids, we kissed under the swing set.* The following two sentences from the second paragraph are both run-on sentences: *For stupid reasons, I have bad table manners according to her and she doesn't like it that I wear a baseball hat indoors. But my family likes Amelia, in fact I think they were more upset than me when we broke up.* The fact that there are no fewer than four run-on sentences shows the readers that this person does not grasp a basic tenet of grammar.

At moments the writer lets the narrative thrust of the story overwhelm him, and he runs into tense problems. For example, these two sentences: *What! I said. I'm shouting into the phone.* The intensity of the memory makes the writer switch abruptly from the past tense (*said*) to the present tense (*I'm shouting*).

Finally, the writer misspells words: he writes *heals* when he means *heels*, and *dessert* when he means *desert*.

Identifying Sentence Errors

1. **(C)** *Subject-Verb Agreement*

Your antennae should tingle when you see a sentence that starts with the word "everyone"—especially when that sentence's subject and verb are separated from each other. Remember that "everyone" is one of those annoying words that sounds plural but is actually singular. Thus, "everyone" should be matched with a singular verb rather than with a plural verb. (C) is your choice, because the plural *have done* is incorrect. The underlined part of the sentence should read *has done*.

In spite of may sound strange, but it's really a correct idiomatic construction that means "despite." *Curve* is the correct word choice because even though it refers to many people, it is one policy, and therefore singular. *Poorly* is also correct because you need an adverb to describe the verb phrase *have done*.

2.   **(C)**   *Pronoun Agreement*

This sentence may look scary, with all its historical information, but remember that when identifying sentence errors, you never need to evaluate content, you only need to evaluate grammar.

The problem here is with the word *it*. What offered soldiers an escape from the machine gun? Foxholes. Since *foxholes* is plural, the sentence must use the plural pronoun "they" to refer back to the foxholes. Instead, it incorrectly uses the singular pronoun *it*. Therefore, (C) is the answer.

3.   **(C)**   *Idiom*

Your ear will help you find the right answer on this one. Hopefully the expression *more medals . . . as any figure skater* sounded odd to you. There's no fancy terminology to explain why that expression is wrong—it's just idiomatically incorrect. We say people win more medals *than* anyone else, not more medals *as* anyone else, so (C) is the answer.

4.   **(E)**   *No Error*

No error.

5.   **(C)**   *Gerund*

You'll probably find the mistake in this question by hearing it. The problem here is with the infinitive *to be*. The phrase *accused to be* isn't an idiom we use in English. If the sentence read something like *the writer was surprised to find himself thought to be a Communist*, the phrase *to be* would be fine. However, because the word used is *accused*, a gerund must follow it: *accused of being*. Thus, (C) is the correct answer.

6.   **(A)**   *Other*

There's no satisfying explanation for why this error is an error, except that in formal English, we don't say *a kind of an*, we say *a kind of*. Corrected, this sentence would begin *the Colonial-period house had a kind of armoire . . . .*

Some of the other answer choices look tempting—(B), for example. It seems as if *rare* is too brief, and maybe the sentence should read something like *a kind of armoire that is rare*. Actually, though, the single word *rare* is grammatically correct and superior to a more wordy phrase because it is so succinct.

If *its* tripped you up because it is apostrophe-free, remember that although you would need an apostrophe if you were talking about "Angel's armoire," if you're talking about something that belongs to "it," you never need an apostrophe, so *its* is correct.

7.   **(D)**   *Parallelism*

Whenever you see a list, you should check it carefully, because lists are prime candidates for parallelism problems. This list, for example, begins with the infinitive *to battle*. Therefore, the entire list must continue with infinitives. The next item in the list is fine: *slow*. It's the third, *giving*, that's a problem. The verb should not be in gerund (-ing) form, but in infinitive form: *give*. Therefore, (D) is the correct answer.

You might have looked twice at (A), thinking *deadliest* would be better than *most deadly*, but *most deadly* is grammatically correct.

(B) can be eliminated because it is grammatically acceptable to use *thousands* as shorthand for *thousands of people*.

8. **(D)** *Pronoun Agreement*

This is one of those sentences that might seem error-free on your first reading. There is a problem, however, with the word *it*. What has been empty for days? The *garbage cans*, a plural subject. This means that the pronoun referring to the garbage cans must also be plural. However, *it*, the pronoun used in the original sentence to refer to the garbage cans, is singular. The answer is (D).

9. **(D)** *Double Negative*

Whenever you spot a word such as "hardly," "scarcely," or "barely," you should be on your guard. All of these words are negative, but they don't necessarily *sound* negative. This makes them favorites of question-writers, who think they will be able to sneak a double negative by you. *Not hardly* is a classic tricky double negative—two negative words used where only one should be used. (D) is the right answer.

Illogical tense switches will crop up on this section of the exam, so you should check underlined verbs carefully. (A) should be checked, but the phrase *that had been unearthed* makes sense in the context of the sentence.

10. **(E)** *No Error*

No error.

11. **(A)** *Tense*

"Know" is the quintessential annoying verb. Annoying verbs are those that never sound quite right in any tense. Familiarize yourself with *know* and all other verbs like it by going over the list provided in the study guide.

Had knew is the problem with this sentence. *Knew* should be replaced with *known*. Technically, to fix the bad conjugation *had knew*, you substitute the simple past form of the verb "to know" with the past participle. You don't really need to know which form is which, or memorize the rules governing their usage. Just review the list in the study guide a few times and you should be fine. And as always, trust your ear and try to "hear" the error.

(D) might strike you as a possible tense error—"become" is another annoying verb—but here, the correct form is used.

12. **(D)** *Adverb*

This error can be tricky to identify because it's one we frequently make in speech. In this sentence we have the adjective *quick* modifying the verb *eating*. This is a problem, because technically, in the land of good grammar, adjectives can't modify verbs. You can get a stomach ache from eating too *quickly*, but it's grammatically impossible to get a stomachache from eating too *quick*. (D) is the answer.

You should look at (B) carefully, because an underlined verb could always mean a tense error. In this case, though, *get* is used logically.

13. **(E)** *No Error*

No error.

14. **(D)** *Faulty Comparison*

This sentence is attempting to compare two things: this year's play, and last year's play. But look at the wording used. We're told that *Hamlet* drew a much larger crowd *than last year*. What the writer means to suggest is that *Hamlet* drew a larger crowd not *than last year*, but *than last year's play*. (D) is the answer because the comparison is faulty.

15. **(A)**   *Subject-Verb Agreement*

The bulk of this sentence refers to plural soldiers: *heavily armored soldiers* who *traveled the countryside*. Only that first phrase, *the medieval knight*, refers to a singular soldier. Because it does not match the rest of the sentence, *the medieval knight* is wrong, and (A) is the correct answer.

16. **(B)**   *Pronoun Agreement*

The trick to spotting the error in this question is to identify the number of the subject *every technician*. Although there are multiple technicians involved in this sentence, when the word "every" is used with any plural noun, that noun phrase is then considered singular. Thus, instead of saying, *every technician . . . took their last look around*, we should say, *every technician . . . took his last look around*, or, in more gender-neutral language, *every technician . . . took his or her last look around*. (B) is the right answer.

17. **(E)**   *No Error*

No error.

18. **(B)**   *Tense*

In this sentence, the phrase *over the past ten years* tells us that the action of the sentence is taking place in the past. But then we get to the words *will have*. These words refer to future action, which is problematic because we already know the sentence is talking about a past event. What we have here is a tense error. (B) is the right answer. Tense errors will crop up on this section of the test, so examine underlined verbs carefully and make sure any tense shifts make sense within the context of the sentence. Remember, it's fine if the tense shifts in one sentence, as long as the shifts are logical.

19. **(C)**   *Gerund*

The difficulty here is that the infinitive *to do* should be the gerund *from doing*. The phrase *stops him to do* violates rules of proper usage for the word *stop* when it means *prevent* rather than *cease*. The rules call for the expression *stops him from doing*, which is what should be used here.

20. **(D)**   *Idiom*

Another idiom question. It's idiomatically correct to discuss solutions *to* something; it's idiomatically impossible to discuss solutions *toward* something. Therefore, (D) is the correct answer.

Improving Sentence Errors

21. **(C)**   *Passive Voice*

Passive voice rears its ugly head in this sentence. That flabby second clause is full of unnecessary phrases. The correct answer, (C), gets rid of the useless phrase *in it's not being known*.

   If you looked askance at that second *its*, you were right to do so. Although it's not dead wrong, it's an undesirable way of using the possessive. Looking for answers that don't include that weird *its* would have been another way of narrowing down the answer choices.

22. **(E)**   *Fragment*

What we have here is a fragment—one that's easily fixed. All you need do is change that *seeming* to *seems*, and the fragment turns into a complete sentence. Thus, (E) is the correct answer.

(B) changes the tense of *seeming*, but not for the better; the change would not fix the fragment problem. (C) is a nice example of why it's important to check answers you think might be right in order to make sure they fit into the sentence. (If you didn't already, check now, and you'll see why it's a crucial step.) (C), like the correct answer, changes *seeming* to *seems*, but it still results in a fragment. The correct answer makes a point: *Stonehenge seems almost like a cliché of a mystery.* (D) sets up an expectation it never fulfills. It suggests to the reader that something else is coming: *Stonehenge, the puzzle that seems almost like a cliché of a mystery . . .* the reader is left thinking, "Yes? What's next?" but the sentence never tells us what's next. If you find yourself asking, "Yes? What's next?" you might be looking at a fragment.

23. **(C)**   *Run-on*

Both halves of this sentence could stand on their own—but the two halves are separated by a mere comma. This means we have a run-on sentence. You cannot have two complete sentences smashed together with only a comma between them. (C) fixes the problem best. It changes the underlined part from a complete sentence to a clause, and it goes the extra mile by making the relationship between the two parts of the sentence more clear.

The other answers don't work because when read back into the original sentence, they don't make sense—which illustrates, again, that when you've picked an answer you think is right, it's crucial to read it with the non-underlined part of the sentence to make sure it actually works.

24. **(B)**   *Misplaced Modifier*

There are two problems with this sentence as it is written. The first is a misplaced modifier. The sentence begins *being one of the premier pianists of his generation.* Immediately following that phrase is the word *critics*, which makes it sound as if the critics are the pianists. We know that Glenn Gould is the pianist in question. When looking for an answer choice, therefore, look for the one that identifies Gould, not the critics, as a pianist.

The other problem with this sentence as it is written is its passivity. Remember, you'll rarely see right answers that include the construction *being that* or something similar.

The answer choice that eradicates both the misplaced modifier problem and the passivity problem is (B). Answer choices (C), (D), and (E) each fix the problem of the misplaced modifier, but they also introduce new problems. Look at (C): *Glenn Gould's status as one of the premier pianists of his generation resulted in the applauding of him by critics.* The construction is so wordy and passive that the phrase sounds exhausted. Also, it suggests that critics gave Gould rave reviews *because* he had such a great reputation, which is not what the original sentence suggests. In (D), the phrase *which meant that* is unnecessary and ungrammatical. And like (C), (D) suggests that critics reviewed Gould not on his merits, but on his reputation. (E), when added to the rest of the original sentence, forms a fragment: *Critics who applauded Glenn Gould being one of the premier pianists of his generation for his definitive recording of the Goldberg Variations.* Not only is it difficult to read, but it starts by saying *critics who . . .* and never tells us what those critics do.

25. **(B)**   *Run-on*

This sentence has two clauses that can stand on their own: *Many older women develop osteoporosis* and *This is largely due to insufficient calcium intake in early years*. Because each clause can stand on its own, it is incorrect to join the two with no punctuation separating them. (B) rightly separates the two clauses with a comma and a conjunction.

The semicolon is used incorrectly in (C). Remember, it's incorrect to include a word like *and* after a semicolon. (D) and (E) both suffer from which/that confusion. (D) uses *which* without a comma, which in this case is incorrect. In answer choice (E), *that* should be *which*.

26. **(B)**   *Run-on*

The conjunction *and* is not ideal for connecting the two parts of this sentence because it does not make clear the relationship between the two parts. (B), the right answer, does make the relationship clear: *there was a long line outside the new club, even though it hadn't received any publicity yet*. The point is now obvious—it's weird that there was such a long line, because the club hadn't been publicized.

(C) turns the sentence into a run-on. (D) has a superfluous comma. (E) gets the meaning of the sentence wrong by suggesting that *because* the club hadn't gotten any publicity, there was a long line.

27. **(A)**   *No Error*

No error.

28. **(E)**   *No Error*

No error.

29. **(C)**   *Passive Voice*

If you ever want to shake a sentence and tell it to stop hemming and hawing, that sentence probably has a passivity problem. The second half of this sentence is way too wordy, and it never names the performer of the action. We're left wondering who is doing this remembering. The right answer, (C), tells us right away that *people* are the ones doing the remembering. It also does away with all unnecessary junk like *and these are the sorts* and *for which she is remembered*.

All of the other answers are wordy. (D) awkwardly puts *Josephine Baker* all the way at the end of the sentence, and (E) makes it sound as if Baker was a professional topless dancer and leopard-walker, when the original sentence refers to these as *escapades*.

30. **(D)**   *Misplaced Modifier*

The problem here is a misplaced modifier. As the original sentence stands, it sounds as if Bing Crosby and Fred Astaire are starring in Connecticut. The sentence intends to say that they are starring in a film. (D) fixes the problem by generating the phrase *which stars both Bing Crosby and Fred Astaire*.

(B) is unnecessarily passive and convoluted. It also sets up a false causal relationship that suggests *because* the film is set in Connecticut, it stars Crosby and Astaire. No such cause-and-effect is set up in the original sentence.

(C) can be eliminated both because it repeats the original problem, and because its tenses are confused. (D) would turn the sentence into a run-on.

31. **(A)**   *No Error*

No error.

32. **(C)** *Coordination*

The word *and* does not capture the relationship between the play and the content of the play. *Alice . . . directed a play and it depicted* makes the story of Plath sound like a secondary, accidental result of the play. The correct answer, (C), makes the relationship more clear. *A play that depicted* suggests that the main purpose of the play was to depict a Plath-like poet. All of the other answers can be eliminated because they don't clarify the relationship, but focus instead on making ineffectual grammatical changes.

33. **(D)** *Parallelism*

The original sentence does not use parallel form. Because it starts out by listing the nouns *lyrics* and *music*, it should list the noun *dancing* on its own, instead of adding the word *his*. Only (D) makes the list parallel.

34. **(C)** *Gerund*

You'll probably catch this error by hearing it. The phrase *to drink* sounds odd. It should be *drinking*, which is why (C) is the right answer. If you don't hear the problem, you can find it by reasoning that if the first half of the sentence uses a gerund, *consuming*, the second half should also use a gerund.

The rest of the answers throw you off the scent by suggesting that the problem is not with the infinitive *to drink*, but with the word *as*.

35. **(A)** *No Error*

No error.

36. **(C)** *Misplaced Modifier*

This is an extremely tricky one. It sounds so good, doesn't it? Unfortunately, what we have here is a misplaced modifier. Although you probably figured out what the sentence is *trying* to say, what it *actually* says is that it was right to oppose the tariff under the circumstances, as if people do their opposing huddled beneath circumstances. Thus, look for an answer that will place the problem modifier in a better place.

(C), the right answer, moves the modifier *under the circumstances* to the beginning of the sentence, where it belongs. (B), (D), and (E) can all be eliminated because they repeat the original problem.

37. **(A)** *No Error*

No error.

38. **(A)** *No Error*

No error.

Improving Paragraphs

39. **(C)** *Addition*

A good way to attack this question is to quickly remind yourself of the gist of the first paragraph. Once you remember that the first paragraph lists examples of how the Internet is used every day, eliminating a few answer choices becomes easy. (A) is about Internet privacy, which sounds good but is never discussed either in the essay in general or this paragraph in particular. (B) can be eliminated because the writer of this essay is promoting use of the Internet, not listing personal reasons why he dislikes it. (E) is about music-sharing, another topic that is not discussed in this essay. (C) and (D) are the most reasonable options. The right answer, (C), is specific and relevant. It talks about using the Internet *on a daily basis*. Don't pick (D) just because it uses the fancy word *ubiquitous*; it's not as specific as (C) because it doesn't mention daily use and it mentions cell phones, which aren't mentioned anywhere else in the paragraph.

40. **(B)** *Revision*

Because you've just answered a question on the general theme of the first paragraph, you'll probably need to glance back at the sentence on electronic papers only briefly. (B), the right answer, fits the bill exactly. The writer brings up electronic papers in order to provide another example of how people use the Internet every day, and the phrase in answer choice (B) clarifies the author's point.

41. **(E)** *Revision*

This question requires you to go back to the sentence in question, along with the ones before and after it. You'll see that the vague *this* is referring back to the previous paragraph, which discussed people's unwillingness to try the Internet. Therefore, (E) is the right answer.

42. **(B)** *Analysis*

Before you look at the answer choices, reread the sentence in question and decide in your own mind why the author asked the question *if we didn't have the Internet, what would happen?*. You don't have to come up with anything fancy. You can think something like, "the writer asks a question, and we know from what he's said before that the answer to the question is yes—if we didn't have the Internet, we would lose a lot." Having an analysis like this in mind will help you tackle the answer choices. (A) is wrong; the writer's initial assertion is that the Internet is good, and the question does not undercut that assertion. (B) is the correct answer. A hypothetical question is one asked for effect, a question to which we know the answer. (C) and (D) are similar to (A) and are wrong for the same reason—the writer is not changing his position that the Internet is a good thing. (E) is not quite as wrong, but it is still wrong. Although the writer is asking a question, he's not really inviting us to question his assertions; it's not a genuine question, it's a setup.

43. **(C)** *Revision*

(C) is the answer choice that best clarifies the relationship between the two clauses. A word like *but* or *however* is definitely needed, and (C) is superior to the other answer choices because its syntax is not awkward.

This is a question for which you probably don't need to return to the actual essay. If you read the reprinted sentence carefully, you'll be fine.

44. **(E)** *Revision*

Again, for this question, you don't need to reread the essay. Reading the reprinted sentence will be sufficient. The initial problem is awkwardness and a pronoun shift. The sentence begins by addressing *you*, but midway through it switches to *we*. The correct answer will marshal pronouns into order. (E) does this by referring to an abstract group of *people*. (B) and (C) do not solve the pronoun problem, and (D) changes the meaning of the sentence to its opposite by suggesting that we *should* be intimidated by the Internet.

45. **(D)** *Combining Sentences*

The issue here is which conjunction to choose. *But* makes the most sense, so (D) is your answer.

46. **(B)**   *Addition*

The phrasing of this question gives you some help: you're looking for a sentence that helps make the transition from the first paragraph to the rest of the essay. (C) and (D) continue with the ballet-bashing of the first paragraph, but they don't gesture toward the rest of the essay, which deals with the revelation that ballet isn't easy after all. Because they don't move beyond that first paragraph, they don't work as transition sentences. (A), although it hints at the next part of the essay, doesn't say anything about it explicitly, so it cannot count as a transition sentence, either. (E) doesn't go with the rest of the essay, since the writer never mentions his sister. (B) is your answer.

47. **(B)**   *Combining Sentences*

In this combination question, all of the answer choices get the relationship between the two sentences right. Your job is to find the answer choice that is grammatical and smooth, and (B) is it. (A) is a run-on. (C) uses the phrase *I'll be feeling guilty*, which is the wrong tense. Tense is also the problem in (E) because of the phrase *I was feeling guilty*. (E) can be eliminated because it is so wordy. The phrase *I'm different from them because* is unnecessary; the right answer conveys the same information more succinctly.

48. **(E)**   *Combining Sentences*

To answer this question, you'll have to go back to the essay and read the sentences before and after the problem sentence. When you do that, you'll see that *I'm surprised at his suggestion* is in the wrong tense. The rest of the story is told in the past tense, and that sentence is in the present. (E) fixes the problem by placing the sentence in the past.

49. **(B)**   *Combining Sentences*

This combination question deals with sequence. The answer choices all convey the same basic idea: the writer decided to take the class, and then he signed up. Only (B) conveys this information well, however. (C) is unnecessarily wordy because of the phrase *then proceeded*. (D) is a fragment. (E) is wordy.

50. **(E)**   *Analysis*

These questions can be tricky because of that capitalized word EXCEPT. Do something to remind yourself that you want to choose whatever the writer *didn't* do. Draw a circle around that EXCEPT, or write a note to yourself by the side of the answer choices: "Choose if writer didn't do." Of these answer choices, the only thing the writer didn't do was set up a hypothetical circumstance, so (E) is your answer. He certainly tells a story, so you can eliminate (A). (B) and (D) are a little vague, but if you can think of even one time he uses examples or draws contrasts, you can eliminate them. He gives an example of his friends' lazy behavior, and he draws a contrast between his friends and himself. So (B) and (D) are gone. (C) sounds fancy, but you can figure out why it's wrong. He does undermine a viewpoint put forth in the first paragraph: in that first paragraph, he talks about his old lack of respect for ballet, and the rest of the essay shows how he was wrong not to respect it. You're left with (E), the right answer. Nowhere in this essay does the writer posit a hypothetical circumstance.

Identifying Sentence Errors

51. (C)   *Pronoun Agreement*

(C) is the correct answer. *It* refers to *paintings*. Since *paintings* is plural, the pronoun that refers to the paintings must be plural as well.

    (A) is also about pronouns; as usual, you want to ask yourself what the pronoun refers to. The pronoun *her* refers to *paintings*, and there's nothing wrong with the phrase *her paintings*. (B) can be eliminated because the preposition *by* is correctly paired with the verb *rejected*. (D) is a straightforward description of the paintings.

52. (E)   *No Error.*

No error.

53. (D)   *Other*

The error in this sentence is difficult to categorize. It's kind of a parallelism problem and kind of a comparison problem. Remember, your ability to use the technical names of grammar problems is not important; it's much more useful to be able to hear what's wrong with a sentence. Your ear should hum, or buzz, or something, when you hit the comparison in this sentence, because when you start a comparison with "more," English idiom dictates that the other side of that comparison will be "than." For example: "I'm *more* competent *than* anyone else in this room." Therefore, the comparison phrase in this particular sentence should read something like *he finds inspiration more from memories of his mother's cooking than from food trends.*

54. (A)   *Subject-Verb Agreement*

There are a number of murky issues in this sentence. The best way to attack it is to try to parse out its clauses. The testers have made matters difficult by linking their answer choices in confusing ways; for example, *whose*, although underlined with the word *fish*, does not really belong to *fish*, but rather to *origins*.

    If you quarantine all prepositional clauses, you will be left with the following central sentence core: *lies the bones*. Does anything sound funny about this? Even if you don't notice anything strange, you'll probably pick up on the fact that the verb precedes the subject. Whenever this happens, your subject-verb agreement bells should go off. Try inverting subject and verb, and you'll probably spot the trick in this sentence. When you invert subject and verb, you get "the bones lies." That sounds wrong, because while "the bones" is a plural phrase, the verb form "lies" is singular. Therefore, your answer is (A).

55. (E)   *No Error*

No error.

56. (B)   *Adverb*

This question tests your knowledge of superlative modifiers (words such as *best, worst, most,* or *least*). Superlatives like *best* can only be used when comparing three or more items. This sentence only compares two items, cats and dogs, so instead of saying *many people like cats best*, it should say *many people like cats better*. (B) is the answer.

    The other tempting answer is (D), simply because the phrase *don't dislike* sounds odd or awkward. It may be unusual, but it's not ungrammatical; it's just another way of saying "like."

57. **(B)** *Wrong Word*

If you missed this one, read over your list of commonly confused words. The problem here is the use of *infamous*, a word that means "notorious" or "known for bad behavior." The writer should have used *famous*, which has no negative connotations. You need to examine the context of this sentence in order to get the answer right. While it's conceivable that someone could describe Eliot as infamous, nothing in this sentence supports such a description. She is described as infamous because of her novel. Since there is nothing scandalous about the novel or its contents, *infamous* is the wrong word to use.

58. **(E)** *No Error*

No error.

59. **(B)** *Subject-Verb Agreement*

The correct choice is (B). In the original text, *delegation* is the subject of *were*. Although this might seem fine at first, *delegation* is one of those tricky words that seems plural but is actually singular. Therefore, it should be matched with the singular verb "was," and (B) is the answer.

60. **(B)** *Faulty Comparison*

Tough question. The problem is that the sentence is technically saying Maria Callas was better known for her dramatic abilities than she was known for her opera singers. Of course, what the writer means is that Callas is better known than other opera singers for her dramatic abilities. This error could have slipped under the radar, since it is perfectly obvious what the writer is *trying* to say, and nothing sounds immediately wrong. Still, the grammar books would call this a faulty comparison, so (B) is your answer.

WRITING TEST II

Part A

Time — 20 minutes

You have twenty minutes to plan and write an essay on the topic assigned below. DO NOT WRITE ON ANOTHER TOPIC. AN ESSAY ON ANOTHER TOPIC IS NOT ACCEPTABLE.

The essay is assigned to give you an opportunity to show how well you can write. You should, therefore, take care to express your thoughts on the topic clearly and effectively. How well you write is much more important than how much you write, but to cover the topic adequately you will probably need to write more than one paragraph. Be specific.

Your essay must be written on the following two pages. You will find that you have enough space if you write on every line, avoid wide margins, and keep your handwriting to a reasonable size. It is important to remember that what you write will be read by someone who is not familiar with your handwriting. Try to write or print so that what you are writing is legible to the reader.

Consider the following statement and assignment. Then write the essay as directed.

"The end always justifies the means."

Assignment: Choose one example from personal experience, current events, or history, literature, or any other discipline and use this example to write an essay in which you agree or disagree with the statement above. Your essay should be specific.

DO NOT WRITE YOUR ESSAY IN YOUR TEST BOOK. You will receive credit only for what you write on your answer sheet.

WHEN YOUR SUPERVISOR ANNOUNCES THAT TWENTY MINUTES HAVE PASSED, YOU MUST STOP WRITING THE ESSAY AND GO ON TO PART B IF YOU HAVE NOT ALREADY DONE SO. IF YOU FINISH YOUR ESSAY BEFORE THIS ANNOUNCEMENT, GO ON TO PART B AT ONCE.

BEGIN WRITING YOUR ESSAY ON THE ANSWER SHEET.

WRITING TEST

Part A

Time — 20 minutes

WRITING TEST

Part A

Time — 20 minutes

WRITING TEST

Part B

Time — 40 minutes

1. Each manuscript in the enormous body of work
                                       A

   left unpublished at the author's death poses their own
        B   C   D

   problems—and pleasures. No error
                             E

2. The characters in Kafka's fiction are so isolated,
                                       A

   and feel so guilty, that from the beginning the reader
     B   C

   feels pessimistic about their chances for happiness.
                             D

   No error
     E

3. Of the dozens of beverages the company makes,
   A   B

   its customers like seltzer water better. No error
     C   D   E

4. Edith Wharton's character Lily Bart can not scarcely
                                        A

   stand to marry a poor man, yet at the same time she
         B   C

   does not wish to marry a rich man she dislikes. No error
                   D   E

5. Today's museums perform several functions: they
            A

   present new works of art, education for visitors, and
     B   C

   exhibit collections. No error
     D   E

GO ON TO THE NEXT PAGE →

6. Radha has <u>decide</u> to <u>go on</u> the camping trip <u>despite</u> the
       A   B   C

    strenuous objections <u>of her</u> friends. <u>No error</u>
                         D   E

7. Before one attempts to take a political stand on the

    issue, <u>you should</u> investigate <u>in depth</u> the <u>pros and cons</u>
             A   B   C

    of <u>both sides</u> of the argument. <u>No error</u>
         D   E

8. The first years of Hank Aaron's pro-baseball career

    <u>were</u> more difficult <u>than</u> <u>other players</u>; he had to endure
    A   B   C

    threats and racist comments from fans and <u>even from</u>
                                          D

    his own teammates. <u>No error</u>
                     E

9. A crucial part <u>of developing</u> <u>an appreciation</u> for
                   A   B

    the work of the novelist Muriel Spark <u>is gaining</u>
                                     C

    <u>an understanding</u> of her dry, subtle humor. <u>No error</u>
      D   E

10. The Eiffel Tower, <u>more than</u> <u>any of</u> Paris's dozens
                     A   B

    <u>of other</u> tourist attractions, <u>have become</u> the symbol of
    C   D

    the city. <u>No error</u>
             E

11. The restaurant owner <u>requires</u> waiters to take <u>both</u> a
                    A   B

    course on wine and a <u>seminar on</u> people skills before
                         C

    <u>he will allow them</u> to serve in his restaurant. <u>No error</u>
    D   E

12. The tour guide cleared <u>his throat</u> and clapped his hands
                        A

    together, <u>his</u> usual sign <u>that</u> the start of the tour was
              B   C

    <u>eminent</u>. <u>No error</u>
    D   E

13. I never expected <u>it could</u> <u>be so</u> difficult to take an exam,
                 A   B

    but this term <u>they have</u> all been very <u>exhausting</u>.
                  C   D

    <u>No error</u>
    E

14. The tenor sang so <u>loud</u> <u>that</u> he completely lost his voice,
                  A   B

    <u>and could not</u> speak for weeks afterwards,
    C

    <u>much less sing</u>. <u>No error</u>
    D   E

15. The teachers' strike <u>continued</u> until someone
                  A

    <u>came up with</u> a plan <u>where</u> the union could work out <u>its</u>
    B   C   D

    differences with the school board. <u>No error</u>
                                E

16. Neither the liberal <u>nor</u> the conservative candidate
                  A

    <u>were prepared</u> at this time <u>to suggest</u> a <u>date for</u> the
    B   C   D

    next debate. <u>No error</u>
                E

GO ON TO THE NEXT PAGE →

17. The amateur-collector kit <u>came complete</u> with
                                    A

    instructions <u>that explained</u> how <u>to prevent</u> the butterfly
                      B   C

    <u>to escape</u> the net. <u>No error</u>
        D   E

18. <u>Wanting to</u> take an active role <u>in public life</u>, Clint
        A   B

    Eastwood <u>ran for and won</u> the position <u>of mayor of</u>
                  C   D

    Carmel, California. <u>No error</u>
                            E

19. The student council, <u>after hearing</u> arguments from both
                              A

    sides and <u>deliberating for</u> an hour, <u>have decided</u> not
                  B   C

    <u>to adopt</u> a new mascot. <u>No error</u>
        D   E

20. Pianos are delicate, sensitive instruments <u>that</u> need to
                                                    A

    <u>have been</u> <u>tuned</u> on a <u>regular basis</u>. <u>No error</u>
        B   C   D   E

GO ON TO THE NEXT PAGE

WRITING TEST

21. Jorge reluctantly agreed to dress up as Santa Claus for the office party, <u>since it involved wearing a heavy, itchy fake belly.</u>

    (A) since it involved wearing a heavy, itchy fake belly
    (B) because it involved wearing a heavy, itchy, fake belly
    (C) but it involved the necessity to wear of a heavy, itchy fake belly
    (D) even though it involved wearing a hot, itchy fake belly
    (E) it involved wearing a hot, itchy fake belly

22. <u>Goya, who began his career painting portraits of royalty, turned</u> to dark, violent subject matter after an illness left him deaf.

    (A) Goya, who began his career painting portraits of royalty, turned
    (B) Goya began his career painting portraits of royalty, he turned
    (C) Goya who once having begun his career painting portraits of royalty, turned
    (D) Goya, because he began his career painting portraits of royalty, turned
    (E) Goya began his career painting portraits of royalty since he turned

23. In advance of the troops, <u>the general who came to scout out the terrain</u> and weigh the tactical benefit of a night attack.

    (A) the general who came to scout out the terrain
    (B) the general, who comes to scout out the terrain
    (C) the general coming to scout out the terrain
    (D) the general came to scout out the terrain
    (E) the general that came to scout out the terrain

24. The would-be novelist <u>in the café with the world-weary smile says he models himself</u> after Hemingway.

    (A) in the café with the world-weary smile says he models himself
    (B) in the café says he models himself, with a world-weary smile
    (C) says he modeled himself, in the café with the world-weary smile,
    (D) says he models himself, with a world-weary smile, in the café,
    (E) with the world-weary smile in the café says he models himself

GO ON TO THE NEXT PAGE →

25. <u>With her rosy cheeks and having a cunning look</u>, the older woman was perfect for the part of a murder suspect.

    (A) With her rosy cheeks and having a cunning look
    (B) Rosy cheeks and a cunning look
    (C) With her rosy cheeks and cunning look
    (D) Rosy cheeks and with her cunning look
    (E) With having a cunning look and rosy cheeks

26. The open call for a new reality show attracted thousands of applicants, <u>each with a desire to become famous</u>.

    (A) each with a desire to become famous
    (B) they each wanted to become famous
    (C) which all had a desire to become famous
    (D) each having a desire to become famous
    (E) when they each had a desire to become famous

27. Paying off your credit card bill in full every month, while sometimes difficult, is <u>better than to pay outrageous interest rates</u>.

    (A) better than to pay outrageous interest rates
    (B) better, still, than it is paying outrageous interest rates
    (C) not as bad as to pay outrageous interest rates
    (D) compared to paying outrageous interest rates, is better
    (E) better than paying outrageous interest rates

28. Isabella Stuart Gardner, Boston socialite, decided in mid-life to become a serious art collector, and as a result <u>an impressive number of European Renaissance paintings began to be purchased</u>.

    (A) an impressive number of European Renaissance paintings began to be purchased
    (B) an impressive number of European Renaissance paintings were purchased by her
    (C) she began to purchase an impressive number of European Renaissance paintings
    (D) beginning to be purchased were an impressive number of European Renaissance paintings
    (E) the purchasing of an impressive number of European Renaissance paintings

29. In 1974 the ballet dancer Mikhail Baryshnikov defected to the United States, <u>leaving behind the Kirov Ballet to join the New York City Ballet</u>.

    (A) leaving behind the Kirov Ballet to join the New York City Ballet
    (B) and joining the New York City Ballet and leaving the Kirov Ballet
    (C) he joined the New York City Ballet after leaving the Kirov Ballet
    (D) for the leaving of the Kirov Ballet in favor of the New York City Ballet
    (E) and as a result was leaving behind the Kirov Ballet, joining the New York City Ballet

30. One of the most inventive and respected dancers in the world, <u>tap dancing was elevated by Fred Astaire</u> from an entertainment to an art.

    (A) tap dancing was elevated by Fred Astaire
    (B) tap dancing, elevated by Fred Astaire
    (C) tap dancing received elevation from Fred Astaire
    (D) Fred Astaire got elevation from tap dancing
    (E) Fred Astaire elevated tap dancing

31. Even though the rain delay lasted for more than three hours, <u>although only a handful of fans</u> left the stadium.

    (A) although only a handful of fans
    (B) only a handful of fans
    (C) yet even so, only a handful of fans
    (D) and yet only a handful of fans
    (E) and it caused only a handful of fans

32. In 1973, the Supreme Court upheld women's right to have abortions, <u>this</u> galvanized groups that opposed abortion and groups that supported it.

    (A) this
    (B) which
    (C) therefore
    (D) that
    (E) in contrast

GO ON TO THE NEXT PAGE

33. For many writers, <u>being applauded by critics is more satisfying</u> than selling lots of books.

    (A) being applauded by critics is more satisfying
    (B) to be applauded by critics is more satisfying
    (C) to have the applause of critics is more satisfying
    (D) applause of critics holds more satisfaction
    (E) having the applause of critics is more satisfying

34. <u>Scene of the historic battle at which Davy Crockett and James Bowie lost their lives, tourists flock to the Alamo.</u>

    (A) Scene of the historic battle at which Davy Crockett and James Bowie lost their lives, tourists flock to the Alamo
    (B) At which Davy Crockett and James Bowie lost their lives, the scene of the historic battle, tourists flock to the Alamo
    (C) The Alamo, the scene of the historic battle at which Davy Crockett and James Bowie lost their lives, to which tourists flock
    (D) Scene of the historic battle, to which tourists flock, is the Alamo, at which Davy Crockett and James Bowie lost their lives
    (E) Tourists flock to the Alamo, scene of the historic battle at which Davy Crockett and James Bowie lost their lives

35. The head chef regularly made a tour of the dining room and <u>stopped to talk to each patron, this cordial atmosphere</u> made the restaurant popular.

    (A) stopped to talk to each patron, this cordial atmosphere
    (B) stopping to talk to each patron, this cordial atmosphere
    (C) created a cordial atmosphere, stopped to talk to each person
    (D) stopped to talk to each patron; this cordial atmosphere
    (E) presented a cordial atmosphere: stopping to talk to each patron

36. As the bus driver sped up, <u>he swerved to avoid, and narrowly missed hitting, a pedestrian</u>.

    (A) he swerved to avoid, and narrowly missed hitting, a pedestrian
    (B) a pedestrian, swerved to avoid, and narrowly missed
    (C) he narrowly missed by the technique of swerving, a pedestrian
    (D) he swerved, narrowly missed, avoided, a pedestrian
    (E) a pedestrian was narrowly missed hitting when he swerved to avoid him

37. The student found his professor boring and aggressive, <u>and these were qualities that were noted</u> on the teacher evaluation form.

    (A) and these were qualities that were noted
    (B) and noted these qualities
    (C) the noting of these qualities was
    (D) her noting of these qualities
    (E) these qualities have been noted

38. The problem with many internships is <u>they don't pay very well, they don't provide valuable work experience, and long hours</u>.

    (A) they don't pay very well, they don't provide valuable work experience, and long hours
    (B) they don't pay very well, they don't provide valuable work experience, they don't work long hours
    (C) they don't pay very well; they don't provide valuable work experience; and long hours
    (D) not paying well, not proving valuable work experience, too many long hours
    (E) low pay, lack of valuable work experience, and long hours

GO ON TO THE NEXT PAGE

WRITING TEST

Directions: Each of the following passages is an early draft of an essay. Some parts of the passages need to be rewritten.

Read each passage and answer the questions that follow. Some questions are about particular sentences or parts of sentences and ask you to improve sentence structure and word choice. Other questions refer to parts of the essay or the entire essay and ask you to consider organization and development. In making your decisions, follow the conventions of standard written English. After you have chosen your answer, fill in the corresponding oval on your answer sheet.

Questions 39–44 are based on the following passage.

(1) *Cafés and restaurants in the United States could benefit by becoming Europeanized in certain ways.* (2) *Living in bustling cities, a slower, more civilized dining and drinking experience would be welcome.* (3) *A few key changes would make a big difference.* (4) *In some cafés, all of the chairs should be turned to face the street, so that patrons could linger and people-watch.* (5) *And café-owners would not have to worry about loss of revenue as a result of this lingering.* (6) *What they lost in quick turnover time they would more than recoup from satisfied customers who would frequently come back for more good treatment.* (7) *Also, waiters should not bring the bill to the table until the customer requests it.* (8) *Then, instead of the customer feeling rushed or harried by his waiter, he would feel relaxed.* (9) *If people were always allowed to linger, and treated with courtesy, they might eat out more.* (10) *The psychological benefits would not be negligible, either.* (11) *It might do real good to stressed city-dwellers to think of restaurants as oases from the hectic pace of regular life.*

(12) *Restaurants should do this because it would increase their revenue and give real pleasure to patrons.* (13) *It may sound like a small thing, but if restaurants model themselves on their European counterparts and they would have slowed down the pace a bit, customers would respond enthusiastically.*

39. Which of the following is the best revision of the underlined part of sentence 2, which is reprinted here?

    Living in bustling cities, a slower, more civilized dining and drinking experience would be welcome.

    (A) Living in a city which is bustling
    (B) Being bustled about in a city
    (C) We live in a city which is bustling
    (D) Especially for people living in bustling cites
    (E) The city bustling around us

40. In context, which of the following is the best replacement for the word *and* at the beginning of sentence 5, reprinted below?

    And café-owners would not have to worry about loss of revenue as a result of this lingering.

    (A) Furthermore,
    (B) Despite this,
    (C) But,
    (D) In contrast,
    (E) Beyond that,

GO ON TO THE NEXT PAGE

41. Considering the context, which of the following is the best revision of the underlined part of sentence 8, reprinted below?

    Then, instead of feeling rushed or harried by his waiter, <u>he would feel</u> relaxed.

    (A) (as it is now)
    (B) he would begin to feel
    (C) the waiter would feel
    (D) he should feel
    (E) the customer would feel

42. Sentence 10 would be improved if the writer

    (A) brought up the European approach to such sanctuaries as museums
    (B) gave his own opinion
    (C) provided a brief description of a café
    (D) discussed other big-city problems
    (E) discussed specific examples

43. In sentence 12, *do this* would be more specific if rewritten as which of the following?

    (A) try new things
    (B) attract patrons
    (C) institute these changes
    (D) have less stress
    (E) accomplish these goals

44. Which of the following is the best version of the underlined portion of sentence 13, which is reprinted here?

    It may sound like a small thing, <u>but if restaurants model themselves on their European counterparts and they would have slowed</u> the pace a bit, customers would respond enthusiastically.

    (A) (as it is)
    (B) however, if restaurants model themselves on their European counterparts, and they are slowing
    (C) but if restaurants model themselves on their European counterparts and slow
    (D) but if restaurants will model themselves on their European counterparts and they will slow
    (E) and if restaurants model themselves on their European counterparts and if they would have slowed

GO ON TO THE NEXT PAGE

Questions 45–50 are based on the following passage.

(1) *Obesity is a big problem in the United States.* (2) *Sixty-one percent of adults suffer from it, but around 300,000 people die every year from diseases directly related to obesity.* (3) *Obesity is related to diabetes, high blood pressure, and getting heart disease.*

(4) *Only a healthy diet combined with a regular exercise program can help people lose weight.* (5) *This sounds simple enough, but it proves nearly impossible for most people.* (6) *Many overweight people go on diets to lose weight, trying everything from pills to shakes and formulas advertised on late-night infomercials.* (7) *You can lose weight by almost any method out there.* (8) *One study showed that ninety-five percent of people who lost weight on diets that didn't include exercise gained back all of the weight after they stop dieting.* (9) *This makes sense, it's unrealistic to expect people to continue drinking only shakes for the rest of their lives.* (10) *Ideally, therefore, reliance on trendy diets would be replaced by a lifelong change in eating and exercise habits.*

(11) *It is not just physical habits that must be changed in order to control obesity.* (12) *Psychology must be considered, too.* (13) *Our intensely weight-conscious society has turned eating from a simple necessity into a loaded psychological endeavor.*

45. Which of the following is the best way to revise the underlined portion of sentence 2, reprinted below?

    Sixty-one percent of adults <u>suffer from it, but around</u> 300,000 people die every year from diseases directly related to obesity.

    (A) suffer from it, but around
    (B) suffer, from it but around
    (C) suffer from it, and
    (D) suffer from it, although
    (E) suffer because of it, but around

46. Which of the following is the best way to revise sentence 3, which is reprinted below?

    Obesity is related to diabetes, high blood pressure, and getting heart disease.

    (A) Obesity is related to diabetes, high blood pressure, and getting heart disease
    (B) Obesity, related to diabetes, high blood pressure, and getting heart disease
    (C) Obesity is related, to diabetes and high blood pressure and to getting heart disease
    (D) Obesity has been related to diabetes high blood pressure, and heart disease
    (E) Obesity is related to diabetes, high blood pressure, and heart disease

47. Which of the following should be inserted at the beginning of the second paragraph, directly before sentence 4?

    (A) On a basic physical level, something must be done about this dangerous problem.
    (B) Faithfully following diets like the Atkins diet can help some people.
    (C) Losing weight and keeping it off turns out to be a fairly manageable proposition.
    (D) It's important to remember that obesity is not simply a physical problem—it's a psychological one, too.
    (E) Obesity poses a serious health risk.

GO ON TO THE NEXT PAGE

48. Which of the following revisions is most needed in sentence 6?

   (A) Replace "from" with a comma
   (B) change "trying" to "they try"
   (C) change "and" to "to"
   (D) omit the word "advertised"
   (E) insert "most of which do not work" after the word "informercials"

49. Which of the following revisions is the best way to combine sentences 7 and 8, reprinted below?

   You can lose weight by almost any method out there. One study showed that ninety-five percent of people who lost weight on diets that didn't include exercise gained back all of the weight after they stop dieting.

   (A) You can lose weight by almost any method out there; studies show that ninety-five percent of people who lost weight on diets that didn't include exercise gained back all of the weight after they stop dieting.
   (B) Studies show that ninety-five percent of people who lost weight on diets that didn't include exercise gained back all of the weight after they stop dieting, but you can lose weight by almost any method out there.
   (C) You can lose weight via almost any method out there; studies show that ninety-five percent of people who lost weight on diets that didn't include exercise gained back all of the weight after they stop dieting.
   (D) Studies show that even though ninety-five percent of people who lost weight on diets that didn't include exercise gained back all of the weight after they stop dieting, you can lose weight by almost any method out there.
   (E) Although you can lose weight by almost any method out there, studies show that ninety-five percent of people who lost weight on diets that didn't include exercise gained back all of the weight after they stop dieting.

50. The underlined part of sentence 9, reprinted below, should be changed in which of the following ways?

   This makes <u>sense, it's unrealistic</u> to expect people to continue drinking only shakes for the rest of their lives.

   (A) sense it's unrealistic
   (B) sense; it's unrealistic
   (C) sense, its unrealistic
   (D) sense, yes it's
   (E) sense it is unrealistic

GO ON TO THE NEXT PAGE

WRITING TEST

Note: The remaining questions are like those at the beginning of Part B.

Directions: For each sentence in which you find an error, select the one underlined part that must be changed to make the sentence correct and fill in the corresponding oval on your answer sheet.

If there is no answer, fill in answer oval Ⓔ.

EXAMPLE:

The other delegates and him immediately
    A   B   C

accepted the resolution drafted by the
                              D

neutral states. No error
               E

SAMPLE ANSWER:

Ⓐ ● Ⓒ Ⓓ Ⓔ

---

51. The scientist said that the purpose of the experiment
                  A   B

is to have found new ways of creating carbon crystals.
        C   D

No error
  E

52. In the realm of oratory, hardly no one can compare to
                        A

Sojourner Truth, who once listed her accomplishments
              B

and punctuated each item on the list with the question
     C   D

"And ain't I a woman?" No error
               E

53. Teachers have found it useful to take their students to
        A   B

the natural history museum, where the exhibits, that
                              C

include an extensive dinosaur fossil collection, are very
                                D

instructive. No error
       E

54. However much we prepare in advance, the statistics
    A

problem sets always prove incredibly challenging for my
              B   C

team and I. No error
    D   E

55. Although London's Scotland Yard is one of the
                      A

most effective police organizations in the world, many
     B

of its cases remain unsolved forever because it is just
                             C

too perplexing. No error
    D   E

GO ON TO THE NEXT PAGE →

56. The Hudson River school of painting, <u>although</u> inspired
                                          A

    by European romanticism, <u>took on</u> a uniquely
                                     B

    American flavor because <u>its</u> disciples painted
                                       C

    <u>such American landscapes</u> as the Hudson River valley,
                     D

    Niagara Falls, the Catskills, and the White Mountains.

    <u>No error</u>
      E

57. The kimono, typically <u>brightly colored robes</u> made
                                   A

    <u>of silk</u> or cotton, <u>has lost</u> popularity among Japanese
      B   C

    women <u>in recent years</u>. <u>No error</u>
            D   E

58. The professors at the <u>physics conference</u> explained
                        A

    <u>his or her</u> <u>research on</u> the issue of <u>cold fusion</u>.
      B   C   D

    <u>No error</u>
      E

59. Ice hockey brawls seem like <u>a harmless</u> and
                              A

    time-honored tradition, <u>but</u> they injure players far
                       B

    <u>more frequently</u> and seriously than you or <u>I</u> realize.
      C   D

    <u>No error</u>
      E

60. There are <u>several important</u> rules to remember when
                 A

    tutoring a student: students should help their clients

    <u>gain an insight for</u> the material <u>at hand</u>,
            B   C

    <u>understand previous mistakes</u>, and give attention
            D

    to upcoming assignments. <u>No error</u>
                   E

S T O P

IF YOU FINISH BEFORE TIME IS CALLED, YOU MAY CHECK YOUR WORK ON THIS TEST ONLY.
DO NOT TURN TO ANY OTHER TEST IN THIS BOOK.

Answers to SAT II Writing Practice Test II

Question Number	Correct Answer	Right	Wrong	Question Number	Correct Answer	Right	Wrong
1.	D	___	___	31.	B	___	___
2.	E	___	___	32.	B	___	___
3.	D	___	___	33.	A	___	___
4.	A	___	___	34.	E	___	___
5.	C	___	___	35.	D	___	___
6.	A	___	___	36.	A	___	___
7.	A	___	___	37.	B	___	___
8.	C	___	___	38.	E	___	___
9.	E	___	___	39.	D	___	___
10.	D	___	___	40.	A	___	___
11.	E	___	___	41.	E	___	___
12.	D	___	___	42.	E	___	___
13.	C	___	___	43.	C	___	___
14.	A	___	___	44.	C	___	___
15.	C	___	___	45.	C	___	___
16.	B	___	___	46.	E	___	___
17.	D	___	___	47.	A	___	___
18.	E	___	___	48.	C	___	___
19.	C	___	___	49.	E	___	___
20.	B	___	___	50.	B	___	___
21.	D	___	___	51.	C	___	___
22.	A	___	___	52.	A	___	___
23.	D	___	___	53.	C	___	___
24.	E	___	___	54.	D	___	___
25.	C	___	___	55.	C	___	___
26.	A	___	___	56.	E	___	___
27.	E	___	___	57.	A	___	___
28.	C	___	___	58.	B	___	___
29.	A	___	___	59.	E	___	___
30.	E	___	___	60.	B	___	___

Calculating Your Score

Your raw score for SAT II Writing test is a composite of your raw score in the multiple-choice section and your score on the essay. Once you have determined your composite score, use the conversion table on page 17 to calculate your scaled score. To Calculate your raw score, count the number of questions you answered correctly on the multiple choice: _____
$$A$$

Count the number of questions you answered incorrectly, and multiply that number by $\frac{1}{4}$:

$$\underline{\hspace{3cm}} \quad X \quad \frac{1}{4} \quad = \quad \underline{\hspace{3cm}}$$
$$B \qquad\qquad\qquad\qquad C$$

Subtract the value in field C from value in field A: _____
$$D$$

Round the number to the nearest whole number: _____
$$E$$

Take your score for the Essay (ask a teacher to grade your essay or grade yourself) and multiply it by 3.43:

$$\underline{\hspace{3cm}} \quad X\ 3.43 = \underline{\hspace{2cm}}$$
$$F \qquad\qquad\qquad G$$

Add the number in field E to the number in Field G: _____
$$H$$

Round the number in field H. This is your Writing SAT II score: _____

Student Essays

Total Score: 12 (each reader gave the essay a 6)

Contrary to the cliché, oftentimes even the most noble end does not justify immoral means. Even when the goal is to end a war or save lives, the process used to achieve those goals must be a worthy one.

In wartime, often leaders explain their bloody actions by saying those actions were necessary in order to achieve a peaceful outcome—but the passage of time often proves that these supposedly necessary means weren't morally justifiable. For example, Hiroshima. The Allied leaders said that in order to end the war, they needed to strike with deadly, overwhelming force. When Hiroshima was bombed, thousands and thousands of people died horrifying deaths. The land and it's people were decimated. It is not clear that striking Hiroshima hurried the end of the war. More importantly, though, it is almost impossible to justify the slaughter of thousands of civilians, even when ending a war is the stated aim.

More recently, lawmakers and scientists have been debating the issue of human cloning. The majority agree that cloning is unethical, but a few scientists say that if cloning was made legal, the research and experimentation that would then be possible would lead to discoveries that could save lives. Some scientists, notably Dr. Antinori, suggest that cloning should be allowed because some people desperately want children. In a news conference, Antinori said that the end (happy parents) justified any means necessary, including cloning. Most lawmakers and scientists agree, though, that even if lives could be saved or people made happy, the moral, psychological, and ethical implications make human cloning impossible. The prospect of "playing God" is too objectionable to justify the potential gains in research.

Sometimes, as in the case of Hiroshima, hindsight makes it clear that the ends don't always justify the means; sometimes, as in the case of cloning, we don't have the luxury of hindsight, and must learn from our past history that no matter how noble the ends, the means should not be morally repugnant.

Discussion:

This is an excellent essay. It is well-structured, well-informed, and, except for a few minor errors, well-written.

The writer has an introductory paragraph that introduces the main idea: the ends don't justify the means. Her first supporting paragraph discusses Hiroshima; her second discusses cloning. Both paragraphs are entirely self-contained. Neither wanders, gets sidetracked, or mentions information from elsewhere in the essay. Perhaps most importantly, both paragraphs will likely impress the readers because of their content. This writer presents herself as someone who is interested in both history and current events. The fact that she comes up with the name of a doctor interested in cloning is excellent. Maybe she read an article on him while eating her bowl of cereal that morning, or maybe she wrote a fifty page paper on him—it doesn't matter where these examples come from. If you can dredge up a specific example from somewhere, do it.

The concluding paragraph is also strong. It comes to a real conclusion, instead of simply summarizing what has come before.

The writer does make a few errors. *For example, Hiroshima* is not a complete sentence. And in the phrase *the land and it's people*, the writer makes the common mistake of using the contraction "it's" (which is short for "it is") instead of using the possessive "its," which is what she should do. However, two small errors that were likely the result of time constraints will not keep a great essay from getting the grade it deserves.

167

Total Score: 4 (each reader gave the essay a 2)

I disagree with the above statement. The end doesn't always justify the means. Sometimes it does, but not always. It all depends on the case in question.

For example, in a Dorothy L. Sayers novel there is a character who wants to get a fortune. Who doesn't? This is a justifiable end. But in order to do it, he has to kill his cousin, whose the one with the fortune. To do this, he eats a little arsenic every day, slowly building up an imunity to it. Finally he can eat doses of arsenic that would be lethal to most, but he can eat them without blinking an eye. Then he serves an ommelette to his cousin that's completely filled with arsenic. He eats the same ommelette, so the police don't think he could be blamed for poisoning his cousin. This was a good end, but an evil means.

Then, there is the recent mayoral election in New York City. Both men wanted to win the race. They both thought they would be the best mayor for New York City. So to them, winning the race is a great end. But in order to get there, in the last days of the campaign they ran a series of mudslinging ads, accusing the other person of sexual harrassment, buying the office, etc. etc. When two politicians lower the tone of a race like that, there is no excuse.

And what about football players who take steroids? They want to make their performance on the field good.

Discussion:

This writer chooses good examples. Talking about a novel in the second paragraph and politics in the third shows the readers that you have read a few books in your day and are reasonably well-informed about current events.

Another good thing is this essay's strong structure. This essay has an opening paragraph, and it devotes its two supporting paragraphs to two different examples. The weak structural point is the last paragraph, which looks as if it was meant to be a third example paragraph. The writer clearly ran out of time, which does not look good to the reader. If you find yourself with only a few minutes left, do not begin a third example. Instead, write a concluding paragraph, even if the paragraph is only a sentence or two.

The main problem with this essay is sophomoric prose. Although the writer's examples are well-chosen, they are not well-developed or written about in an elegant way. The essay reads a bit like a transcript of the writer's spoken ramblings on the statement.

One consistent flaw is the author's tendency to rely on vague words like "this" and "it": *in order to do it, to do this, this was a good end, in order to get there.* Overuse of "this" and "there" and "it" means that you're making reference to something that is perhaps clear to you, but is probably not clear to the reader. Instead of saying something like *in order to do it*, for example, the writer should say *in order to gain the fortune.* This will orient readers, and prevent them from suspecting that you're a lazy or vague writer.

The abbreviation "etc." should not appear in a formal essay, and it certainly should not appear back to back, as it does in the third paragraph.

Identifying Sentence Errors

1.   **(D)**   *Pronoun Agreement*

When the writer of this sentence refers back to *each manuscript*, he talks about *their own problems*. This is incorrect, because we're talking about *each manuscript* on its own. Therefore, the singular word *manuscript* should be matched with the singular phrase *its own problems*. (D) is your answer.

Choice (A) is fine; *each* is singular, so it goes with the singular word *manuscript*. (B) and (C) might look odd at first, since they use jargon with which you might not be familiar. But unless you can find a concrete reason why the underlined phrases might be wrong, you cannot pick (B) or (C).

2. (E) *No Error*

No error.

3. (D) *Adverb*

If you're comparing three or more items, you need a superlative, a word that usually ends in -*st*, such as *juiciest*, *lamest*, or *jolliest*. Comparative words, which often end in -*er*, such as *better*, can only compare two items. Since *dozens* of items are being considered in this sentence, you need a superlative, not a comparative. Since *better* is a comparative, it is wrong, and (D) is the answer.

Whenever you encounter a verb, such as *like* in (C), you'll want to make sure that its tense makes sense in the context of the sentence as a whole. Illogical tense switches will undoubtedly be tested on this section of the exam, so it's really important to scrutinize the tense of an underlined verb. *Like* does make sense in this sentence, so (C) is not the answer.

4. (A) *Double Negative*

Whenever you see a word such as "scarcely," you should be alert to the possible presence of a double negative. Two negative words jammed next to each other almost invariably form a double negative. *Cannot* is obviously a negative word. *Scarcely* is also negative, but less obviously so. Be careful around "scarcely," and its cousins "hardly" and "barely"; they are all negative without sounding negative, and it's easier to miss a double negative when one of those negative-but-doesn't-sound-it words is in the mix.

So the right answer is (A); *cannot scarcely* should be either *cannot* or *scarcely*. Besides the fact that *scarcely* is not obviously a negative word, there's another difficulty in identifying the right answer: the language of this sentence is a bit snooty. Don't be intimidated because this sentence sounds like it should be read in an English accent; a double negative is a double negative.

5. (C) *Parallelism*

When you see a list, you should check it carefully for errors of parallelism. This list begins and ends with verb phrases (*present new works* and *exhibit collections*), but the middle item is a noun (*education*). Remember, items in a list must take parallel form. Therefore, *education for visitors* should be changed to something like *provide education for visitors* or *offer education to visitors*, and (C) is the correct answer.

Today's might look strange, but the apostrophe-s is in fact correct. The museums belong to today — hence the possessive.

6. (A) *Tense*

Your ear is the most reliable way of finding tense errors. Hopefully as you read through this sentence, you'll notice that the phrase *has decide* does not sound right; it should be *has decided*. (A) is the correct answer.

(B) doesn't present any problems; it's a straightforward way of describing Radha's plan. (C), the preposition *despite*, is used correctly. (D) is a possessive pronoun, also used correctly.

7. (A) *Pronoun Shift*

If a sentence begins with "one" as its subject, it can't switch to a "you" subject halfway through — and vice versa. This sentence begins with the phrase *before one attempts*, but midway through, it switches pronouns: *you should investigate*. (A) is the answer.

8. (C) *Faulty Comparison*

This sentence has a faulty comparison. Technically, this sentence says that other players weren't as difficult for Hank Aaron as were the first years of his career. What the writer means to say is that the first years of Aaron's career were more difficult than the first years of other players' careers. (C) is your answer.

9.   **(E)**   *No Error*

No error.

10.   **(D)**   *Subject/Verb Agreement*

The key to spotting the error in this sentence is to notice how far apart the subject (*The Eiffel Tower*) is from its verb (*have become*). If we eliminate the intervening clause *more than any of Paris's dozens of other tourist attractions*, we get *The Eiffel Tower have become*. Sound wrong? It is. *The Eiffel Tower* is a single subject, while the verb form *have become* is plural. (D) is the right answer.

Whenever you see a long, descriptive clause intervening between subject and verb, try to read the sentence without it. This is especially important when the subject is singular, and whatever noun comes inside the clause is plural. In this sentence, for example, the intervening clause talks about *dozens of other tourist attractions*, so you might make the mistake of thinking the plural *have become* refers to the plural tourists. Don't be fooled! Make sure you're matching subject and verb correctly.

11.   **(E)**   *No Error*

No error.

12.   **(D)**   *Wrong Word*

Eminent means "prominent, well-known." *Imminent* means "impending, about to begin." This writer wanted the latter word and used the former. Unfortunately, barring a lucky guess, the only way to get this question right is to study that list of pesky commonly confused words.

13.   **(C)**   *Pronoun Agreement*

This sentence might sound fine on first reading, but you should always look carefully at pronoun usage. We use pronouns incorrectly in speech so frequently that it can be difficult to notice pronoun errors on the test. In this sentence, the problematic pronoun is *they*. Because the sentence starts out by talking about *an exam* (singular) it cannot refer to that one exam as *they*. Instead of *they have all been exhausting*, the sentence should read something like *each one has been exhausting*. Alternatively, the sentence could use plurals throughout: *I never expected it could be so difficult to take exams, but this semester they have all been very exhausting.*

Eliminating (A) and (B) might be a little tricky because of the choppy underlining. It's fairly easy to tell that *it could* is a grammatical phrase, but *be so* looks odd because of the way it's underlined. When you're unsure of an answer choice, try to step back and read the phrase in the context of the entire sentence.

14.   **(A)**   *Adverb*

Look at the first clause, *the tenor sang so loud that he completely lost his voice. Sang* is a verb, and it is described by the adjective *loud*. This is a problem, because adjectives can't describe verbs. A corrected version of the sentence would read *the tenor sang so loudly. Loudly* is grammatically correct; it is an adverb, and adverbs exist specifically to describe verbs. (A) is your answer.

The phrase *much less sing* might sound strange to you, or even ungrammatical; it's one of those idiomatic expressions that cannot really be explained. Hopefully you've heard it or read it a few times and know that it's fine.

15. (C)   *Other*

The problem here is with the word *where*. Unfortunately, there's no satisfying grammatical explanation for why we can't use *where* in this context; it's just idiomatically sloppy. The sentence should read something like *someone came up with a plan by which the union could work out its differences.*

That *its* looks vaguely wrong, but indeed, the school board, although comprised of many members, is a single entity. Therefore we must refer to it as *it*, not *they*. And strange as it seems, there is no missing apostrophe. The differences belong to the school board, so the possessive *its* is correct.

16. (B)   *Subject/Verb Agreement*

When you see a neither/nor sentence, mental bells should ring. Try to remember that neither/nor constructions are tricky. If you don't remember that rule, you might get this question wrong. Why? Because the sentence sounds so darn good—and it sounds so darn good because we always get neither/nor wrong in conversation. Remember: when the subject attached to the "neither" is singular, and the subject attached to the "nor" is singular, the verb form must be in the singular as well. The verb *were* in this sentence is incorrect because it is plural. *Liberal* is singular, and *conservative* is singular, so the verb form should be the singular "was." Conceptually, it may help to think of it like this: we are not being given a group with one group property (the liberal *and* conservative candidates are this way)—rather, both are being considered singly.

17. (D)   *Gerund*

The infinitive *to prevent* demands to be followed by a gerund. If those grammar terms give you the willies, think of it like this: you can't have the phrase *to prevent to escape*. The rules of English dictate that instead, we say *to prevent from escaping*. (D) is the answer.

18. (E)   *No Error*

No error.

19. (C)   *Subject/Verb Agreement*

Whenever the subject of a sentence is separated from its verb, you should check the sentence's subject-verb agreement. Try taking out the long clause in between the subject and verb and see if the sentence starts to sound funny. If you take out the clause *after hearing arguments from both sides and deliberating for an hour*, you're left with the bare bones of the sentence: *the council have decided*.

If you don't hear anything strange yet, take a closer look at the subject. This sentence's subject happens to be the noun *council*, one of those tricky words that sounds plural but is actually singular. *Have decided* is a plural verb form, which is incorrect because it is paired with the singular *council*. The sentence should say *the student council* has *decided not to adopt the new mascot*. The right answer is (D).

20. (B)   *Tense*

Your ear is one of your most valuable tools on this test, and if *have been* sounds a little weird to you, congratulations. You've found the right answer. This sentence starts in the present tense, and there is no logical reason to switch tenses. Therefore, *have been* is incorrect. The sentence should read something like *Pianos are delicate, sensitive instruments that are tuned on a regular basis.*

Pronouns are frequently tested on this part of the exam, so it's always a good idea to check them. ETS will sometimes test to see if you know when to use *that* and when to use *which*. In this case, *that* is correct (remember, nonrestrictive clauses are followed by *that*, not *which*).

You might be thrown a bit by (C), since verbs ending in -*ed* tend to be thought of as past tense verbs, and you know that the sentence takes place in the present. In this example, however, *tuned* is just fine (the technical reason is because it is part of a verb phrase, so it functions as an infinitive).

Improving Sentence Errors

21. (D)   *Conjunction*

We know that Jorge wasn't keen on the idea of playing Santa, so why would he do it *since* it involved wearing an uncomfortable costume? That does not make sense. We need a more logical conjunction between the two clauses, a conjunction like *even though*. There it is in (D).

(B) has the same problem as the original sentence. (C) includes the phrase *necessity to wear*, and *necessity* is one of those words that must be followed by a gerund like *of wearing*. (E), when added to the original sentence, makes a run-on.

22. (A)   *No Error*

No error.

23. (D)   *Fragment*

Fragment. Remember, if you feel like the sentence grinds to a halt before it's made its point, it might be a fragment. Here, we're left thinking, "The general did what?" The sentence never finishes what it begins. The correct answer, (D), tells us what the general did: he came to scout out the terrain.

24. (E)   *Misplaced Modifier*

This sentence is incorrect because of a misplaced modifier. Look at the problem: *the café with the world-weary smile*. When it stands on its own like that, you can probably see the problem: the sentence makes it sound like the café has the world-weary smile, when it means to say the would-be novelist has the world-weary smile. (E) corrects the problem.

(B) is a bit strange. It makes it sound as if the novelist's technique for modeling himself after Hemingway is to employ a world-weary smile. This is not what the original sentence suggests.

(C) repeats the original problem. The phrases in (D) are arranged so that they completely obscure logical meaning.

25. (C)   *Parallelism*

Parallelism is the issue here. We're talking about two qualities of this woman: *rosy cheeks* and *having a cunning look*. Because that first quality is described as a noun, the second quality must be described as a noun, too. In (C), it is: *cunning look*.

26. (A)   *No Error*

No error.

27. (E)   *Gerund*

The infinitive *to pay* is incorrect. The sentence begins with the gerund *paying*, and for the sake of parallelism, the second half of the sentence should also use a gerund. Therefore, (E) is the correct answer.

(C) can be eliminated because it does not fix the infinitive problem. (B) is not the right answer because of its wordiness. There's no reason for that *still* or the phrase *it is*. (D) must be eliminated simply because it is so awkward. The phrase *is better* shouldn't be tacked onto the end of the sentence like that unless it's absolutely necessary—which, in this case, it's not.

28. **(C)**   *Passive Voice*

The second half of the sentence uses the passive voice. Although we can figure it out from context, we're never told the identity of the performer of the action: who is buying the paintings? The right answer, (C), makes explicit the fact that *she* (Gardner) was the one buying the paintings.

29. **(A)**   *No Error*

No error.

30. **(E)**   *Misplace Modifier*

The problem here is a misplaced modifier. Look at the problem in isolation: *One of the most inventive and respected dancers in the world, tap dancing*. Tap dancing is not a respected dancer, Fred Astaire is. The answer choice that best expresses this is (E).

(B) makes the sentence into a run-on and doesn't fix the misplaced modifier. (C) does not fix the misplaced modifier. (D) changes the meaning of the sentence; it suggests that Fred Astaire benefited from tap dancing, whereas the original sentence suggests that tap dancing benefited from Fred Astaire.

31. **(B)**   *Coordination*

This sentence suffers from bad coordination. The coordinating word, *although*, muddles the meaning of the sentence and makes it sound as if the rain delay continued despite the fact that only a few fans departed. The correct answer, (B), simply removes the incorrect *although*, thereby making the meaning of the sentence clear: most fans stuck it out and stayed on through the long rain delay.

Answers (C) and (D) use phrases synonymous with the original, problematic *although*. (E), even though it changes *although* to *and*, does not solve the problem. It makes the relationship between the two clauses just as strange as it is in the original sentence.

32. **(B)**   *Run-on*

Here we have a run-on sentence. Both sides of the equation, on either side of the comma, can stand alone as complete sentences. Therefore, they cannot be joined by a comma. (B) tidily fixes the problem by changing *this* to *which*.

33. **(A)**   *No Error*

No error.

34. **(E)**   *Misplaced Modifier*

The misplaced modifier in the question makes it sound as if tourists are the scene of the historic battle. (E) correctly identifies the Alamo as the battle site.

(B), besides being a mess, repeats the original problem. (C) introduces a new misplaced modifier: this one makes it sound as if tourists flock to the lives of Bowie and Crockett. (D) is okay but unnecessarily complicated. There's no reason that the phrase *the Alamo* should be so far away from the phrase that describes it, *scene of the historic battle*.

35. **(D)**   *Run-on*

The initial problem is a run-on sentence. Two complete sentences are joined together by no more than a comma. This does not work. (D) solves the problem by inserting a semicolon between the two clauses.

36. **(A)**   *No Error*

No error.

37. **(B)** *Passive Voice*

Passive voice is the culprit that avoids naming the performer of an action. In this sentence, we never find out *who* noted the professor's qualities—the class? The faculty board? It turns out it was the student, as we see in (B). Although (B) does not include the words *the student*, if you read it back into the original sentence, it's clear that it was the student making the notes. (D), the only other answer choice that names a performer, is not the best answer because it is phrased very awkwardly.

38. **(E)** *Parallelism*

In order to fix this error of parallelism, all of the items on this list of problems with internships must be named in similar fashion. Thus, if you're going to talk about *long hours*, the other two items on the list must be nouns, too. And if you're going to talk about *they don't pay very well*, the other two items on the list must be internship actions. The correct answer, (E), turns all of the items into noun phrases. Don't be scared off by the fact that it changes the underlined part significantly. It is the only answer choice that passes muster.

Improving Paragraphs

39. **(D)** *Revision*

The real problem with the sentence as it stands is that *living in bustling cities* is very vague. Who is doing the living? What is the relationship of that phrase to the rest of the sentence? (D) identifies who is doing the living: *people*. It also relates the phrase to the rest of the sentence with the word *especially*.

Some of the other answers sound okay until you read them back into the original sentence. Never omit that crucial read-back step.

40. **(A)** *Revision*

For this question, it's important to go back to the essay and read a few sentences before and after the problem sentence. Simply realizing that you shouldn't start sentences with "and" won't help you get the right answer on this question. Context matters here. It turns out that the sentence in question is an attempt to support the idea that cafés should be Europeanized. This means that the two likely answer choices are (A) and (E). (E) can be eliminated, though, because the phrase *beyond that* suggests that the writer is talking further about the same example, when actually what he's doing is introducing a new point. (A) it is.

41. **(E)** *Revision*

It's an obvious point, but remember that whenever the question explicitly mentions context, it's a good idea to go back to the essay and figure out why context is important. Here it's important because they're trying to get you to realize that the pronoun *he* is vague. Only if you go back to the essay can you confirm that the *he* in question is the customer, not the waiter. (E) is the right answer. Even if you recognize the pronoun problem, if you don't go back to the essay, you risk choosing (D) simply because it's specific.

42. **(E)** *Analysis*

Again, context matters for this question. If you go back and look at the paragraph in question, you'll see that the writer says *the psychological benefits would not be negligible, either*. This begs the question: what are some of those psychological benefits? The writer zooms on without naming any, but specific examples of benefits would be a good idea. Therefore, (E) is the answer.

43. (C) *Revision*

Another context question. If you look at a few sentences before and after the problem sentence, you'll see that just prior to the start of that new paragraph, the writer was talking about all of the changes that should be instituted in cafés. (B) is too specific, and (D) is about people, not cafés. (A), (C), and (E) aren't bad, but (A) and (E) are a little vague. *Goals* and *new things* aren't really what's being discussed in this paper; changes are. (C) is your answer.

44. (C) *Revision*

Tense is all over the place in the original sentence. The phrase that begins *if restaurants model themselves* continues with *they would have slowed*. It starts in the present tense, so it should continue in the present tense. For this question, it's especially important to prepare your own answer before looking at the answer choices, because after you read a few, they are hard to keep straight.

You're looking for the answer choice that uses only present tense. That leaves you with (C).

45. (C) *Revision*

The word *but* is not correct in the original sentence. *But* makes the fact that 300,000 people die from obesity sound like it *contradicts* the fact that sixty-one percent of people suffer from obesity. Actually, these two facts make perfect sense when considered together. Therefore, the connecting word should be *and*, as it is in (C).

46. (E) *Revision*

In order to correct the faulty parallelism of the original sentence, the items in the list must be all noun phrases or all gerunds. In the original sentence, the first two items are noun phrases, but the third is a gerund. (E) turns the gerund *getting heart disease* into the noun phrase *heart disease*, fixing the problem.

47. (A) *Addition*

Before you go about choosing an answer, examine the essay and see what's missing from the beginning of that second paragraph. The second paragraph begins abruptly, jumping right from talking about the problems that obesity causes to talking about how people should diet. A transition would be useful—and you should remember, too, that transitions are favorite additions on this section of the test. (A) is the correct answer. It provides a transition, and it also foreshadows the last paragraph, in which pyschological concerns will be discussed.

48. (C) *Revision*

These kinds of questions are a serious pain, and the best way to deal with them is to figure out the problem with the sentence on your own. If you have to try out every suggested change, you're going to be working on this question for too long. It happens that the problem is in the list of things people try. If you're saying something like *from fish to soup to nuts*, you must use the word *to* in between each item. You can't throw in an *and* every so often. (C) is the correct answer.

49. (E) *Combination*

Another annoying question, and again, the best way to deal with it is to figure out the answer before you look at the answer choices. Ask yourself how the two sentences relate to one another. Basically, they're saying that even though you can lose weight, you'll gain it back once you stop dieting. That's all you need to figure out on your own. Even though that sentence doesn't sound exactly like the right answer, (E), the idea is the same, so you'll recognize the right answer when you see it.

50. **(B)** *Revision*

The problem with this sentence: it's a run-on. In order to correct the problem, the right answer choice, (C), throws a semicolon between the two clauses. This is a common method of run-on correction on this test.

Identifying Sentence Errors

51. **(C)** *Tense*

Have found is a correct combination of words on its own, but in the context of this sentence, it's incorrect. The scientist is explaining the current (present tense) purpose of his project. The fact that his experiment is happening now means that the results will come in the future. Therefore, the phrase *have found*, which suggests the past, is illogical. (C) is the correct answer.

52. **(A)** *Double Negative*

Be wary when you spot words such as "hardly," "barely," and "scarcely." Although they do not necessarily sound negative, they are; therefore, when placed next to another negative word, they form the grammatically illegal double negative. *Hardly* and *no* cannot be placed next to one another as they are in this sentence. Thus, (A) is the answer. This sentence could be fixed either by removing one of the negative words (*no one can compare*) or changing one of the negative words (*hardly anyone can compare*).

53. **(C)** *Other*

This question is a bit daunting because there are so many clauses winding their way around. The problem is that one of them is a restrictive clause, but it's followed by *that*. This is not right. When you have a restrictive clause, it should be followed by *which*, not *that*. In plain English: if you have a comma, that comma must be followed not by *that*, but by *which*. Corrected, this part of the sentence would read, *the exhibits, which include an extensive dinosaur fossil collection . . . .*

The other answers that look likely for this question are those that underline tenses. Tense switches around a bit in this sentence, but it's never illogical; the teachers *have found it useful* in the past; the exhibits are there in the present tense, so they *are* very instructive.

54. **(D)** *Pronoun Case*

Don't make the mistake of thinking that because they sound more formal or proper, phrases like *my team and I* are always better than phrases like *my team and me*. Sometimes, as in this sentence, "me" is the right word to use. If you're not sure whether "I" or "me" is correct, try taking out the noun that proceeds the "I" (or "me") and see how the sentence sounds. Here we get, *the statistics problem sets always prove incredibly challenging for I*. That sounds pretty terrible. (D) is the answer.

The verb *prove* is used in a slightly unusual way in this sentence, but it is correct.

55. **(C)** *Pronoun Agreement*

As always, you want to examine pronouns with an eagle eye. Look at (C): what is the subject of the verb *is*? If it was *Scotland Yard*, we'd be in the clear; however, the subject of *is* is actually *cases*.

You can figure out that (A) is the right answer using either grammar or logic. Grammatically, since *cases* is plural, referring to cases as *it* is incorrect; *they* would have been the appropriate pronoun. Logically, cases probably remain unsolved not because Scotland Yard is too perplexing, but because the cases are too perplexing.

56. **(E)** *No Error*

No error.

57. **(A)** *Subject/Descriptor Agreement*

The issue here is the relation between the subject, *kimono*, and the descriptor in the clause, brightly colored robes. Compare *kimono* to *brightly colored robes*—the describing phrase is plural, while *kimono*, your subject, is singular. We have a winner: (A).

58. **(B)** *Pronoun Agreement*

Don't panic: you don't have to know anything about science to answer this question. You just have to know a little something about pronoun agreement. We're talking about *professors*, multiple professors—so why are they referred to by the singular phrase *his or her*? They should be referred to by the plural word *they*.

(A) might trick you if you're working quickly—it looks as if there might be a missing apostrophe there. Maybe this is a conference that *belongs* to physics? If you're not sure, try substituting another word for *physics*: "biology conference"? "Chemistry conference"? Nothing wrong there. What about "biology's conference" or "chemistry's conference"? Those sound wrong. There's no apostrophe missing.

(C) might trip you up if you're not familiar with the correct preposition to use after the word *research*. As with most prepositions, this is really a question of idiom that can only be answered by simple memorization. The *cold fusion* bit is probably thrown in just to intimidate the nervous test-taker. Keep in mind that it's just a plain old adjective correctly modifying a plain old noun, and then you can successfully eliminate (D).

59. **(E)** *No Error*

No error.

60. **(B)** *Idiom*

Bravo if your first instinct upon seeing this question was to check the list for parallelism errors. That is the most obvious place to check first, but it turns out there aren't any parallelism errors. The problem here is with idiom. English idiom says that we cannot write *gain an insight for*. There's no real reason for this; that's just the way it is. In English, we say, *gain an insight into*. Therefore, (B) is the correct answer.

WRITING TEST III

Part A

Time — 20 minutes

You have twenty minutes to plan and write an essay on the topic assigned below. DO NOT WRITE ON ANOTHER TOPIC. AN ESSAY ON ANOTHER TOPIC IS NOT ACCEPTABLE.

The essay is assigned to give you an opportunity to show how well you can write. You should, therefore, take care to express your thoughts on the topic clearly and effectively. How well you write is much more important than how much you write, but to cover the topic adequately you will probably need to write more than one paragraph. Be specific.

Your essay must be written on the following two pages. You will find that you have enough space if you write on every line, avoid wide margins, and keep your handwriting to a reasonable size. It is important to remember that what you write will be read by someone who is not familiar with your handwriting. Try to write or print so that what you are writing is legible to the reader.

Consider the following statement and assignment. Then write the essay as directed.

"With age comes wisdom."

Assignment: Choose one example from personal experience, current events, or history, literature, or any other discipline and use this example to write an essay in which you agree or disagree with the statement above. Your essay should be specific.

DO NOT WRITE YOUR ESSAY IN YOUR TEST BOOK. You will receive credit only for what you write on your answer sheet.

WHEN YOUR SUPERVISOR ANNOUNCES THAT TWENTY MINUTES HAVE PASSED, YOU MUST STOP WRITING THE ESSAY AND GO ON TO PART B IF YOU HAVE NOT ALREADY DONE SO. IF YOU FINISH YOUR ESSAY BEFORE THIS ANNOUNCEMENT, GO ON TO PART B AT ONCE.

BEGIN WRITING YOUR ESSAY ON THE ANSWER SHEET.

WRITING TEST

Part A

Time — 20 minutes

WRITING TEST

Part A

Time — 20 minutes

WRITING TEST

Part B

Time — 40 minutes

1. The teachers did not expect a complete victory, but they
   A
had counted on the university granting at least some of
     B   C
his or her main requests. No error
  D   E

2. To everyone's astonishment, the chairperson of the

PTA was arrested to be drunk and disorderly on the
    A   B   C
streets of the town. No error
     D   E

3. Strewn around his playpen was the toddler's favorite
   A   B   C
toys, including a miniature car and a set of alphabet
                    D
blocks. No error
    E

4. The mayor issued a statement declaring that increased
                  A   B
taxation is not hardly an acceptable solution to the
        C
problems of the city. No error
      D   E

5. If you are going to Beijing in December, it is

essential to bring along clothing that works in layers,
   A   B
as the sudden changes of temperature there can
                        C
catch one off guard. No error
  D   E

GO ON TO THE NEXT PAGE

6. The unconscious, <u>according to</u> Freud, <u>is divided into</u>
        A   B
the *id*, <u>which</u> consists of instincts and desires, and
        C
the *superego*, <u>which</u> controls the id. <u>No error</u>
        D   E

7. At the school assembly, one candidate for student

council made a speech <u>where</u> <u>he</u> proposed <u>holding</u> a
                          A   B   C
blood drive <u>in the fall</u>. <u>No error</u>
              D   E

8. Peter <u>swum</u> ten laps <u>in record time</u>, <u>and</u> won first
          A   B   C
prize <u>in the competition</u>. <u>No error</u>
        D   E

9. More <u>devotedly</u> <u>as any</u> nun in the church, Mother
          A   B
Teresa worked <u>long hours</u> to restore the health of
                    C
her patients <u>in the hospital</u>. <u>No error</u>
                  D   E

10. The appeal <u>of new technology</u> lies in its ability to
                    A
perform new functions; new machines <u>are faster</u>,
                                          B
<u>more efficient</u>, and <u>cheap</u> than ever before. <u>No error</u>
    C   D   E

11. The typical American high school student has to

<u>take out</u> several loans <u>in order to</u> attend college
    A   B
because <u>in the last</u> thirty years <u>they have</u> grown
              C   D
extremely expensive. <u>No error</u>
                          E

12. The *Tao te Ching*, <u>an</u> ancient Chinese philosophical
                          A
text <u>that</u> advises simplicity and <u>lack of desire</u>, <u>has had</u>
        B   C   D
a profound influence on Chinese art and literature.

<u>No error</u>
    E

13. The governor, as well as all fifty members <u>of his staff</u>,
                                                    A
<u>have been</u> working <u>nonstop</u> on the <u>reelection</u>
    B   C   D
campaign. <u>No error</u>
              E

14. <u>Despite</u> several heavy-handed <u>illusions</u> to <u>the lateness</u>
    A   B   C
of the hour, <u>Ms. Wong's</u> date didn't realize that she
                  D
wanted to leave. <u>No error</u>
                      E

15. The professor asserted he could <u>not scarcely</u> imagine a
                                        A
better <u>role model</u> for Sarah Lawrence students <u>than</u>
          B   C
Alice Walker, <u>herself</u> a Sarah Lawrence alumna.
                  D
<u>No error</u>
    E

16. After <u>drinking</u> glasses of pink lemonade, yellow
              A
lemonade, and limeade, <u>the taste-tester</u> could not
                          B
decide <u>which</u> drink tasted <u>sweeter</u>. <u>No error</u>
          C   D   E

GO ON TO THE NEXT PAGE

17. The month of July <u>has</u> so often <u>been associated</u>
                    A   B

    with vacations that <u>the very mention</u> of the month
                             C

    conjures up visions of barbecues, fireworks, and

    <u>the beach</u>. <u>No error</u>
      D   E

18. <u>Before</u> she became president of the <u>entire company</u>, she
     A   B

    <u>has been</u> a vice president <u>for many</u> years. <u>No error</u>
     C   D   E

19. A <u>learned</u> Buddhist priest should help his followers
       A

    <u>gain an insight for</u> not only <u>how to reach enlightenment</u>
        B   C

    but also how <u>to meditate correctly</u>. <u>No error</u>
                   D   E

20. The guest lecturer <u>strode up</u> to the podium, put down
                      A

    his papers, <u>and without</u> introduction <u>began</u> to read
                   B   C

    <u>from it</u>. <u>No error</u>
      D   E

GO ON TO THE NEXT PAGE

WRITING TEST

Directions: The following sentences test correctness and effectiveness of expression. In choosing answers, follow the requirements of standard written English; that is, pay attention to grammar, choice of words, sentence construction, and punctuation.

In each of the following sentences, part of the sentence or the entire sentence is underlined. Beneath each sentence you will find five ways of phrasing the underlined part. Choice A repeats the original; the other four are different.

Choose the answer that best expresses the meaning of the original sentence. If you think the original is better than any of the alternatives, choose it; otherwise choose one of the others. Your choice should produce the most effective sentence—clear and precise, without awkwardness or ambiguity.

EXAMPLE:

Laura Ingalls Wilder published her first book <u>and she was sixty-five years old then.</u>

(A) and she was sixty-five years old then
(B) when she was sixty-five
(C) at age sixty-five years old
(D) upon the reaching of sixty-five years
(E) at the time when she was sixty-five

SAMPLE ANSWER:

21. In the past, quarreling men were accompanied to their duels by men called "seconds," <u>a practice that is strange to us now.</u>

    (A) a practice that is strange to us now
    (B) and since they did that practice, it is strange to us now
    (C) which is strange to us and it was a practice
    (D) a practice that is strange to them then
    (E) this is strange to us in practice

22. Initially, Frannie was unwilling to start jogging, <u>and she tried it anyway</u> and soon it became an enjoyable part of her morning routine.

    (A) and she tried it anyway
    (B) even though she tried it anyway
    (C) she tried it anyway
    (D) but she tried it anyway
    (E) thus she tried it anyway

23. In difficult economic times, people try to spend less, <u>plan ahead, and relying on family support is oftentimes helpful</u>.

    (A) plan ahead, and relying on family support
    (B) planning ahead, and relying on family support is oftentimes helpful
    (C) planning ahead and rely on family support is oftentimes helpful
    (D) and it's oftentimes helpful, planning ahead and to rely on family support
    (E) plan ahead, and rely on family support

GO ON TO THE NEXT PAGE

24. By telling rueful, funny, and cerebral stories set in New York City, <u>the popular conception of Manhattan has been changed by Woody Allen</u>.

    (A) the popular conception of Manhattan has been changed by Woody Allen
    (B) Manhattan as it is popularly conceived has been changed by Woody Allen
    (C) Woody Allen's popular conception of Manhattan has been changed
    (D) the popular conception of Manhattan were changed for Woody Allen
    (E) Woody Allen changed the popular conception of Manhattan

25. <u>Although they were revered by the Egyptians, cats were feared in the Middle Ages, when they were often burned as witches</u>.

    (A) Although they were revered by the Egyptians, cats were feared in the Middle Ages, when they were often burned as witches
    (B) Cats were feared in the Middle Ages, although they were revered by the Egyptians, when they were often burned as witches
    (C) Although they were often burned as witches, cats were revered by the Egyptians, although they were feared in the Middle Ages
    (D) Cats were revered by the Egyptians and feared in the Middle Ages, although they were often burned as witches
    (E) Although they were revered by the Egyptians, fearing them in the Middle Ages, people often burned cats as witches

26. With admirable resolve, many young people have flocked to New York City in search of fame or <u>a new life, in the process they cause a glut in the real estate market</u>.

    (A) a new life, in the process they cause a glut in the real estate market
    (B) a new life, a glut in the real estate market being the result
    (C) a new life and in the process have caused a glut in the real estate market
    (D) a new life: and in the process, they are causing a glut in the real estate market
    (E) a new life, the real estate market has been glutted by this

27. The prisoner expressed no <u>repentance, the judge was angered</u> and imposed a heavy sentence.

    (A) repentance, the judge was angered
    (B) repentance, so the judge was angered
    (C) repentance; so the judge was angered
    (D) repentance that angered the judge
    (E) repentance angering the judge

28. When casting a musical, directors consider not only voice and acting ability, <u>but does the person look good</u>.

    (A) but does the person look good
    (B) but looks
    (C) but whether or not the person looks good
    (D) and if the person looks good
    (E) however good the person looks

29. Benjamin Franklin wrote an accomplished autobiography, owned and edited a newspaper, and invented <u>bifocals; he is most widely known, however,</u> for his great work as a diplomat and statesmen.

    (A) bifocals; he is most widely known, however,
    (B) bifocals, but is most widely known, however,
    (C) bifocals, having been most widely known
    (D) bifocals: however, known most widely
    (E) bifocals, since he is most widely known

30. <u>Side effects of the drug, such as dizziness, loss of appetite, and nausea, are listed</u> on the side of the bottle.

    (A) Side effects of the drug, such as dizziness, loss of appetite, and nausea, are listed
    (B) Side effects of the drug, such as dizziness, loss of appetite, and nausea, is listed
    (C) Dizziness, loss of appetite, and nausea, side effects of the drug, is listed
    (D) Dizziness, loss of appetite, and nausea, for example, are listed and are side effects
    (E) Side effects are listed, such as dizziness, loss of appetite, and nausea

GO ON TO THE NEXT PAGE ➤

31. <u>An urban legend, much repeated and embellished, that</u> enormous crocodiles prowl the sewers of Manhattan.

    (A) An urban legend, much repeated and embellished, that
    (B) That much repeated and embellished urban legend
    (C) An urban legend, much repeated and embellished, says that
    (D) Repeating and embellishing the urban legend, that
    (E) That urban legend was much repeated and embellished

32. Poets Elizabeth Barrett and Robert Browning had a <u>dramatic courtship, being that they had to</u> keep their love secret from Barrett's domineering father.

    (A) dramatic courtship, being that they had to
    (B) dramatic courtship although they had to
    (C) dramatic courtship: they had to
    (D) dramatic courtship; since they had to
    (E) dramatic courtship: part of which was that they had to

33. In her work as a modern dance choreographer, <u>Martha Graham drew inspiration from mythology and from Freudian themes</u>.

    (A) Martha Graham drew inspiration from mythology and from Freudian themes
    (B) inspiration was found by Martha Graham from mythology and from Freudian themes
    (C) the themes of mythology and Freud provided Martha Graham with inspiration on which to draw
    (D) Martha Graham drew inspiration, first from mythology, and then from Freudian themes
    (E) Freudian themes, and mythology, inspired Martha Graham

34. The town was deluged with a record amount of rain, <u>but some of the rivers flooded</u>.

    (A) but some of the rivers flooded
    (B) but some of the rivers began to flood
    (C) still some of the rivers started flooding
    (D) yet some of the rivers flooded
    (E) and some of the rivers flooded

35. <u>A warning was issued about the student parking lot violations by the principal</u>.

    (A) A warning was issued about the student parking lot violations by the principal
    (B) A warning, issued about the student parking lot violations, was by the principal
    (C) The student parking lot violations, issued by the principal, were warned
    (D) The principal issued a warning about the student parking lot violations
    (E) The student parking lot violations warning, by the principal, was issued

36. John Milton's treatise on divorce advocates realizing that not all marriages are perfect, and <u>to end marriages that are desperately unhappy</u>.

    (A) to end marriages that are desperately unhappy
    (B) ending marriages that are desperately unhappy
    (C) to, if marriages are desperately unhappy, leave them
    (D) ending them, if the marriages are desperately unhappy
    (E) to end those marriages that make both parties desperately unhappy

GO ON TO THE NEXT PAGE

37. <u>An amazing prodigy, a German operetta, an Italian opera buffa, symphonies, sonatas, and concertos were written by Bach by the time he was thirteen.</u>

    (A) An amazing prodigy, a German operetta, an Italian opera buffa, symphonies, sonatas, and concertos were written by Bach by the time he was thirteen
    (B) By the time he was thirteen, Bach, an amazing prodigy, had written a German operetta, an Italian opera buffa, symphonies, sonatas, and concertos
    (C) A German operetta, an Italian opera buffa, symphonies, sonatas, and concertos were written by Bach, an amazing prodigy, by the time he was thirteen
    (D) A German operetta, an Italian opera buffa, symphonies, sonatas, and concertos, an amazing prodigy, were written by Bach by the time he was thirteen
    (E) By the time he was thirteen, a German operetta, an Italian opera buffa, symphonies, sonatas, and concertos had been written by an amazing prodigy, Bach

38. The referee was known for his fairness and calmness, <u>qualities that were consciously cultivated</u>.

    (A) qualities that were consciously cultivated
    (B) qualities that he consciously cultivated
    (C) which were qualities having to be consciously cultivated
    (D) known also for qualities that had to be consciously cultivated
    (E) and those he consciously cultivated

GO ON TO THE NEXT PAGE

WRITING TEST

Questions 39-44 are based on the following passage.

(1) *People frequently associate rap with violence, misogyny, and materialism.* (2) *Some rap music glorifies all three.* (3) *Not all rap music does.*

(4) *Jay-Z is a hip-hop artist whose music frequently demeans women.* (5) *In his song "Anything," he praises his mother.* (6) *He raps, "As a man, I apologize for my dad," and "the most important lesson in life was when you said 'Strive for what you believe in, set goals and you can achieve them.'"* (7) *With the first lyric, he takes on the role of protector, apologizing for the bad behavior of his father.* (8) *With this lyric he implies that he will do better in his own adult personal life.* (9) *With the second lyric, he credited his mother for his success in life.*

(10) *DMX is another well-known rapper.* (11) *He often raps about the violence of life on the streets.* (12) *He raps about inflicting violent death on his detractors.* (13) *Some of his songs, however, bristle with nonviolent political commentary.* (14) *His song "Who We Be" addresses the misunderstanding from which the black community suffers.* (15) *Lyrics like, "the suffering young mothers—it happens too often" express an understanding of the toll taken on wives and mothers when their husbands and sons face prison.*

(16) *Even rappers whose songs reflect and sometimes glorify the violence that they knew in their young lives often write songs that reveal the real respect they feel for women, and the revulsion they feel for violence.* (17) *It is a common misperception that hip-hop turns its back on what some call family values.*

39. In the context of the first paragraph, which of the following best revises and combines sentences 2 and 3, which are reprinted below?

    Some rap music glorifies all three. Not all rap music does.

    (A) Some rap music glorifies all three, however not all rap music does.
    (B) It is true that some rap music glorifies all three, and some rap music doesn't.
    (C) While some rap music glorifies all three, not all rap music does.
    (D) In point of fact, some rap music glorifies all three, some rap music does not.
    (E) While some rap music glorifies all three and not all rap music does.

40. Which of the following sentences, added after sentence 3, is the best topic sentence for the second paragraph?

    (A) Let me tell you about a personal encounter I had with a rapper.
    (B) One such rapper is Jay-Z.
    (C) Even some music-industry executives secretly think this way.
    (D) This misguided perception is held by most people.
    (E) Many well-known rappers occasionally speak up for surprisingly traditional values.

GO ON TO THE NEXT PAGE

41. Which of the following is the best way to revise and combine sentences 4 and 5, which are reprinted below?

    Jay-Z is a hip-hop artist whose music frequently demeans women. In his song "Anything," he praises his mother.

    (A) In his song "Anything," Jay-Z, a hip-hop artist whose music frequently demeans women, praises his mother.
    (B) Jay-Z is a hip-hop artist whose music frequently demeans women, and in his song "Anything," he praises his mother.
    (C) Although Jay-Z is a hip-hop artist whose music frequently demeans women, in his song "Anything," he praises his mother.
    (D) Praising his mother in his song "Anything," Jay-Z is a hip-hop artist whose music frequently demeans women.
    (E) Jay-Z is a hip-hop artist who frequently demeans women and creates a song like "Anything," which praises his mother.

42. In context, which of the following best revises the underlined part of sentence 9, which is reprinted here?

    With the second lyric, he credited his mother for his success in life.

    (A) (as it is)
    (B) he is crediting his mother
    (C) he credits his mother
    (D) his mother, who is to be credited
    (E) his mother got the credit

43. In order to change the repetitive nature of sentences 11 and 12 (reprinted here), which of the following is the best revision and combination of the underlined parts of the sentence?

    He often raps about the violence of life on the streets. He raps about inflicting violent death on his detractors.

    (A) life on the streets and about
    (B) street life, however he discusses
    (C) life on the streets but he raps about
    (D) life on the streets thus about
    (E) street life, moreover he raps about

44. The writer uses all of the following techniques EXCEPT:

    (A) telling a personal story
    (B) debunking a commonly held belief
    (C) concluding with a summary
    (D) citing specific examples
    (E) analyzing lyrics

GO ON TO THE NEXT PAGE

Questions 45–50 are based on the following passage.

(1) *Last summer, I decided to get a fun job.* (2) *I wanted to make a lot of money, meet interesting people, and work irregular hours.* (3) *I decided to wait on tables.* (4) *Although this decision seemed smart at the time, now it was clear that I couldn't have made a more unwise choice.*

(5) *I envisioned working at a ritzy, elegant restaurant with linen napkins and little lamps on every table.* (6) *In my imagination, I saw myself opening bottles of wine and presenting plates with a flourish.* (7) *When it came time to apply for jobs, the only opening was at the local fish and chips joint.* (8) *I decided maybe working at the fish and chips place would be fun, so I applied.* (9) *On my first day of work, I realized that instead of linen napkins and little lamps, I was going to be surrounded by crusty ketchup bottles and plastic place mats.* (10) *And the clientele wasn't exactly what I had in mind, either.* (11) *The worst part was that on the very first day, as I carried a heavy tray of food to a table, I tripped over a fork, and fried scallops and clams went flying everywhere.*

(12) *It never improved.* (13) *The customers left terrible tips, my feet hurt all the time, and I constantly smelled like fish, even after going home and taking a shower.* (14) *My mother wouldn't let me quit, because she said I had made a commitment to work all summer and I had to fulfill it.* (15) *Because of this, I kept my awful job until the end of August.* (16) *Waiting tables, not only did I smell like fish, I started fighting with my mother!*

45. Which of the following revisions of the underlined part of sentence 4 (reprinted here) is best?

    Although this decision seemed smart at the time, now it was clear that I couldn't have made a more unwise choice.

    (A) (as it is now)
    (B) now it became clear that I couldn't have
    (C) now, I couldn't have made, clearly,
    (D) now it is clear that I couldn't have
    (E) now it would become clear that I couldn't have

46. Which of the following words, added at the beginning of sentence 7 would clarify the relationship of the sentence to the rest of the paragraph?

    (A) so
    (B) but
    (C) still
    (D) and
    (E) however

47. How could the writer best improve sentence 10, reprinted here?

    And the clientele wasn't exactly what I had in mind, either.

    (A) Define "clientele"
    (B) Give specific examples of the clientele
    (C) Mention the most popular entrees
    (D) Ask a hypothetical question
    (E) Discuss more problems

48. In context, which would be the best replacement for the word *it* at the beginning of sentence 12?

    (A) My job
    (B) My food-carrying skills
    (C) The tips
    (D) The clientele
    (E) My skills

49. Which of the following is the best revision of the underlined part of sentence 15 (reprinted here)?

    Because of this, I kept my awful job until the end of August.

    (A) In spite of this,
    (B) However,
    (C) Because of my mother,
    (D) Because of that,
    (E) In conclusion,

50. Which of the following is the best revision of sentence 16, which is reprinted here?

    Waiting tables, not only did I smell like fish, I started fighting with my mother!

    (A) (as it is)
    (B) Not only did I smell like fish, I started fighting with my mother after the onset of waiting tables.
    (C) I started fighting with my mother and smelling like fish because I waited tables.
    (D) Not only did waiting tables make me smell like fish, it made me start fighting with my mother.
    (E) Waiting tables was the reason why I was smelling like fish and would fight with my mother.

GO ON TO THE NEXT PAGE

WRITING TEST

51. <u>Not only</u> is skiing expensive, but <u>it is</u> difficult to learn
    A   B

    <u>and</u> it <u>often leads</u> to knee injuries. <u>No error</u>
    C   D   E

52. Since he had <u>drove</u> twenty miles <u>just</u> to hear her speak,
               A   B

    Thomas was annoyed to learn <u>that</u> the professor
                              C

    <u>had cancelled</u> her lecture. <u>No error</u>
    D   E

53. Before television <u>was invented</u>, the radio was the
                   A

    primary <u>source of</u> entertainment for American families,
             B

    and <u>they were</u> frequently listened to in the majority
             C

    <u>of households</u>. <u>No error</u>
    D   E

54. As he <u>exited</u> the building, the curator <u>remarked</u> that
          A   B

    the arms collection <u>was not</u> as extensive as
                  C

    the Metropolitan Museum of Art. <u>No error</u>
            D   E

55. A brilliant artist, Vincent van Gogh <u>brought together</u>
                                A

    <u>distinctly</u> different painting techniques as effortlessly
    B

    <u>than any</u> Renaissance painter <u>ever had</u>. <u>No error</u>
    C   D   E

56. After sitting <u>in the back</u> of an <u>overcrowded</u> lecture hall
                  A   B

    <u>for</u> three hours, I became <u>real</u> bored. <u>No error</u>
    C   D   E

57. Some students of architecture <u>have argued</u> that Frank
                          A

    Gehry's design of the Guggenheim Museum in Bilbao,

    Spain, <u>is</u> <u>more technically astonishing than</u> Frank Lloyd
          B   C

    Wright's <u>design of the</u> Guggenheim Museum in New
             D

    York. <u>No error</u>
          E

GO ON TO THE NEXT PAGE

WRITING TEST—*Continued*

58. Josephine Baker's <u>style of</u> entertainment was
                           A

considerably <u>more elegant</u> and refined than many of
                 B

her <u>fellow performers</u>, and <u>she became</u> the toast of
     C   D

sophisticated Paris. <u>No error</u>
               E

59. Neither fame nor <u>the spirit of</u> adventure <u>were enough</u>
              A   B

<u>to tempt</u> the explorer's crew to join the expedition
C

<u>to the North Pole.</u> <u>No error</u>
  D   E

60. <u>Because</u> in the past left-handed children <u>were taught</u>
   A   B

that there was something wrong with them because of

<u>their left-handedness</u>, and were sometimes even forced
    C

to write with their right hands, modern-day teachers

are careful not to make left-handed children feel

<u>self-conscious.</u> <u>No error</u>
  D   E

S T O P

IF YOU FINISH BEFORE TIME IS CALLED, YOU MAY CHECK YOUR WORK ON THIS TEST ONLY.
DO NOT TURN TO ANY OTHER TEST IN THIS BOOK.

Answers to SAT II Writing Practice Test III

Question Number	Correct Answer	Right	Wrong	Question Number	Correct Answer	Right	Wrong
1.	D	——	——	31.	C	——	——
2.	B	——	——	32.	C	——	——
3.	B	——	——	33.	A	——	——
4.	C	——	——	34.	E	——	——
5.	D	——	——	35.	D	——	——
6.	E	——	——	36.	B	——	——
7.	A	——	——	37.	B	——	——
8.	A	——	——	38.	B	——	——
9.	B	——	——	39.	C	——	——
10.	D	——	——	40.	E	——	——
11.	D	——	——	41.	C	——	——
12.	E	——	——	42.	C	——	——
13.	B	——	——	43.	A	——	——
14.	B	——	——	44.	A	——	——
15.	A	——	——	45.	D	——	——
16.	D	——	——	46.	E	——	——
17.	E	——	——	47.	B	——	——
18.	C	——	——	48.	A	——	——
19.	B	——	——	49.	C	——	——
20.	D	——	——	50.	D	——	——
21.	A	——	——	51.	E	——	——
22.	D	——	——	52.	A	——	——
23.	E	——	——	53.	C	——	——
24.	E	——	——	54.	D	——	——
25.	A	——	——	55.	C	——	——
26.	C	——	——	56.	D	——	——
27.	B	——	——	57.	E	——	——
28.	B	——	——	58.	C	——	——
29.	A	——	——	59.	B	——	——
30.	A	——	——	60.	E	——	——

Calculating Your Score

Your raw score for SAT II Writing test is a composite of your raw score in the multiple-choice section and your score on the essay. Once you have determined your composite score, use the conversion table on page 17 to calculate your scaled score. To Calculate your raw score, count the number of questions you answered correctly on the multiple choice: _____
A

Count the number of questions you answered incorrectly, and multiply that number by $\frac{1}{4}$:

_____ X $\frac{1}{4}$ = _____
B   C

Subtract the value in field C from value in field A: _____
D

Round the number to the nearest whole number: _____
E

Take your score for the Essay (ask a teacher to grade your essay or grade yourself) and multiply it by 3.43:

_____ X 3.43 = _____
F   G

Add the number in field E to the number in Field G: _____
H

Round the number in field H. This is your Writing SAT II score: _____

Student Essays

Total Score: 12 (each reader gave the essay a 6)

It is not always true that wisdom only comes with age. Often children and young people demonstrate wisdom. You can see this in Henry James's novel What Maisie Knew; *you can also see it in Martin Amis's novel* The Rachel Papers. *In both of these novels, the extremely young characters demonstrate wisdom beyond their years.*

What Maisie Knew is about a very young girl whose parents are in the process of a messy, acrimonious divorce. Although she does not fully grasp what is going on, nevertheless Maisie sees human relationships with a much keener and kinder eye than the adults around her. James points out that it is not the ability to grasp the concepts of divorce and alimony and adultery that makes someone wise; rather, it is the ability to understand people's behavior. Maisie senses every twitch and change in mood in everyone around her. This is in stark contrast to the adults, who act in blind selfishness, paying no attention to the feelings and thoughts of those around them because they are so busy paying attention to themselves. (Maisie would probably have something valuable to say to modern children whose parents are divorced.)

The Rachel Papers stars a character named Charles. Much of his pursuits are typical of any teenager's; he is mostly interested in sleeping with the girl he is dating, and he pays painfully close attention to his pimples and music and journal. However, at the same time, he demonstrates more wisdom than any of the adults around him. He examines his human relationships in a way that eludes his own father. Charles is extremely concerned with treating people with kindness, whereas his father cheats on Charles's mother and finds nothing wrong with that behavior. Charles makes close notes of every important conversation he has with his family, and studies his papers for clues to their significance.

Wisdom is not simply the kind owned by the stereotypical wise old sage who strokes his beard and ruminates on the world. Henry James and Martin Amis show their readers a different kind of wisdom—a thoughtfulness and insight into human relations that young people possess, and older people can lack.

Discussion:

This essay, while it contains a few errors and problems, not all of which can be ascribed to the hurried way the writer had to work, nonetheless demonstrates strong overall ability. It is well-organized, uses relevant examples, and conveys its message via clear prose.

The writer organizes effectively; she devotes the first paragraph to an introduction and a brief mention of the examples she'll use, the second paragraph to a discussion of the Henry James novel, the third paragraph to a discussion of a Martin Amis novel, and the last paragraph to a summary and a little rule: part of the reason the cliché isn't true is because wisdom is not a monolithic concept.

Her examples are well-chosen; readers will be impressed to see that this writer has read and understood two works of merit.

There are a few problems, none of which are major enough to affect the writer's score. Remember, the readers do not expect perfection, and a few mistakes will not prevent you from getting a 12.

This sentence presents a comparison difficulty: *Maisie sees human relationships with a much keener and kinder eye than the adults around her.* This faulty comparison suggests that Maisie sees relationships more clearly than she sees adults; what the writer means to suggest, however, is that Maisie sees relationships more clearly than adults see relationships.

The sentence at the end of paragraph 2 is gratuitous and it clashes in tone with the rest of the essay: *Maisie would probably have something valuable to say to modern children whose parents are divorced.* This parenthetical remark adds nothing to the substance of the essay and it takes the reader away from the critique of the book and into contemporary sociological issues.

Finally, the writer relies too heavily on the word *wisdom*. Of course, since this word appears in the prompt, it can be difficult to avoid using it. Still, especially in the last paragraph, the writing would have sounded stronger had the writer used a synonym.

Total Score: 2 (each reader gave the essay a 1)

I'm not sure what can be said about such a wise old saying in such a short space of time and room to right!!! I think, to me, this statement is saying that you can only be smart, wise, knowladgeble, etc., if you are older/ getting on in years. And if that person is older, than he/she will really know what kind of advice to give somone like me a high school student, like what to do to have a good life or how to get the most out of life. I think this statement is usually true. For example, I have a grandmother, Grandma Ruth, who helps me so much. You look at her and your not sure if she's really "with it" because she's really old, but she's sharp as a tack! She remembers all our birthdays and how old we are. She always gives me good advise whenever I have a problem.

Then sometimes its not true, though. Because my little brother is the smartest, and he's defenately not old!! Sometimes I'll bring a friend home and he'll say something that seems wierd at the time, like Oh I don't like that person, but in the end it always turns out that he was right, I shouldn't have trusted that person.

So on both sides of this argument there are things to say.

Discussion:

Essays that get a total score of 2 are those essays that demonstrate incompetence. They have serious flaws: poor or no organization, badly developed examples, and grammatical errors, among others.

One of the initial difficulties here is that this writer does not take a stance on the statement. At the end of the meandering first paragraph, it seems as if he will agree with the statement, but the second paragraph begins with waffling: sometimes the statement is not true. And the writer emphasizes his own failure to pick a side by ending his essay with the unfortunate sentence *So on both sides of the argument there are things to say.*

Another big problem here is the examples, which are poorly chosen. Both examples concern the writer's personal life. He mentions his grandmother and his little brother, thereby missing an opportunity to wow the readers with evidence of his great learning.

Among the most glaring mistakes here are the constant spelling errors: *room to right* should be *room to write, knowladgeble* should be *knowledgeable, somone* should be *someone, your not sure* should be *you're not sure, advise* should be *advice, sometimes its not true* should be *sometimes it's not true, defenately* should be *definitely,* and *wierd* should be *weird.* You get the picture: this writer has made it obvious that he has a real problem spelling words correctly.

Identifying Sentence Errors

---

1. **(D)**   *Pronoun Agreement*

Bells should go off whenever you see the phrase "his or her" in an Identifying Sentence Errors question. Remember, just as you'll see some sentences with an incorrect use of the plural "their" (*everybody put on their shoes*), you'll also see a few incorrectly singular "his or her" possessives. *The teachers* is a plural subject, and therefore should be replaced with the plural pronoun *their.*

2. **(B)**   *Gerund*

Because of the vagaries of the English language, we cannot say *arrested to be.* We must say *arrested for being.* Therefore, (B) is the answer.

3. **(B)**   *Subject-Verb Agreement*

There's something unusual about the way this sentence is constructed: its verb precedes its subject. Whenever this happens, you should be concerned about subject-verb agreement, because inverting subject and verb makes it easier to miss hearing an error in number. *Strewn around the playpen was... the toys* may not sound funny to you, but flip things around so that the subject precedes the verb, as it does conventionally: now you get *the toys was strewn around the playpen.* That construction makes it easier to see that the verb form *was* should actually be in the plural form "were," to match the plural word *toys.* Your answer is (B).

Strewn may look odd, but that really is the correct past tense of the verb "to strew." You may be hung up on strange-sounding past tense verb forms on the test; the best way to avoid this problem is to go over your list of "Annoying Verbs" in the Identifying Sentence Errors section of the guide.

4.   (C)   *Double Negative*

Mental sirens should wail when you see a word like *hardly*. It's one of those words that is negative despite the fact that it doesn't sound negative. And a negative word, even one that doesn't sound negative, cannot be placed next to another negative word. This means that (C) is the answer. A corrected version of the sentence would read either *taxation is not an acceptable solution* or *taxation is hardly an acceptable solution*.

(A) involves the correct form of the verb "to declare." Problems with verbs in this section of the exam will mostly involve tense and subject-verb agreement, and *declaring* involves neither.

5.   (D)   *Pronoun Shift*

This is an especially tricky case of pronoun shift because the two pronouns involved—*you* and *one*—are placed so far apart. Sentences that have long intervening clauses, as this sentence does, should be checked carefully for problems with both subject-verb agreement and pronoun agreement. Here, the writer begins by talking about "you" (*if you are going to Beijing*), but shifts to "one" at the end of the sentence (*catch one off guard*). Remember, if you start with "you," you cannot switch to "one" in mid-sentence.

6.   (E)   *No Error*

No error.

7.   (A)   *Other*

There's no specific grammar rule that explains why you can't use *where* in this context, but think about it this way: a speech isn't a location, and the word *where* should only be used in association with locations. In corrected form, this part of the sentence would read *one candidate for student council made a speech in which he proposed holding a blood drive*.

8.   (A)   *Tense*

"Swim" is a classic annoying verb. You should familiarize yourself with all of the annoying verbs listed in the study guide, as these will account for some of the tense errors on this section of the test. In this sentence, *swum* should be *swam*. If you've successfully trained your ear, *swum* might have sounded incorrect. The answer is (A).

9.   (B)   *Idiom*

In English, the phrase *more devotedly as* is a violation of the rules of idiom. We say *more devotedly than*. (B) is the answer.

10.   (D)   *Parallelism*

This list, which explains the appeal of new technology, starts with the comparing words *faster* and *more efficient*. Both imply that new technology is faster and more efficient than something (most likely old technology). Even though the subject of comparison isn't named, it is implied. The third item on the list, however, poses a problem. The word *cheap* does not imply a comparison. Instead of *cheap*, the third item in the list should be *cheaper*.

Although this is technically a parallelism problem, you can also figure out the right answer by using your technique for identifying faulty comparisons: extend the comparison as far as you can, and see what happens. By extending the implied comparison, you get *new machines are faster than old machines, more efficient than old machines, and cheap than old machines*. In that extended form, it becomes even more clear that (D) is the right answer.

11. **(D)** *Pronoun Agreement*

As you examine your pronouns, you might notice that in the phrase *they have grown extremely expensive*, *they*, a plural word, refers not to loans, another plural word, but to college, a singular word. As you know, plural pronouns like *they* cannot be used to refer to singular subjects. Therefore, (D) is the answer. Always be scrupulous when checking your pronouns; if you rush, it's easy to assume that *they* refers to loans, and decide that the sentence is error-free.

12. **(E)** *No Error*

No error.

13. **(B)** *Subject-Verb Agreement*

The important thing to spot right away is the use of the construction *as well as*. This is one of those terrible, tricky phrases, like "along with" and "in addition to," that sound as if they make their subject plural, but in fact *do not*. No matter who else is working *as well as* the governor, the governor is still our sentence's subject—and so it's the governor who determines the sentence's verb form. And since *the governor* is a singular subject, the verb should be singular as well. The correct answer is (B).

If you haven't already, go over the section called "Singular Subject that Looks Plural" in the Subject-Verb Agreement section of Identifying Subject Errors. The only way to deal with these tricky phrases is to memorize them.

14. **(B)** *Wrong Word*

Illusions are "tricks" or "false images." *Allusions* are "references." Ms. Wong was making allusions, not illusions, to the late hour. This is a straightforward case of wrong word usage, and in order to nail these questions, it's important to read over the list of commonly confused words in your study guide.

15. **(A)** *Double Negative*

Always be alert to the possible presence of a double negative when you encounter a word that is negative but doesn't sound it, like *scarcely*. In this question, (A) is the answer because it is incorrect to place the negative word *not* directly beside the negative word *scarcely*. To solve the problem, the phrase would have to be rewritten as *he could not imagine* or *he could scarcely imagine*.

That *herself* might sound a little odd, but it is in fact a grammatically correct construction.

16. **(D)** *Adverb*

Sweeter is a special type of adverb called a comparative modifier. You don't need to remember the phrase "comparative modifier." What you do need to remember is that when comparing two items, you must use a word like *uglier, shorter,* or *sweeter*, and when comparing three or more items you must use a word like *ugliest, shortest,* or *sweetest*. Since this sentence compares three items, that *sweeter* should be a *sweetest*. (D) it is.

(B) is not the answer because taste-tester does indeed require a hyphen. Even if you're looking at a hyphen with suspicion, remember: you're trying to find the *most wrong* part of the sentence. If you have something like *sweeter*, which you're pretty sure is wrong, and something like *taste-tester*, which you kind of think might be wrong, go with the one that seems more wrong.

(C) correctly uses the pronoun "which."

17. **(E)** *No Error*

No error.

18. **(C)**   *Tense*

The first part of the sentence, *before she became president of the entire company*, makes us expect the second half of the sentence to explain what happened before this woman became president of the company. The second half of the sentence, therefore, should use the past tense. Instead, the phrase *has been* suggests an action that continues to the present time. This doesn't make any sense. The verb phrase should be *had been*, not *has been*.

19. **(B)**   *Idiom*

The problem here is an unidiomatic construction. *Gain insight for* should be *gain insight into*. (B) is the correct answer.

20. **(D)**   *Pronoun Agreement*

Whenever you see a pronoun separated from the noun it replaces, as in answer choice (D), you should take notice. What does *it* refer to? *His papers*. Because this guy has more than one paper, the pronoun that refers to those plural papers should be plural (*they*) not singular (*it*).

Strode up, although it certainly sounds strange, is actually the correct past tense form of the verb "to stride." If you missed this one, check out the list of irregular verbs, and study the ones with which you're unfamiliar.

Improving Sentence Errors

21. **(A)**   *No Error*
No error.

22. **(D)**   *Coordination*

Here we have a case of faulty coordination. The word *and* does a bad job of expressing the relationship between *Frannie was unwilling to start jogging* and *she tried it anyway*. Whatever word connects the two clauses should suggest that Frannie had to overcome her own unwillingness before she started jogging. (D) does that. The phrase *Frannie was unwilling to start jogging, but she tried it anyway* makes sense.

(B) is an improvement on the original, but it doesn't work as well as (D). Remember, the directions instruct you to choose the *best* answer.

(C) leaves out a coordinating word altogether. This is no solution. As some officious adult has no doubt explained to you, ignoring a problem does not make it go away. (E) sets up precisely the wrong relationship between the two clauses by saying that because Frannie didn't want to jog, she jogged.

23. **(E)**   *Parallelism*

In order to fix the error of parallelism in the original sentence, you need to describe all of the actions using infinitives, as (E) does. Getting rid of that phrase *oftentimes helpful* is fine. Even if you worried about getting rid of that phrase, though, the two answer choices that include it, (B) and (C), both have big grammatical problems that make them wrong. (B) uses two gerunds, which makes that first infinitive *to spend* the odd man out. (C) uses one infinitive, *rely*, but it still has that problematic gerund *planning*.

24. **(E)**   *Passive Voice*

There's no egregious error in this sentence, but there is an error: passive voice. The second half of the sentence wastes time getting to the point, which is that Woody Allen is the guy changing the conception. We don't find out that it is he who performs the action until the very end of the sentence. The right answer, (E), tells the reader right away that Allen is the performer.

25. **(A)**   *No Error*

No error.

26. **(C)**   *Run-on*

Here we have a run-on sentence. It is easily fixed, as you can see from the right answer, (C); all you need do is utilize that popular run-on fixing technique of inserting "and." Problem solved.

27. **(B)**   *Run-on*

The original sentence is a run-on. The correct answer, (B), simply adds the conjunction *so*, which turns the second half of the sentence into a dependent clause and fixes the problem.

28. **(B)**   *Parallelism*

This is a slightly deceptive one; you know to look for parallelism errors in lists, and this is a list, but it's not an obvious one because it's broken into two parts. However, a list it is—a list with a parallelism problem. We're told that directors consider *voice* and *acting ability* and *does the person look good*. That third consideration sticks out like a sore thumb because it is not a noun. The right answer choice, (B), makes *does the person look good* into a noun: *looks*. (B) might sound a little abrupt to you as you're reading through the answer choices, but if you read it back into the sentence, you'll see that it sounds right.

29. **(A)**   *No Error*

No error.

30. **(A)**   *No Error*

No error.

31. **(C)**   *Fragment*

There is no verb pulling the weight in this sentence. Sure, rumors are getting *repeated* and *embellished*, but there is no verb explaining what the urban legends are doing. According to the right answer, (C), the urban legend is *saying*. That's enough. Fixing fragments doesn't mean you have to change the meaning of the sentence entirely, you just need a verb in there pulling its weight.

32. **(C)**   *Misplaced Modifier*

You should be instantly suspicious when you see the phrase *being that*, either in a question or in an answer. It's a grammatically flabby phrase and it will almost always be wrong on this test. Here, the phrase *being that* is symptomatic of a larger problem: a misplaced modifier. The modifier *being that they had to keep their love secret* is misplaced because in its current location, it doesn't accurately express the relationship between the courtship and the domineering father. After reading the sentence, we're left wondering why

202 • Improving Sentence Errors

they had to keep their courtship secret. Was it because Barrett's father disapproved? Was it because it gave them a thrill to sneak around? Answer choice (C) makes the relationship more clear. As you suspected, yes, they snuck around *because* her father disapproved. That colon, by the way, is a shorthand way of saying, "and here's the reason."

(B) does make the relationship between the two clauses more clear, but you can gather even from the imprecise original sentence that the courtship wasn't dramatic *although* the father disapproved, but *because* he disapproved. Therefore, although (B) clarifies, it clarifies incorrectly.

The sentiment behind (D) is correct, but the use of the semicolon is not. If the semicolon was replaced with a comma, (D) would be unobjectionable.

You can eliminate (E) not only because it uses the colon incorrectly (again, replacing the colon with a comma would be grammatically correct) but because it is just too darn wordy.

33. **(A)** *No Error*

No error.

34. **(E)** *Conjunction*

The conjunction *but* is wrong for this sentence. It's not surprising, as *but* suggests, that when record amounts of rain fell, rivers should flood. It's natural that flooding should occur. Therefore the conjunction *and* is what's needed, and (E) is your answer.

35. **(D)** *Misplaced Modifier*

Unless this is a particularly rebellious principal we're talking about, she's probably not the one violating the student parking lot rules. That, however, is what the construction of the sentence suggests. The phrase *student parking lot violations by the principal* changes the intended meaning of the sentence. The right answer choice, (D), fixes the misplaced modifier by moving it to the front of the sentence. In the corrected version, the principal is the one issuing the warnings, not violating the rules.

(B) fixes the problematic suggestion that the principal is the rule-breaker, but it is unnecessarily awkward, and we don't find out until the end of the sentence who's doing the warning.

(C) introduces a new misplaced modifier; this time, the suggestion is that the principal is issuing the parking lot violations.

(E), like the original sentence, casts the principal as rule-breaker.

36. **(B)** *Gerund*

This sentence begins by saying Milton's treatise advocates __ and __. Those two blanks must be filled up by parallel words, and in the sentence as it is presented, they are not. The first word is a gerund, *realizing*, so the second word should also be a gerund, *ending*, not the infinitive *to end*. Therefore, (B) is the right way to correct the sentence.

(C) separates *to* from *leave* with that intervening clause, but *to leave* is an infinitive clause nonetheless, and therefore means another problem of parallelism. (D) must be eliminated because it is so awkward, and (E) repeats the original problem.

Test III Explanations

37. **(B)**   *Misplaced Modifier*

This question makes it sound as if the German operetta is the amazing prodigy. Look at the phrase by itself, and the problem becomes clear: *An amazing prodigy, a German operetta.* Bach is the prodigy, not the operetta.

Look at (B), the correct answer, and compare it to (C). Although (B) and (C) are similar, (C) is too passive. You don't find out until the end of the sentence that we're talking about Bach and what he wrote. (B) is the better answer because right away, it identifies the important ideas and tells you who is performing the action.

(D) and (E) both contain misplaced modifiers.

38. **(B)**   *Passive Voice*

It sounds from the original sentence as if no one in particular cultivated the referee's good qualities. (B) makes it clear that the cultivator was *he*, the ref. In your own writing and on this portion of the test, expunge passive voice whenever you can. Passive voice avoids naming the performer of the action, and it's important to give credit (or blame) where it's due.

Improving Paragraphs

39. **(C)**   *Combing Sentences*

All of the answer choices here express the same basic meaning: Even though some rap glorifies all three, some rap does not. Therefore, you'll have to eliminate answers based on grammar, rather than content. Only (C) is grammatically correct. (A) and (D) are run-on sentences. (B) is awkward. (E) uses the conjunction *and* in an illogical way.

40. **(E)**   *Addition*

Before you answer this question, it's important to go back and remind yourself of the main idea of the second paragraph. The correct answer, (E), is the one that provides the most appropriate introduction to the second paragraph by talking about well-known rappers and traditional values.

A few of the other answers are easily eliminated: (A) is out in left field, since no *personal encounters with rappers* are discussed anywhere in the essay. (C) is also pretty easy to get rid of, since industry executives aren't mentioned in the second paragraph or elsewhere. (B) looks good, because it mentions Jay-Z, and Jay-Z is the focus of the second paragraph. Compared to the right answer, however, (B) is vague, and the phrase *one such rapper* is not appropriate. No picture of a rapper has been painted previous to the second paragraph, so *one such rapper* doesn't refer to anything. (D) also looks good, and it might be a contender for right answer if the question asked you about a transition sentence. But (D) really refers to the first paragraph more than it does to the second, so (E) is the better answer.

41. **(C)**   *Combining Sentences*

Before looking at the answer choices, figure out the problem with the two sentences as they stand. These sentences might have made you pause the first time you read the essay, because they present two seemingly contradictory ideas, with no explanation of the contradiction. How can Jay-Z simultaneously demean women and praise his mother? Look for the answer choice that resolves this conundrum.

Only (D) makes the paradox clear by using the word *although*. All of the other answer choices combine the two sentences but don't acknowledge the fact that it's strange that a sometimes-misogynist rapper would write an ode to his mom.

42. **(C)** *Revising Sentences*

Context matters on this one. If you don't go back and reread a few sentences before, after, and including the problem sentence, you might be tempted to choose (A). Out of context, that sentence is grammatically perfect. If you go back and reread, however, you'll see that *credited* should not be in the past tense because the rest of the paragraph is in the present tense. Therefore, (C) is the answer.

43. **(A)** *Combining Sentences*

Once you decide how these two sentences relate to each other, it's your job to figure out which of the connecting words posited by the answer choices is the right one. It's not *however* or *but*; those imply that rapping about violence and rapping about violent death are somehow opposed to one another. *Thus* or *moreover* make more sense, but both (D) and (E) have grammar problems. (A), the right answer, uses the simple but serviceable word *and*, and is grammatically correct.

44. **(A)** *Analysis*

On these questions, be sure to remind yourself of what you're doing. Throw a big circle around that word *EXCEPT*, or write a note to yourself in the margin: "choose the answer that's NOT in the essay." Because you're so used to picking the sentence that should be in the essay, it requires an adjustment to remember that on "except" questions, the right answer is the one that's *not* in the essay.

Here, the one thing the writer does not do is tell a personal story. This is a fairly formal essay on rap, and the writer does not introduce her own favorite songs, or talk about how she came to appreciate rap. (B) is incorrect because the entire essay debunks the myth that rappers are violent misogynists. (C) can be eliminated, because the last paragraph does indeed constitute a summary. (D) is a little vague, but the writer does talk about specific rappers and lyrics, so it's safe to eliminate (D). (E) is wrong because the bulk of the essay is spent analyzing lyrics.

45. **(D)** *Revising Sentences*

You can go back and read a few sentences surrounding the problem sentence if you want to, but happily, this question is one you can safely answer without rereading the essay. The problem is tense switch. The sentence talks about how the decision seemed in the past, and how it seems now. It's the how it seems now part that sounds funny. Try to fix the sentence in your own mind before you look at the answer choices. Hopefully you'll come up with something close to (D), the right answer. The change makes sense: because the second half of the sentence is talking about the present, the verb form *was* doesn't make sense. The verb form *is* does make sense.

46. **(E)** *Revising Sentences*

The phrasing of this question is intimidating, but it's actually a manageable question. Go back and reread the relevant portion of the second paragraph and you'll find that the sentence in question sounds abrupt. The writer is talking about working at a fancy restaurant, and then suddenly she's talking about applying to a fish and chips place. By adding the conjunction *however*, as (E) does, the writer clarifies for the reader that her application to the fish and chips place was in opposition to her desire to work at a swanky place. The rest of the answers, other than (B), don't convey this opposition. (B) is serviceable, but as one of your English teachers probably told you, it's not ideal to begin a sentence with *but*. Because you have the synonymous and more snazzy *however* as a choice, (B) is not the best answer.

47. **(B)** *Analysis*

(B) is the right answer because when the writer tells us that the clientele wasn't what she had in mind, we instantly long to hear some good stories about really nasty, rude clients.

Even if you didn't long to hear nasty stories, you could have found the right answer to this question by eliminating wrong answers. (A) doesn't make much sense because *clientele* is a fairly well-known word, and there's not much reason to screech to a halt and define it. Mentioning the most popular entrees is not appropriate at this juncture, since the writer is airing her grievances about the restaurant, not telling us about its merits. (D) and (E) are both too vague. What kind of hypothetical question should she ask? Why should she discuss more problems?

48. **(A)** *Revising Sentences*

You'll need to go back and reread the relevant portion of the essay in order to answer this question. The problem with the word *it* is that it's too vague, especially when used in the topic sentence of a new paragraph. The best replacement for *it* is *my job*. What follows that topic sentence whining about *it never improved* is a list of horrible things about the job. Therefore, all of the other answers besides (A) are too specific. Only *my job* is sufficiently all-encompassing.

49. **(C)** *Revising Sentences*

This sentence suffers from vagueness. The phrase *because of this* could mean a number of things, and a good answer choice will make that phrase more specific. Context is important here, so be sure to go back and reread a little. The writer is talking about her mother's wishes, which were the reason she stayed at her hated job. Therefore, (C) is a good answer. It was because of her mother that the writer kept on at the restaurant. Don't be thrown off by the other answer choices; vagueness is the issue, not choice of conjunctions, as the other answer choices suggest.

50. **(D)** *Revising Sentences*

These answer choices are a bit knotty, because they're all basically okay. You have to determine the right answer based on which is the least awkward and makes the most sense. The only one that really fits the bill is (D). The phrase *not only* is a crucial one, because it helps the reader understand what's going on. And (D) is a much more stylishly written than (B), the only other answer choice that uses *not only*.

Identifying Sentence Errors

51. **(E)**   *No Error*

No error.

52. **(A)**   *Tense*

It's always a good idea to try to hear the error by reading through the sentence; frequently some aspect of the sentence will simply sound wrong. Take a look at the first clause, *since he had drove twenty miles just to hear her speak. Drove* might sound a bit funny to you. It should. Remember that "drive" is one of the annoying verbs listed in your study guide. Annoying verbs, which never sound quite right in any tense, account for a large portion of all tense errors, so it's a good idea to memorize that list. Try substituting *had driven* for *had drove*. It sounds much better. (A) is the right answer.

   If you weren't sure that (A) was the answer, the second clause might have made you pause, because there are some potential tense land mines in the phrase *Thomas was annoyed to learn that the professor had cancelled her lecture.* However, the underlined phrase *had cancelled* is fine. Thomas *was annoyed* in the past, because the professor *had cancelled* in the even-more-distant past. The tenses express the logical sequence of events.

53. **(C)**   *Pronoun Agreement*

(C), *they*, refers to *the radio*. Don't be tricked into thinking that the abstract term *the radio* should be treated as a plural. Although it does refer to the general radios listened to by the American people, it is still a singular word and must be treated as such. It must be paired, therefore, not with the plural *they*, but with the singular *it*.

54. **(D)**   *Faulty Comparison*

Although you can probably figure out what this sentence is *trying* to say, what it *actually* says is that the Museum was not as extensive as the arms collection. The intended meaning, though, is that the according to the snooty curator, the arms collection at one museum was not as extensive as the arms collection at the Metropolitan Museum of Art. We have a case of faulty comparison here, and (D) is the answer.

55. **(C)**   *Idiom*

The idiom goes: "As ___ as." So you say things like, "As purple as," "As disgusting as," "as cheesy as." Here we have the unidiomatic expression *as effortlessly than*. (C) is the answer.

56. **(D)**   *Adverb*

(D) uses an adjective where an adverb is needed. Remember, adjectives can be used only to describe people or places; you must use adverbs to describe actions. Thus, the action of being bored can only be described by the adverb *really*, not by the adjective *real*. In standard English, you cannot be *real bored*, you can only be *really bored*. You can also be "really bored" *by* standard English, but that's a different story.

   You might have considered (B), but believe it or not, that really is the correct way of spelling *overcrowded*.

57. **(E)**   *No Error*

No error.

58. **(C)**   *Faulty Comparison*

This is an example of faulty comparison. The sentence means to say that Baker's style was more elegant than the style of her contemporaries, but it actually says that her style was more elegant than the contemporaries themselves. This is a subtle difference, yes, but it's an important one. (C) is the answer.

59. **(B)**   *Subject-Verb Agreement*

Spotting the error in this sentence will not be difficult if you've gone over your list of tricky constructions in the "Subject-Verb Agreement" section of the guide. If you have, that "neither/nor" construction will catch your eye right away. Remember that in this kind of construction, the nouns that follow the *neither* and the *nor* are considered separate, dual subjects—so if the noun following *neither* is singular, and the noun following *nor* is singular, your verb form should be singular as well. It may help to quickly break the sentence into two separate sentences: could you say, *Neither fame were enough* or *Nor fortune were enough*? No; the correct verb form would be *was enough*, and therefore (B) is your answer.

60. **(E)**   *No Error*

No error.

SparkNotes Literature Study Guides:

1984
The Adventures of
   Huckleberry Finn
The Adventures of
   Tom Sawyer
The Aeneid
All Quiet on the
   Western Front
And Then There
   Were None
Angela's Ashes
Animal Farm
Anne of Green Gables
Antony and Cleopatra
As I Lay Dying
As You Like It
The Awakening
The Bean Trees
The Bell Jar
Beloved
Beowulf
Billy Budd
Black Boy
Bless Me, Ultima
The Bluest Eye
Brave New World
The Brothers Karamazov
The Call of the Wild
Candide
The Canterbury Tales
Catch-22
The Catcher in the Rye
The Chosen
Cold Mountain
Cold Sassy Tree
The Color Purple
The Count of Monte Cristo
Crime and Punishment
The Crucible
Cry, the Beloved Country
Cyrano de Bergerac

Death of a Salesman
The Diary of a Young Girl
Doctor Faustus
A Doll's House
Don Quixote
Dr. Jekyll and Mr. Hyde
Dracula
Dune
Emma
Ethan Frome
Fahrenheit 451
Fallen Angels
A Farewell to Arms
Flowers for Algernon
The Fountainhead
Frankenstein
The Glass Menagerie
Gone With the Wind
The Good Earth
The Grapes of Wrath
Great Expectations
The Great Gatsby
Gulliver's Travels
Hamlet
The Handmaid's Tale
Hard Times
Harry Potter and the
   Sorcerer's Stone
Heart of Darkness
Henry IV, Part I
Henry V
Hiroshima
The Hobbit
The House of the
   Seven Gables
I Know Why the
Caged Bird Sings
The Iliad
Inferno
Invisible Man
Jane Eyre

Johnny Tremain
The Joy Luck Club
Julius Caesar
The Jungle
The Killer Angels
King Lear
The Last of the Mohicans
Les Misérables
A Lesson Before Dying
The Little Prince
Little Women
Lord of the Flies
Macbeth
Madame Bovary
A Man for All Seasons
The Mayor of Casterbridge
The Merchant of Venice
A Midsummer
   Night's Dream
Moby-Dick
Much Ado About Nothing
My Ántonia
Mythology
Native Son
The New Testament
Night
The Odyssey
The Oedipus Plays
Of Mice and Men
The Old Man and the Sea
The Old Testament
Oliver Twist
The Once and Future King
One Flew Over the
   Cuckoo's Nest
One Hundred Years
   of Solitude
Othello
Our Town
The Outsiders
Paradise Lost

The Pearl
The Picture of Dorian Gray
A Portrait of the Artist as a
   Young Man
Pride and Prejudice
The Prince
A Raisin in the Sun
The Red Badge of Courage
The Republic
Richard III
Robinson Crusoe
Romeo and Juliet
The Scarlet Letter
A Separate Peace
Silas Marner
Sir Gawain and the
   Green Knight
Slaughterhouse-Five
Snow Falling on Cedars
The Sound and the Fury
Steppenwolf
The Stranger
A Streetcar Named Desire
The Sun Also Rises
A Tale of Two Cities
The Taming of the Shrew
The Tempest
Tess of the d'Urbervilles
Their Eyes Were
   Watching God
Things Fall Apart
To Kill a Mockingbird
To the Lighthouse
Treasure Island
Twelfth Night
Ulysses
Uncle Tom's Cabin
Walden
Wuthering Heights
A Yellow Raft in
   Blue Water